YOUR MONEY OR
YOUR HEALTH

YOUR MONEY OR YOUR HEALTH

America's Cruel, Bureaucratic, and Horrendously Expensive Health Care System:

How It Got That Way and What To Do About It

NEIL ROLDE

PARAGON HOUSE
NEW YORK

First edition, 1992

Published in the United States by

Paragon House
90 Fifth Avenue
New York, N.Y. 10011

Library of Congress Cataloging-in-Publication Data
Rolde, Neil
Your money or your health: America's cruel, bureaucratic, and horrendously expensive health care system: how it got that way and what to do about it / Neil Rolde.—1st ed.
    p.   cm.
Includes bibliographical references and index.
ISBN 1-55778-520-1
1. Medical care—United States.
2. Medical policy—United States.
3. Medical economics—United States.   I. Title.
RA395. A3R65 1992
362.1'0973—dc20

                                                        92-11904
                                                        CIP

Manufactured in the United States of America

To the many millions of Americans who do not have proper access to health care, in the hope that this scandalous situation may soon be changed.

CONTENTS

ACKNOWLEDGMENTS

A politician's nightmare is that in thanking people for their help, he will leave someone out. With instincts honed by more than twenty years of active participation in politics, I will thereby forego listing the individual names of persons who helped me in the preparation of this book, because there were so many of them and my memory, no doubt, has flaws. A number of my sources *have been* cited in these pages. So I will simply rely on expressing a generic debt of gratitude to all who took the time to share their expertise with me, whether in Canada or Washington, D.C. or Hawaii or Maine or California or in other parts of the U.S., and who wrote to me from England, France, Germany, etc.

Some exceptions to this rule: a loud chorus of thanks to Shep Welsh of Bath, Maine, for his invaluable assistance, friendship, and encouragement; also an expression of appreciation to my editor, P J Dempsey, for her help and support; and a word of gratitude to my old friend Seymour Kurtz, who helped make this book possible

INTRODUCTION

Songs and legends from England's eighteenth century celebrate daring highwaymen who intercepted unwary stage coaches and, at pistol point, offered passengers an unappetizing one-sided bargain: "Your money or your life."

With far less panache, modern Americans are being presented with a similarly distasteful choice by a rich and powerful medical establishment that demands the toughest of all decisions: "Your money or your health."

Two stark, unpleasant facts have at last galvanized a serious national debate about the future of our medical care system.

1. We Americans now lay out a greater proportion of our Gross National Product for health care than do any other people in the entire world. As of 1989, the U.S. spent 12 percent per year of its national income on health care. Canada and France (both of whom provide their people universal health care) pay the next highest percentage—about 8.6 percent.[1]

2. A constantly growing number of working Americans have utterly no access to health care. This is because they can no longer pay ever-rising insurance premiums and are neither poor enough nor old enough to qualify for government programs. Others—even wealthy people when they're sick—are finding that insurance companies flatly refuse to protect them at any cost. The figure most often quoted to account for such Americans is 37 million,

but estimates range as high as 40 million, and no lower than 31 million (the figure put forth by the American Medical Association).[2] And the number goes up every month.

Other facts cited in the national debate deal with the efficiency of our health care system. Critics ask where the United States ranks in key areas such as infant mortality and population longevity—and the answers are not what you'd expect from a system whose champions proudly trumpet it to be "the best in the world."

In the United States, ten babies out of every one thousand successfully delivered die before they reach their first birthdays. On a world scale, that places us in twenty-second place, behind such countries as Singapore, Spain, and Ireland.[3]

People in other major industrialized nations live longer, too. Our average life span (in 1987) of 78.3 years lags behind those of Japan, France, Sweden, Canada and Germany.[4]

Such hard statistics have been called shameful by those seeking a change in our system, particularly when they are measured against results from nations that manage to provide health care to *all* their people.

Critics seldom fail to point out that the U.S. is the only industrialized nation in the world without universal health care. They usually follow by adding that the only other industrialized society with the same deficiency is the Republic of South Africa—frequently failing to mention that even this apartheid state does provide such services to its entire white population. As an ironic aside, they may also mention that in the Persian Gulf war, the U.S. went into battle to defend two "helpless" nations—Saudi Arabia and Kuwait—both of whom manage to offer universal health care. And so, by the way, does Iraq.

All this hullabaloo over the failures and inadequacies of the American health care system is far from new. As long ago as 1970, the Health Law Project of the University of Pennsylvania published a book declaring, "the crisis in medical care has arrived as an American public issue." It noted with alarm that the country was spending more of its GNP on health care than any other nation. (At that time we were almost on a par with Canada, which had not yet instituted its single-payer system.)[5] At the end of the same decade, the *Congressional Quarterly* gasped in alarm as it reported that our health care expenditures had risen 350 percent between 1965 and 1978.

The problem has not been totally ignored. Recent efforts at all levels of government—from the U.S. Congress to scores of state legislatures—have tried to remedy bits and pieces of these ills. The results have been infuriatingly unsuccessful. Panaceas have been proposed, debated, and enacted (including Medicare and cost-containment schemes and catastrophic illness protection) only to be found wanting. Nothing has ever worked. Costs keep rising for harried American taxpayers as they cope with rising taxes, soaring out-of-pocket costs for their health insurance premiums, tricky co-payments and deductibles, etc. The situation has become so onerous and burdensome that it seems, to many, a new and more esoteric form of highway robbery.

Despite the constantly worsening situation, opponents of any proposed system of universal health care have beaten back any real change with the argument, among others, that "we can't afford such a thing. It will bankrupt the country." These critics conveniently ignore the fact that many American families have been literally bankrupted by the present system—the most expensive in the world.

A major new element in the growing debate, not heard earlier because it did not exist, is the experience of our neighbor to the north. The Canadians have provided a controversial yardstick by which many Americans are beginning to measure our own health care system.

How did we get into such a fix? Why has the United States found itself on such a singular track for providing health care and why do we remain on it? What forces created the current patchwork system, and what influences do they exert today? And, finally, what do all the various pressure groups and special interests want, and what do their aspirations bode for our national future?

The aim of this book is to answer these questions and to suggest a possible course of action. It will try to blaze a purposeful path through the thicket of what may be the most confusing public issue facing the nation, as well as the most threatening to the security and well-being of millions of Americans.

We drink to the health of our friends. We pray for the health of our families and ourselves. And if the worst should happen, we yearn to know that we will survive not only our ills, but also their financial consequences. This is a double burden that is unique to Americans. It is an unnecessary burden. There is no reason at all that "your money or your health" must be the bitter choice of the American people.

1 THE FIRESTORM

"All's for the best in the best of all possible worlds."

This was the platitude continually repeated by Dr. Pangloss, the ridiculous, ever-optimistic philosopher in Voltaire's *Candide*, as he viewed a world full of murder, tragedy, and deceit. Pangloss would be the perfect defender for today's American health care system.

Against the "best medical system in the world" echo the daily cries of anguish from ordinary citizens. The outcry, reflected in the media, is building to a deafening crescendo, which bids fair to become a key issue of the nineties as the problems of the tottering health care system multiply and become increasingly obvious.

As Voltaire wrote of the constantly worsening conditions that were to erupt and sweep away the old regimes in Europe, so critics fear that the potential disintegration of the American health care system is reaching firestorm proportions that may well do serious damage to our republic. The firestorm is being fanned by the growing perception that costs are totally out of control and that the middle class, once complacent, is now threatened by a relentless juggernaut—a health care system that is indeed "broke," and urgently needs "fixing."

A good example of the qualitative change from past crises of a similar sort can be seen in a recent article in the *New York Times*.[1] Appearing on the business page, the headline read:

1

BLUE CROSS
ENDS PLAN
FOR GROUPS

100,000 MEMBERS
OF NEW YORK STATE
ASSOCIATIONS CUT

The story reported that the groups losing their health insurance included lawyers, chamber of commerce personnel, professional women, journalists, private school employees—in short, middle-class people who had, no doubt, thought themselves well insulated against such a dire eventuality.

Those affected were offered the option of buying individual replacement policies. However, if any of the individuals had serious health problems, they would face astronomical increases in cost. One lawyer, suffering from a chronic illness, found that his premiums would rise from three thousand dollars to eleven thousand dollars a year. Even in cases where the desperate groups were able to find new carriers, they learned that their members would have to pass physical examinations.

Empire Blue Cross, the company in question, was candid about the reason for the cancellations. As their premiums had risen and risen, younger, healthier members of the affected groups had dropped out to take less expensive options. That left Empire with "older, sicker members who do not have other choices." Empire Blue Cross was losing money on the deal. A company vice-president said the company "had to guard against letting its pool of individual policyholders be dominated by people who were poor health risks."

The lesson is plain: In the 1990s, not only the working poor but also the upper middle class were facing the prospect of being left unprotected against medical care bills. And this is happening in a world where serious operations cost hundreds of thousands of dollars, hospitals beds are being charged out at seven hundred dollars to one thousand dollars a day, and the stack of bills accumulating over an extended illness can literally be an inch thick.

Some of the upper-middle-class professionals cut by Empire Blue Cross would be forced to join the ranks of the "invisibles"—those myriad victims of the systems who fall through the cracks, and whose pathetic stories have fallen on deaf ears for decades. It is worth noting that when the Canadian system fouls up, when someone reportedly dies for lack of care, American critics of universal national health care grab the incident and howl about the inefficiency that permits such a thing to happen. At the same time, they choose to ignore the fact that the identical thing happens in this country on a regular basis. The horror stories about our health care system have become so common that they frequently seem to lose their power to stir emotions. Or is it the case, as some have suggested, that vestiges of an old American ethic linger on and insist that those who can't pay for their own health care are little better than deadbeats?

Frightening stories of the failure to care for Americans come from all across the nation.

In Tennessee, the Young family, Tommy and Pamela, left without health insurance when Tommy lost his job, had to separate so Pamela could apply for Medicaid because their daughter needed surgery.[2]

In California, Charles William Jones died eighteen days before surgery scheduled to relieve his congestive heart failure. The surgery had been postponed for more than four months because Jones had been dropped from Medi-Cal, the state's version of Medicaid, and it took Contra Costa County that long to arrange an operation.[3]

In Ohio, an anguished parent wrote to a disabilities task force: "Shannon was in the hospital for surgery in July of 1988. Her bills totaled over $103,000. Our insurance has a $200,000 for life maximum on it. We hardly have any left on her and she is going to have more surgery in August. Shannon is only 12 years old and if she lives we will not have any insurance at all for her."[4]

In Louisiana, Belinda Sanchez of Baton Rouge saw her insurance rates go from $250 to $1,000 a month after her husband was diagnosed with cancer.[5]

Vermont chimes in with stories of people who couldn't buy insurance for any price, including a thirty-eight-year-old man in Burlington, recovering from heart bypass surgery, whose insurer dropped him and all the other members of his small business group.[6]

Mr. and Mrs. Charles Alexander of Duncanville, Texas, face more than $180,000 in medical bills because their Dallas health insurance company, Miller Leasing, suddenly went out of business.[7]

In New Hampshire, the family of Eugenia Skinner Shorrock, age ninety-five, auctioned off her locally famous museum collection, con-

3

taining such items as books autographed by Albert Schweitzer and Helen Hayes and vintage Barnum and Bailey memorabilia, in order to pay her health care expenses.[8]

In Florida, Anna Marie Lane was turned away from Jackson Memorial Hospital, Dade County's only public hospital, because she didn't have a two hundred dollar deposit for an operation on a huge fibrous tumor in her uterus. Bertha Dalger, suffering from breast cancer, was rejected because she didn't have three hundred dollars.[9]

Case after case is recorded by the Massachusetts consumer organization Health Care For All: The family of Mary P. loses their down payment for a home when her three-year-old daughter becomes ill; Jacob M. dies of a burst aneurysm while waiting six months to be eligible for Medicare and an operation; Phillip R.'s stomach cancer becomes inoperable because, without insurance, he couldn't afford early tests.[10]

Richard Lincoln of Wayne, Maine, an older man who lost his executive's job but was afraid not to continue the $217 monthly payments on his health insurance, wrote me, "It's almost a choice between buying food and lights and heat and giving up Blue Cross and ending up in the poverty line."[11]

David Chittim, a small-businessman in Sabattus, Maine, canceled his insurance policy with an angry outburst: "You have finally lost me. I hung on as long as I could, given the obscene increases in premiums over the last three years, but you have at last succeeded in breaking me. I can no longer afford your monthly extortion."

Lorraine Matthews and her husband, an elderly couple in Waldoboro, Maine, found themselves $160 over the limit to qualify for Medicaid. Both age 72, they contemplated divorce.

Margaret Squires of Augusta, Maine, the mother of a special needs child, exploded in exasperation at Blue Cross-Blue Shield: "You have processed the same claim three times, three different ways, and a different claim for the same service on a different day was processed a fourth way."

The ultimate comment on the firestorm raging over health care in the U.S. may well have been provided in July 1991 by William Benefield of Amarillo, Texas. Outside the Veterans Hospital in that Panhandle city, Benefield, a veteran, set himself afire and died to protest cuts in veterans' benefits.[12] Or perhaps an even greater indictment of the shortcomings of our "free-market" health care system is found in the story of Theresa Walsh of New York City, whom I met not long ago. Injured in an accident, she was left crippled, presumably wheelchair-bound for life, when her insurance money ran out. Undaunted, she left the United States and went to a Third World country, where doctors restored her ability to walk. That country was Cuba—Communist Cuba.

All of these individual nightmares are the real drama behind a mounting pile of baleful statistics about U.S. health care. Put in human terms, they make it clear that something must be done, and done quickly.

Whoever, like Mrs. Squires, has wrestled with the Kafkaesque irrationality of an insurance company bureaucracy, or, like old Lorraine Matthews, has been isolated on the wrong side of a Federal means test, will not be cheered at all to learn the cost of such paperwork. Two new studies document the immense waste of our health care system.

The General Accounting Office in Washington—neither a branch of Congress nor an arm of the presidential administration, but an independent body with no political axe to grind—has confirmed what many students of the Canadian system have long maintained: the administrative savings of a single-payer system are astronomical. A key paragraph of the report spells out the astounding fact that "if the universal coverage and single-payer features of the Canadian system were applied in the United States, the savings in administrative costs alone would be more than enough to finance insurance coverage for the millions of Americans who are currently uninsured. There would be enough left over to permit a reduction, or possibly even the elimination, of copayments and deductibles, if that were deemed appropriate."[13]

Other points made by the GAO were that a U.S. single-payer system could constrain the growth in long-term health costs; that such costs have risen at a slower pace in Canada ("measured either on a per capita basis or a share of gross national product"); and that there are more physicians per capita in Canada than in the U.S., but the cost of medical services is one-third less.

The second study, although it was performed by a less objective group (doctors who advocate a single-payer system), reinforced the GAO findings with specific figures, for example, that nearly one-quarter of all health expenditures in the U.S. are devoted to administration. With total health spending now more than $800 billion a year, those administrative costs total over $200 billion! This study, by members of the Physicians For A National Health Program, also predicts that by the year 2020, half of all health care costs in our country will be for administration if the present growth rate of administrative overhead continues. An extraordinary observation included in the study is that Massachusetts Blue Cross-Blue Shield alone employs 6,682 workers to service 2.7 million subscribers—a greater number than all of Canada uses to serve 25 million people.[14]

Opponents of a Canadian-style health care system for the U.S. usually riposte with the argument that patients there have to wait for treatment—which is sometimes true for elective procedures, but never for emergencies. Increasingly, however, Americans are beginning to see the "invisibles" in our own society—those who have to wait for care because of lack of money, often with fatal results: Charles William Jones, dead in California; Jacob M., dead in Massachusetts; Anne Marie Lane, turned away from a hospital in Florida for lack of a two-hundred-dollar deposit.

Confirmation of the extent to which Americans are forced to wait for health care was reduced to cold statistics by the noted polling firm of Lou Harris and Associates in a 1989 survey. They were presented by the organization's president, Humphrey Taylor, at a colloquium of the National Committee for Quality Health, a group of hospital, drug company, and medical supply house executives—hardly an audience wishing to hear favorable comments about Canada's health care system.

The Harris poll found that when citizens in three countries—Canada, Great Britain, and the United States—were asked if they had at any time in the past twelve months failed to receive health care services they thought they needed, the figures were 4 percent for Canada, 5 percent for Great Britain, and 13 percent for the United States. In releasing these results, Taylor pointed out that the 13 percent in the U.S. represented more than twenty-four million Americans.

He also estimated 40 to 50 million Americans were underinsured or had no health insurance at all, and that his firm's soundings indicated a decline in satisfaction with the U.S. health care system. The "very satisfied" category had dropped from 52 percent in 1980 to 35 percent in 1989. The same poll showed that 29 percent believed the

6

system needed to be completely rebuilt and 60 percent believed it needed substantial change.[15]

One of the positive factors that buoys up the system is that many Americans still have health insurance provided by their employers. But the cases of Richard Lincoln of Maine and Tommy Young of Tennessee show how vulnerable working people can become if they lose their jobs. Their security vis-à-vis health care is threatened when hard times strike.

For retirees who believed their health benefits would continue for the rest of their lives, the problem is particularly acute. Eastern Airlines' bankruptcy, for example, jeopardized ten thousand retirees, many not old enough for Medicare—like Connie Patterson, an Eastern flight attendant for thirty-five years...who now suffers from Parkinson's disease, or Jean Rae, a chief agent in Eastern's baggage service for twenty-eight years, who has had open heart surgery and a kidney transplant.[16]

Lawyers for retirees have argued before the bankruptcy court that claims for promised health care services should come first because they are often a matter of life and death. Jean Rae needs $350 a month for anti-rejection medications because of her transplant. Will she end up having to pauperize herself in order to qualify for Medicaid? And the retirees are not the only ones who have lost their health care. There are also thirty thousand Eastern workers who have been pushed out of their jobs and now face a world where insurance carriers may not wish to sell them coverage.

Another part of the new reality is that company-financed group insurance increasingly asks the worker to pay more. Policies that once paid 100 percent of all health costs are now routinely trimmed to from 80 percent to 20 percent. A recent poll of executives of the nation's largest companies showed 75 percent opposed to national health care despite the pressures of rising insurance costs. When asked how they intended to deal with those pressures, they blandly asserted they would require workers to pay more out of their own pockets. It should come as no surprise then that 73 percent of the strikes in the U.S. in the last three years have been over health care benefits—the most notable being the recent strike against AT&T by electrical workers around the country.

Labor has reacted because unions have always believed health care benefits were a substitute for wage increases—so, in turn, cutting those benefits is the same as cutting a worker's paycheck. Until fairly recently, this arrangement, which began during World War II when wages were frozen, was a bargain for employers. As late as 1979, health benefits were a mere 8 percent of pre-tax corporate profits. A decade later, they account for 56 percent of the gross bottom line. Going up at the rate of 17 percent a year, the actual cost of health benefits is approaching four thousand dollars per worker.

Some large corporations are beginning to conclude that the system is outmoded and needs replacement. The most celebrated industrial convert to a Canadian-style single-payer system is Chrysler. Its President, Lee Iacocca, has compared health care costs at his Michigan plants with those across the border in Ontario. The difference amounts to about five hundred dollars additional per American-made car. Faced with the fact that Japan's universal health care is the cheapest among industrial nations, and that Germany's is also much cheaper, the competitive disadvantage for American car-makers is obvious.

A change in Federal accounting rules will soon make a dire situation even worse. Companies will have to carry the full future cost of health care for their retirees on their books as a liability, thus creating a dampening effect on profits. This will cause a particular hardship at places like Chrysler and Bethlehem Steel and Caterpillar Tractor, which have an older workforce and large numbers of retirees.

An additional problem with job-linked health insurance is that many small businesses cannot afford it. Only a third of those businesses with fewer than ten employees provide coverage. The extent of the difficulty can be seen in the statistic that states that 87 percent of American companies have fewer than twenty employees. Moreover, small companies, if they do offer health insurance, generally have to pay more than companies with large blocs of workers—who can use this leverage to demand better rates—and who also have better tax advantages. Business spending for health care has grown eight-fold since 1970, and small businesses have borne the lion's share of those costs. In 1988, costs for companies with fewer than twenty-five employees rose 33 percent—one and one half times the increase for large corporations. A National Federation of Independent Businesses survey of its members revealed 89 percent felt health insurance costs were "profoundly expensive."[18] Various schemes have been proposed to protect small businesses against mandates to supply employee health insurance and most of these plans, like that of the NFIB, predictably would have the costs picked up by the taxpayers. They want to avoid a situation such as in Hawaii, when the state, through an exemption from Federal law, has forced *all* business to cover its workers. Clearly, it is uncertain how long job-linked health insurance can remain the linchpin of American health care.

The chaos of the health care system is also having a tremendous negative effect on physicians. They are being overwhelmed by paper. The maze of bureaucracies they face has grown progressively more burdensome. And it is not only with the government, but also fifteen hundred separate private insurers. In only two years, from 1988 to 1990, American doctors were forced to hire 74,700 new clerical workers simply to cope with the mountains of paper.[19]

In a system that is supposed to represent "free enterprise," physicians are increasingly handcuffed by the ever-increasing red tape created by the government and the insurance companies. A Gallup poll taken in 1989 among practicing doctors revealed 40 percent so discouraged that they said they would not go to medical school if they were back in college. The principal reason was the bewildering array of rules and regulations now governing their practices.[20]

Medicare accentuated this trend in 1983 when it adopted a payment policy called DRGs (Diagnostic Related Groups), a series of 467 categories of illness diagnoses, each with the total price the government will pay. Insurance companies soon followed with similar lists. To cope with the confusion, doctors found they had to hire practice consultants to advise them how to make a living amid this thicket of red tape. Again, a Gallup study of doctor's attitudes showed an increasing number, 63 percent, who felt they were losing control of patient treatment.

The latest "layer of bureaucracy" is being crafted by Congress and has been nicknamed ET (expenditure targets). It will be a new schedule of fees with a built-in mechanism for avoiding the excess billing that has permitted some doctors to escape the restraints of previous Medicare cost controls. Under ET, the Department of Health and Human Services would—much as the Canadians do—set a national target for overall payments to physicians.

Of course, Medicare is not the only game in town, and many doctors are fighting the system. They flatly refuse to accept patients under the program who do not—or cannot—pay additional fees. They complain they have no choice. Not only are they paid less than normal (many claim they do not even cover their overhead costs), but the paperwork is a nightmare and payments are often delayed. Currently, Medicare will pay only 80 percent of the standard fee it sets. Many doctors now demand up-front cash from patients before they will even examine them.

Confusion breeds confusion, and some consumer groups now publish lists of doctors willing to accept Medicare and Medicaid "assignment." In Massachusetts, a new law requires doctors to accept all Medicare patients at the established rates. Federal law, written to deal with a similar access problem, forbids "patient dumping" that occurs when hospitals turn away emergency patients who cannot offer proof they can pay for care. The first test of this law occurred in Victoria, Texas. Dr. Michael Burditt refused to care for a pregnant woman about to give birth. He sent patient Rosa Rivera to a hospital in Galveston over the protests of his own nurses. The baby was born in the ambulance while still forty miles from its destination. Burditt, appealing the twenty-thousand-dollar fine imposed, said Mrs. Rivera's extraordinarily high blood pressure created a situation beyond his ability and he feared complications could lead to a malpractice suit.

The fragmentation of the nation's health care system has resulted in some doctors becoming "medical entrepreneurs." They invest in new high-tech equipment that regulatory bodies have not allowed hospitals to purchase. MRI (magnetic resonance imaging) machines are an example. These are new diagnostic devices far more effective than X-rays and infinitely more expensive. Federal cost controls, and even more stringent state controls of capital expenditures, have tried to limit their numbers. But none of these restrictions apply to doctors' offices. As a result, using Florida as an example, three-quarters of the imaging machines currently in use are owned by doctors or groups in which doctors have invested. This has inevitably led to charges of conflict of interest, since the doctors are the very ones who order the expensive tests.

Congress has taken action to control cases where doctors own an interest in clinical laboratories. This action was prompted by findings of the Inspector General of the Department of Health and Human Services, who determined that patients of doctors with such investments received 45 percent more testing than others. In 1987, this resulted in extra Medicare costs of $28 million. A new law attempting to control clinical labs takes effect in 1992, and similar legislation is contemplated to control MRIs and other high-tech gadgetry.

While a few American doctors earn incomes in the millions of dollars, others do not do financially well at all. High overhead costs are particularly draining on internists, general practitioners, pediatricians, and others who are paid mostly for advice rather than costly procedures. These doctors are forced to hire additional clerks to keep up with the required paperwork while their fees are kept relatively low by the reimbursing bodies that eventually pay them. A New Jersey doctor, Melvin P. Vigman, wrote to the *New York Times* to point out that a family doctor who questions, examines, and counsels a patient for half an hour or longer will be lucky to receive a sixty-dollar fee, while a radiologist who takes fifteen to twenty minutes to read an MRI test can bill two hundred dollars.[21]

The plight of the profession was aptly illustrated by Dr. Gordon Guyatt, an Ontario, Canada, physician who told me that in his hospital in Hamilton a few years ago, a number of doctors talked of emigrating the the U.S. to make more money. "You don't hear that kind of talk any longer," Dr. Guyatt said. "The word has gotten back of how miserable it is for doctors to practice in the U.S."[22]

In recent years a number of American doctors have formed Physicians for a National Health Care Program, an organization that urgently promotes a Canadian-style single-payer national health care system. They operate in open defiance of the American Medical Association. In Vermont, 10 percent of the state's physicians recently signed a petition advocating universal health care coverage financed by a broad-based tax. Even the once ultra-reactionary AMA has softened its position, raising eyebrows and getting attention with calls for an overhaul of the country's health care system. An editorial in the *Journal of the American Medical Association (JAMA)* states emphatically that "it is no longer acceptable morally, ethically or economically for so many of our people to be medically uninsured or seriously underinsured."

Predictably, the suggested AMA solution, "Health Access America," is self-serving and would, in their words, "build on our current system's strengths and repair its weaknesses." It would also avoid the problems of cost containment, and instead pour more taxpayer money at the problem. Even so, the very fact that the nation's best-known defender of the status quo admits that our system is failing has added a new dimension to the firestorm.

Hospitals, too, are feeling the heat. Many are losing money. "Operating margins," the major source of funds for facility improvements and payment for uncompensated care in our nation's mostly not-for-profit hospitals, are dropping at an alarming rate. More than a few hospitals have had to close their doors—almost 150 community hospitals vanished between 1980 and 1986. At least half of the country's public hospitals, traditionally run by municipal or county governments for the care of the poor and uninsured, were running at a loss when the 1980s began, and their financial situations have steadily worsened. Almost a quarter of our privately run non-profit hospitals also reported they were running in the red. Even more chilling is the estimate that by the year 2000, 40 percent of American hospitals will be closed or converted to other uses.[23]

Rural hospitals are particularly vulnerable. Under the Medicare system, they are paid about 20 percent less than urban hospitals, on the theory that everything costs less in the boondocks. The result is that of the 150 hospital closures since 1980, eighty-six were in rural areas. And when a rural hospital closes it is a disaster. In some small towns it is the equivalent of losing the biggest employer. In terms of service it can be even worse. In six of the closures, the institution was the only one in the entire county.

The urban community hospital is usually the only hope for the poor and uninsured. These public hospitals have been stuck with the costs of uncompensated care at a rate more than double that of other hospitals. In the past those losses could be passed along in fee increases to paying patients—but no longer. Insurance now balks at paying hospitals on the old cost-plus basis, and in a mere six years, uncompensated care debts assumed by hospitals rose from $3.5 billion in 1980 to $8.4 billion in 1986. In highly regulated states, more and more hospitals are being forced to dip into their endowments simply to survive.

The bureaucracy strangling doctors is doing the same to hospitals. Large expensive staffs needed to handle billing contrast with the skeleton crews in Canadian hospitals (where most of them deal mostly with charges for visiting Americans). The U.S. government, and some state governments, continually monitor even the minutest details of hospital operation and subject them to the worst sort of bureaucratic nit-picking, including a citation because a doctor initialed a record instead of writing out his full name.

Insurance companies would seem unlikely victims of the present system since they appear to have such a vested interest in its maintenance. But they, too, have problems. Some health insurers are in real trouble—both small companies like Great Republic Insurance of California, with twenty-five thousand policyholders, recently seized by state regulators, and giants like Blue Cross-Blue Shield of New Jersey, covering nearly one-third of the state population. The latter has a deficit of $124 million and stands to lose the right to use the Blue Cross-Blue Shield name and insignia if it does not correct that condition. One strategy under consideration was to pressure the state to change its rules to allow the company to eliminate more of its poor health risks.[24]

The existence of a two-tiered health care system in the U.S. has been documented by several dramatic findings. A nationwide analysis of 600,000 hospital records by the Center for Health Policy Studies of Georgetown University School of Medicine revealed that hospital patients without insurance die at three times the rate of their insured countrymen. It found doctors less likely to order expensive or optional procedures for them. A Massachusetts study revealed that even in a state with an uncompensated care pool that picks up costs at public expense that insurers won't, the uninsured are far less likely to have access to three important (and expensive) techniques for coping with heart disease: angiography (a diagnostic test), coronary bypass surgery, and angioplasty (a non-surgical artery-reaming procedure).[25] Rationing of health care by financial consideration is clearly alive and well in the American health care system.

One reaction to this news was an editorial in the *Daily Utah Chronicle*, a student newspaper at the presumably conservative University of Utah. The following words ran cheek by jowl with ads urging students to become Naval officers and promoting the Temple and Family History Week of the Mormon Church: "...In a world where technological advances enable us not only to conduct 'advanced' wars in the distant sands of the Middle East but also to save and improve the lives of patients afflicted with a variety of ailments, there is no excuse for the indirect extermination of one segment of the population simply because it is unable to pay for insurance."[26]

13

There seems no end to the litany of discontent when Americans discuss health care. The elderly, whose problems were supposed to have vanished with Medicare, find they have to spend more and more of their fixed incomes on supplementary insurance to cover what the program omits. Talk about firestorms! Nothing in American public life quite matched the fury of the elderly when told that the well-off among them would have to pay for less fortunate seniors under provisions of the Catastrophic Illness Bill Congress passed and then hastened to repeal. The poor were supposed to have their needs met by Medicaid, but it is estimated that only 40 percent of them are presently covered.

Every day seems to bring headlines of new atrocities on the heath care front:

COURT BACKS CUT IN BENEFITS
FOR CATASTROPHIC ILLNESSES

HOSPITALS MAY GET AN ADDED
BURDEN ON MEDICARE BILLS

UTILITIES WANT RATES
TO COVER HEALTH COSTS

THE SHAME OF EMERGENCY CARE FOR KIDS

MENTAL HOSPITAL CHAINS ARE ACCUSED
OF CHEATING ON INSURANCE

A GROWING U.S. AFFLICTION:
WORTHLESS HEALTH POLICIES

DEBATE FLARES ON PHYSICIAN
EARNINGS FROM REFERRALS

SPENDING IN '91 ON HEALTH
CARE UP 11% IN U.S.

The situation grows progressively more untenable. Business is unhappy. Doctors are unhappy. Hospitals are unhappy. And hanging

14

over every one of us, save a handful of multimillionaires, is a terrible insecurity. What happens if I get sick? Or a member of my family does? Will a lifetime of hard work and savings be wiped out? Almost all of us know of someone who has had to shoulder intolerable financial burdens. Who will be next?

As cost-shifting continues unabated, with the Federal government repeatedly cutting Medicare and Medicaid and leaving others to pick up the differential, the result is a steep, never-ending rise in insurance rates. Consequently, more and more of us drop our coverage and this vicious cycle feeds on itself. Meanwhile, no effective mechanism exists to control providers' costs. Physicians raise their rates because their expenses climb. Expensive new technologies are promoted and must be paid for. We see our health care system in dire straits and believe that it cannot get any worse. And yet it does.

Cries for action come from all sides with increasing urgency. Payers, providers, consumers—all demand change.

How did we ever get ourselves into such a fix?

Why is it that our country is really the only industrialized nation on the planet without a universal health care system? Do we care less for our fellow countrymen? Are we out of step, or is the rest of the world wrong, while we alone are right?

A look into the American past sheds light on this puzzling state of affairs, and also indicates a possible path for the future.

2 HOW WE GOT WHERE WE ARE, PART I

THE BEGINNING

The world's first national health care system was the result of pure political cynicism. It happened in Germany, shortly after a hodge-podge of separate states was united under Prussia following a successful war with France. The author of this new law providing workers with sickness benefits was none other than the "Blood and Iron" chancellor of the new Reich, Otto von Bismarck. On November 17, 1881, Bismarck persuaded Kaiser Wilhelm I to proclaim a government plan for a series of measures to ease the life of Germany's industrial workers. The three measures were the forerunners of today's health insurance, workers' compensation, and social security.

Bismarck was not moved by any deep consideration for working men. The Prussian Junker was, even for those days, an arch conservative. His purpose was purely political; he wanted to head off what he considered the growing threat in Germany of socialism—a movement exemplified by the spectacular growth of the quasi-Marxist Social Democrat party. The Iron Chancellor had already bullied the Reichstag into enacting a group of laws repressing the Social Democrats, and had made it plain that he had no interest in measures that would alleviate workers' hours or working conditions, regulate child and female labor, or allow unions to organize. The bow to "state socialism," as he referred to it, was pure political opportunism.

The Sickness Insurance Law, enacted in 1883, protected most German workers, who paid into local "sickness funds" on a ratio of two-thirds to their employers' one-third. The law fixed payments for medical treatment, and sick pay was limited to thirteen weeks. The program was run by regional health bureaus to which workers could be elected.[1]

Bismarck's calculated liberalism didn't work. German socialism was not pre-empted. But the unintended consequences of his innovations were to echo through Europe and the United States during the years before World War I. For, according to Bismarck biographer Hajo Holborn, "it is certainly true that the very substantial health program removed much misery from the worker's life."[2]

In 1908, David Lloyd George, the fiery Welshman who was a leader of England's Liberal party, visited Germany and was impressed with the results of Bismarck's health care program. Three years later, as chancellor of the exchequer, he convinced Parliament to pass the British National Insurance Act, a pure copycat measure that secured compulsory health coverage for all British workers between sixteen and seventy who earned less than two pounds a week. While it was not quite as blatant a political sop as Bismarck's measure, the law was enacted in 1911, a year of unparalleled labor unrest in Britain, with almost one million workers on strike and over ten million working days lost. Even more to the point for Lloyd George, a new Labour party had come into being and was making gains. The Liberals had to do something.

Strife in coal mines, the transport industry, shipbuilding, railroads, etc. helped accelerate a new political strategy. Writing about the Health Insurance Act, the sardonic British historian George Dangerfield noted that "the Liberals produced [the bill] after a period of prolonged and difficult gestation in the gritty and inscrutable way of an oyster with a pearl," and added that it was "not designed to advance the worker, but to propitiate him."[3]

Under the act's provisions, for four pence a week, workers would receive medical, sickness, disability, maternity, and sanatorium benefits. Dependents weren't covered, but were urged to buy insurance from the newly established voluntary insurance companies, who were also given the right under law to administer the program. This was part one of the law, which went into effect in July 1912. Part two, an experimental scheme of unemployment insurance restricted to certain trades, did not go on line until 1920. The Liberals were disappointed when workers—as they had been in Germany in Bismarck's time—were unimpressed. They wanted wage increases more than health care coverage.

Despite the lack of political success, Bismarck's idea took hold, and by the outbreak of World War I, ten European nations had adopted some form of compulsory health insurance.[4]

AMERICA'S "FIRST WAVE"

Interest in a health care program was also rising in America. The same after-effects of industrialization that were changing Europe were at work in the United States—if anything, they were even more pronounced. In America, unregulated capitalism, and the conditions it brought, created not the great wave of socialism that convulsed Europe, but a backlash of reformism that led to "the Progressive Era," the decade before World War I. One historian of the times, Mark Sullivan, preferred to call the period "the Roosevelt Era," in acknowledgment of the impact of ex-President Theodore Roosevelt.[5] In 1912, Teddy returned to the political arena as the candidate of the new Progressive party he had helped found after being denied the Republican presidential nomination. Part of his appeal was based on a European-style health plan.

The Progressive platform, adopted at its Chicago convention on August 7, 1912, contained the following plank: "The protection of home life against the hazards of sickness, irregular employment and old age through the adoption of a system of social insurance adapted to American use."[6]

The night before the platform was adopted, Teddy Roosevelt included the following plug for that plank in a rousing speech to the delegates: "What Germany has done in the way of old-age pensions or insurance should be studied by us, and the system adapted to our uses."[7]

Roosevelt was continuing what he had already started. Both as governor of New York and as president of the United States, he had overcome strong resistance from business interests and pushed through workers' compensation laws. The endorsement of health insurance by the Progressive party was to be the first recognition of the need of such a program by any major political party in the U.S.

The Progressives, however, were not the first Americans to seek a health insurance program. An effort had already been underway for at least a half-dozen years. In 1906, a group of economists, political scientists, and statisticians organized the American Association for Labor Legislation with precisely that intent. The Russell Sage Foundation financed a trip for them to Europe to study the effects of Bismarck's program. The result was the publication of *Workingmen's Insurance in Europe,* which added impetus to the AALL effort. Despite Roosevelt's defeat in 1912, the AALL soon afterward went ahead and formally launched its drive by creating a Committee of Social Insurance. Included on it were Dr. Isaac M. Rubinow, a prominent member of the American Medical Association, and Dr. Alexander Lambert, who was one day to become the AMA's president. Dr. Lambert had also been Teddy Roosevelt's personal physician, and was said to be the guiding force behind the universal health insurance plank in the Progressive party platform.

The AALL was determined to create a model bill in favor of compulsory health insurance. It took them three years to draft standards, and by 1916 the proposed legislation was ready. It covered all employed persons earning less than twelve hundred dollars a year; made provision for other workers to join; took care of all medical, surgical, and nursing costs for up to twenty-six weeks; and offered maternity benefits and even funeral expenses.

Support for the AALL plan grew quickly. Governors Hiram W. Johnson of California and Samuel W. McCall of Massachusetts immediately jumped on the bandwagon, along with several key labor leaders. Two unlikely organizations—the National Convention of State Insurance Commissioners and the National Association of Manufacturers—had committees endorse the proposal even though their reports were never accepted by their parent groups. The New York State Medical Society was initially in favor of the plan and they, along with the AMA—eventually to be among the fiercest opponents of any form of national health care—became virtual allies of the movement!

The AMA had been loosely organized in 1847, and had already been on the scene for more than half a century. It became active in politics in 1899, when it opened a lobbying office in Washington, D.C. Initially there was a definite "progressive" cast to its activities, and it played a leading role in urging passage of the Pure Food and Drug Act of 1906. The AMA also worked closely with Dr. Abraham Flexner, whose 1910 report resulted in significant revamping and

19

upgrading of medical education in the nation.

The symbiosis between the AMA and the AALL in the promotion of compulsory health insurance received a major boost at the 1915 AMA convention in San Francisco. Until then the *Journal of the American Medical Association (JAMA)* had been printing reports from a London correspondent who wrote disparagingly about the result of Britain's health insurance law. But Dr. Lambert, addressing the San Francisco convention, presented an entirely different outlook. He reported that not only had millions of Britons received adequate health care for the first time, but, of even more interest, the incomes of British physicians had increased by anywhere from the equivalent of $750 to $2,000 a year. The very next year, a report presented by Dr. Rubinow's committee to the AMA's highest body, the House of Delegates, strongly endorsed a compulsory rather than a voluntary health insurance system.

When the AALL bill was introduced in state legislatures, *JAMA* called it it "the inauguration of a great movement."[8] This "Standard Bill" was eventually presented in fifteen states between 1916 and 1920, and nine of those states created commissions to study the issue. Five reported favorably on the idea of compulsory health insurance. Even Congress scheduled hearings on the subject in 1916.

But opposition was growing. Until this time, the commercial insurance industry had barely dipped a toe into the waters of health insurance. Their first move was in 1911, when group coverage was offered for accident and sickness for large industrial populations. That policy was usually connected to life insurance. There was also some self-insuring by a few industries, railroads, unions, and fraternal organizations. And there were even experimental prepaid HMO-type plans at Johns Hopkins and the Massachusetts General Hospital.

Small as their stake was, the powerful insurance companies wanted to protect their possible futures, and so they led the fight against any American adoption of European plans for universal health care. A.E. Forrest, President of the Health and Accident Underwriters Conference, blasted the idea at a 1917 social work conference as "a compulsory, communistic system that is repugnant to American minds and destructive of American initiative and individuality."[9] The Prudential Life Insurance Company added its august voice as well.

Most surprising, however, was the vociferous opposition of the country's leading labor leader, American Federation of Labor chief Samuel Gompers. At times the venerable labor pioneer sounded apoplectic as he damned the entire concept of compulsory health insurance. In his testimony before a Congressional committee considering a national insurance fund, Gompers railed, "I would rather help in the inauguration of a revolution against compulsory insurance..."[10]

The depth of opposition of this gruff English-born offspring of Dutch Jews, who had emigrated to New York as a boy, can be glimpsed in the title of a 1916 AFL publication: *Voluntary Social Insurance vs. Compulsion: Shall the Toilers Surrender Their Freedom for a Few Crumbs?*[11]

To this day Gompers is quoted by opponents of national health care. Dr. Harry Gross, in a 1983 polemic, *National Health Insurance: A Pragmatic Perspective,*[12] quotes the labor leader as asking, "Is it wise to open up opportunities for government agents to interfere lawfully with the privacy of wage earners?" Gross then notes, almost gleefully, that the AFL Executive Committee in 1916 voted unanimously against compulsory health insurance.

By way of explanation, the pioneer labor leader also opposed old age pensions and workers' compensation. He did not like to see the labor movement taking a legislative route to realize its aims. His experience had been that laws ostensibly passed to help workers were too often turned around by the courts and used to bash unions. The prime example had been the 1890 Sherman Antitrust Act, which had come within an ace of putting the AFL out of business. Finally, from a personal point of view, the labor leader had been raised in the dog-eat-dog world of New York's lower east side, had trained as a cigar-maker, and was a relatively uneducated man who mistrusted and scorned the academics promoting the AALL legislation.

In time voices were raised within the AMA in opposition to doctors Lambert and Rubinow. Eden V. Delphey, a New York physician, wrote a blistering attack on the AALL bill in *JAMA,* listing eighteen objections to compulsory health insurance. The journal also printed, in 1917, a letter from Frederick L. Hoffman, chief statistician of the Prudential Life Insurance Company, claiming the health level of Americans was as good as that in European nations with compulsory insurance. Therefore, such a program was "wholly unnecessary."

American entry into World War I added a new dimension to the discussion. Since the entire concept had been fathered by Bismarck, critics could now attack the idea as "pro-German" and "anti-American." It would mean, according to a participant at an Ohio Hospital Association meeting, the "Germanizing of American medical care."

Internally the AMA position slowly changed. Dr. Rubinow was eased out of his position and replaced by an outspoken opponent, Dr. Malcolm L. Harris. The extent of the change in the AMA attitude can be seen in the fact that in 1918 the organization had supported a $1.24 billion Federal grant to the states for infant and maternal care, but three years later, in 1921, such programs were called "a form of federal bureaucratic interference with the sacred rights of the American home." At their 1920 convention, AMA delegates resolved to strenuously oppose any form of compulsory health insurance, reputedly chanting "Get Lambert" as they voted.

The AALL Standard Bill failed to pass any state legislature. Its 1920 defeat in the last of them, New York, is seen as the last gasp of the "first wave"—the initial concerted effort to bring national health care to the United States.

THE FDR YEARS

In an introduction to an attack on national health insurance, John Goodman, Director of the Center for Health Policy Studies at the University of Dallas, warned (in 1980) that the issue "threatens to be a recurring specter" on the political scene.[13]

And so it has been, rising phoenix-like from the ashes of each defeat it has suffered since it first surfaced during the Progressive Era.

The second wave of activism reached its height in 1935, interest in it spurred by the Great Depression. Franklin Roosevelt was in the White House grappling with the monumental problems resulting from an economic collapse that left 28 percent of the workforce unemployed. His frenetic "one hundred days" at the start of his administration created a mixed bag of programs—some successful and popular, like the Civilian Conservation Corps (CCC), others of doubtful efficacy, like the soon-to-be-declared-unconstitutional National Recovery Act (NRA).

"Franklin had become convinced," wrote one member of his "brain trust," Rexford Tugwell, "that the shaking up people had experienced repeatedly during the past five years had induced a longing for certainty that transcended all other desires."[14] FDR's reply to that longing was Social Security—"the broadly appealing issue," according to Tugwell, "which, in spite of disappointments with NRA, AAA, and PWA, carried conviction that Franklin would keep trying until he found the means for ensuring permanent well-being for the people of the United States." FDR was also feeling congressional pressure as a result of the Townsend Plan, a scheme concocted by a California physician that would distribute two hundred dollars a month to every American over age sixty.

Social Security could be stretched to include a compulsory health insurance plan to cover the millions of Americans no longer able to pay for health care. The idea appealed to Roosevelt. He turned to Frances Perkins, his secretary of labor, the nation's first woman cabinet member, and entrusted her with the formulation of the Social Security program.

Frances Perkin's Cabinet Committee on Economic Security included an advisory council. Part of that group was a Medical Advisory Board, and it was understood by all that the parlous state of the country's health services was certain to be a topic of major consideration.

That American health care was in bad shape had already been documented by what was considered the most comprehensive study ever made on the subject. It was the work of the Committee on the Costs of Medical Care (CCMC), appointed in 1927 by Calvin Coolidge and funded privately by a consortium of eight foundations. Five years of work had produced no less than twenty-eight reports, and they concluded that no one in the country was receiving enough health care, not even those who could easily afford it. Even before the market crash in 1929 and the onset of the depression, 25 percent of patients in the country were unable to pay for their care. Doctor-patient ratios and the availability of hospital beds were woefully inadequate in many states.

With the CCMC report as a base, Perkins and her group debated what to do about the issue as part of Social Security. FDR told the group, in a November 15, 1934, meeting, that health insurance would be highly desirable.[15] But when Perkins, in a radio speech, hinted that health insurance was being considered, the AMA took the offensive. The president was bombarded with calls and telegrams opposing the idea, and the Perkins Committee reluctantly retreated. Harry

Hopkins, head of the WPA and close advisor to FDR, had been the loudest advocate of national health insurance, but had to be content with a weak recommendation for a "study" of the subject. Yet even this mildest of suggestions drew such heavy political fire that it, too, was eventually deleted.

Dr. Morris Fishbein, the ultraconservative editor of *JAMA*, credits famed neurosurgeon Harvey Cushing with having swayed Roosevelt. Cushing's daughter was married to the president's son, and despite the fact the two fathers were of different political parties, they maintained a close personal relationship. A member of Perkins's Medical Advisory Committee, Cushing was no fan of universal health insurance, but nowhere near as reactionary as Fishbein and other AMA rightwingers. He warned that the doctors' lobby had to prepare a positive response to the issue.

The AMA ignored Cushing. It called an extraordinary special session of its House of Delegates less than a month after the Social Security bill was sent to Congress and sought vainly to strike Federal aid for child and maternal health from the law. The extremes of AMA power were exerted against Albert G. Milbank, Chairman of the Board of the Borden Company. His Milbank Fund had financed studies of preventive medicine, and the fund's director had criticized the AMA for its position on Social Security. In response the word went out advising doctors to stop recommending Borden's evaporated milk for babies. Milbank caved in; he fired the director of the fund and denied he had ever endorsed any kind of health insurance.

For the rest of his administration, FDR's position on health insurance was, at best, uneven. In July of 1938 he organized a National Health Conference to consider yet another committee's report detailing the nation's unmet health needs. Enthused by the conference's call for compulsory health insurance, FDR tentatively gave support to a bill by New York senator Robert F. Wagner, Sr., which incorporated a variation of the proposal. But with the 1940 election approaching, the president soon withdrew his support and let the Wagner Bill die.

In 1943 another Wagner Bill, this time co-sponsored by Montana's Senator James E. Murray and Representative John E. Dingell of Michigan, also failed to get strong White House support. FDR's announced position was that he planned to put the issue on the back burner and push for national health care once the war was won.

TRUMAN AND BEYOND

On November 19, 1945, President Harry S. Truman delivered a health message to Congress. The Missourian had been chief executive for about seven months and made no bones at all about what he wanted: expansion of Social Security to include medical insurance.

Four times during his speech he emphasized that his plan was not socialized medicine. He stated, "Socialized medicine means that all doctors work as employees of the government. The American people want no such system. No such system is here proposed." Truman added his belief that the American people were the most insurance-minded in the world, and would not be "frightened off from health insurance because some people have misnamed it 'socialized medicine.'"[16]

In his optimism, Harry Truman woefully underestimated the AMA.

It was not until his come-from-behind re-election in 1948 that the AMA began to worry in earnest about Truman's intentions. The AMA had a front group in Washington, the National Physicians Committee. It had been set up to lobby, to propagandize, and to safeguard the AMA's tax-exempt status. Now it took on a new challenge, and spent $1 million over seven years to brand national health insurance as "socialized medicine."

NPC methods were often crude and distorted. In a pamphlet attacking one of the Wagner-Murray-Dingell bills, they screamed that the issue was one of "human rights as opposed to slavery." With typical exaggeration, they titled their effort *Abolishing Private Medical Practice or $13,048,000,000 of Political Medicine Yearly in the United States*. They bought ads in *Editor and Publisher* and *Publisher's Auxiliary* magazines, offering three thousand dollars to cartoonists who would pillory the idea of national health insurance. That effort drew strong unfavorable comment even from the magazines that carried the ads. But their biggest gaffe was to pay three thousand dollars for a letter from a Reverend Dan Gilbert which was circulated to AMA members and thousands of Protestant clergymen. What the AMA did not know, until too late, was that Gilbert had been associated with the notorious anti-Semite William Dudley Pelley and his fascist Silver Shirts.

Before long the respected public relations firm of Rich and Associates resigned the AMA account because they would not tone down their hysterical attacks. The doctor's group then turned to of Clem Whitaker and Leone Baxter, a California husband-wife PR team. They were hired a month after Truman's re-election in expectation of a hard push for national health care.

Whitaker and Baxter were no neophytes. They'd helped defeat California governor Earl Warren's proposed bill for universal health care—this despite the fact that the two had earlier helped run Warren's campaign for governor. Provided with insurance company funding, they had helped create an unprecedented avalanche of advertising and unremitting pressure on media and lawmakers, which had paid off in 1945 when Warren's bill failed by a single vote.

Whitaker and Baxter knew the campaign they had to wage for the AMA was going to be difficult—and expensive. Truman was back in office and effectively using a Federal Security Administration report revealing that 325,000 Americans were dying needlessly every year for lack of health care. Prior to Whitaker and Baxter, the AMA had no better answer to Truman's charge of unnecessary deaths than the general and unsatisfying statement that "the true measure of medical progress is not how many die, but how long they live before they die." And, on top of this, the British, with international fanfare, had just instituted their all-encompassing National Health Service.

Preparing to do battle, the California PR firm moved to the Chicago headquarters of the AMA and hired a staff of thirty-seven. The AMA raised money for the battle by levying a twenty-five-dollar tax on every member. Those who resisted paying the levy were soon in trouble with local medical societies who controlled licenses.

The result was a war chest of $2.25 million. It paid for 55 million pamphlets that warned: "Guard your health, guard your pocketbook, socialized medicine would rob both." There were also ninety thousand posters showing a kindly bearded doctor treating a sickly little girl and captioned, "Keep politics out of this picture." Other materials included a fabricated slogan attributed to Lenin claiming, "Socialized medicine is the keystone of the arch of the socialist state."

The AMA's PR gurus were smart enough not to rely solely on negatives. Their strategy became instrumental in affecting a major change in the financing of American health care when they convinced their masters to support *voluntary* health insurance. Until then the AMA had opposed group hospitalization plans such as Blue Cross-Blue Shield. Morris Fishbein had set the tone when he referred to them as "medical soviets." Now, under the slogan "The Voluntary Way is the American Way," the AMA dropped its opposition and even gave support to such plans. As a result, the 1940s saw an 89 percent increase in enrollment in hospitalization plans, to 66 million.

Not content with having made passage of a health bill politically impossible, the AMA sent their PR team out to get their enemies in the 1950 elections. Spending generously, they helped defeat Senator Claude Pepper in a Florida primary and replaced Senate Majority Leader Scott Lucas of Illinois with conservative Everett Dirksen.

Turning their attention inward, Whitaker and Baxter polished the AMA image, presenting their employers as a modern, up-to-date organization. As part of their program, they forced the retirement of *JAMA's* curmudgeon editor Fishbein, long the spokesman for American doctors.

Beaten on the legislative front, the stubborn Truman did not surrender. He set his staff to finding a less comprehensive means of dealing with health care—one that would be less vulnerable to frontal attack. A new strategy was devised by two executives at Social Security, I.S. Falk and Wilbur Cohen. Their plan was to provide sixty days of free hospital care to those sixty-five or older already covered by Social Security.

From the ashes of defeat Truman became the father of Medicare. The program would not come to pass during his administration, but the old fighter from Missouri would live to see the concept signed into law.

JFK AND MEDICARE

The sixth plank in the 1960 Democratic Party Platform called for "the right to adequate medical care and opportunity to achieve and enjoy good health." More specifically, it also stated, "We shall provide medical care benefits for the aged as part of the time-tested Social Security insurance system. We reject any proposal, which would require such citizens to submit to the indignity of a means test—a 'pauper's oath.'"

Once in the White House, President John F. Kennedy sought to make good on the Democrats' promise. He chose Lincoln's Birthday in 1961 to ask Congress "to set up a system of health insurance for the aged tied to Social Security."

The issue had not been totally dormant since Truman's days. While the intervening Eisenhower years had seen no major presidential initiatives, Congress had not been idle. Representative Aime Forand of Rhode Island had been pushing since 1957 for a modified version of the Falk-Cohen plan, and had slowly gathered support—or at least promises of neutrality—from formerly hostile groups such as the American Nurses Association and the American Hospital Association.

The *New York Times* commented that "health insurance was easily the number one issue in the 1960 session and it provoked some of the most intense lobbying ... to be seen in years," and that Forand had become a household word.[17] The day before Kennedy's announcement, the *Times* had editorialized about the cost of Blue Cross insurance, increases totaling 33.4 percent and 26.9 percent in two years.

Like Truman, Kennedy made it clear that his program was not socialized medicine. "It is a program of prepayment of health costs with absolute freedom of choice guaranteed. Every person will choose his own doctor and hospital."

Response was swift. Less than a week later, on February 18, 1961, a *Times* headline read:

AMA MAPS FIGHT
ON AGED-CARE BILL

Calling the Kennedy proposal "the most deadly challenge ever faced by the medical profession," the AMA announced a campaign in its usual hyperbolic fashion, beginning with posters reading "Socialized Medicine and You," to be placed in every doctor's office. They gathered allies: Arthur Motley, president of the national Chamber of Commerce, announced to the annual luncheon of the Group Insurance Forum of the Health Insurance Association of America (no doubt to ringing cheers from the four hundred assembled members) the strong opposition of the business community to the president's proposal.

The familiar pattern repeated itself, but Kennedy was prepared to fight. In May of 1962, he spoke to a giant rally in New York's Madison Square Garden supporting Medicare. It was one of thirty-three such rallies held simultaneously across the country. The president said he considered health care the only item in his "New Frontier" program that could compare in magnitude with the issues confronted by the New Deal. He openly expressed his disappointment over his failure to push the program through Congress. Yet, as biographer Arthur Schlesinger, Jr. wrote, "I doubt whether he really counted on getting Medicare in 1961 or 1962."[18] More likely dates were 1964 or 1965.

The Kennedy assassination in Dallas on November 22, 1963, put an end to all JFK timetables.

Much has been made of the skill with which JFK's successor, Lyndon Johnson, manipulated public sentiment for the martyred president into a successful package of "Great Society" measures. One of those was Medicare, enacted within the purported Kennedy timetable, in 1965. But it was no easy matter, nor was the end product the simple measure envisaged when New Mexico Senator Clinton B. Anderson and California Representative Cecil King introduced the original bill for the late president.

The problem was the House of Representatives, and the autocratic chairman of its Ways and Means Committee, Wilbur Mills. The Anderson-King Bill passed the Senate in 1964, but was held by Mills in a House-Senate committee. The chairman had his own agenda, embodied in a bill that had been enacted in 1960, at the end of the Eisenhower administration. The Kerr-Mills Act provided Federal grants to the states to subsidize health care for indigent elderly who could not meet their medical expenses. It was the inspiration of the pledge in the 1960 platform that the Democratic health program would not include "means tests" or "pauper's oaths," since such were included in the Kerr-Mills Act. It was also a program that the AMA, despite some grumbling, had accepted.

The logjam was broken by the 1964 presidential election. Not only did Johnson trounce Barry Goldwater, but Democrats made significant gains in Congress (forty-four new House members alone). The new members of the House Ways and Means Committee provided a majority for Medicare, and the politically astute Mills promptly changed his position.

The importance attached to Medicare by the Johnson administration is underlined by the fact that the legislation became the first bill on the Congressional docket in the new term. On January 7, 1965, LBJ publicly called for passage of the Anderson-King Bill, and a cooperative Wilbur Mills promised swift action.

While the AMA had not been idle, the organization had lost some of its clout. Working through a new front, the American Medical Political Action Committee (AMPAC), it frequently found itself in trouble. AMPAC was successfully sued for misidentifying a United Steelworkers Union executive in one attack, and was caught using false financial figures in its advertising. Perhaps the biggest mistake of the AMA, the one that lost it a great deal of credibility, was the acceptance of a $10 million grant from leading cigarette manufacturers to study the effects of smoking on health—a study planned in response to the Surgeon General's report of January 1964, linking heart disease to smoking.

Congressional hearings soon established that the Kerr-Mills Act was not an effective substitute for Medicare. The law had been in effect for four years and was still being used by only twenty-eight states. The AMA hurriedly came up with its own alternative, "Eldercare." This was a Federal-state program to subsidize private health insurance for the elderly. It failed, but a similar bill was sponsored by John W. Byrnes of Wisconsin, the ranking minority party member of the House Ways and Means Committee. The Byrnes plan, labeled "Bettercare," was pre-empted by Mills in favor of the package eventually reported out of his committee.

The three-part result of Mills's effort was the genesis of modern Medicare and Medicaid. It contained the following provisions:

1. The original Anderson-King provisions for hospitalization benefits for the elderly through Social Security—now Medicare, Part A.
2. The Byrnes "Bettercare" proposal to pay physicians' costs for the elderly—now Medicare, Part B.
3. An expanded Kerr-Mills Federal-state program to pick up the medical expenses of the poor—now Medicaid.

On April 8, 1965, the House approved the measure and gave Wilbur Mills a standing ovation. On July 9, the Senate approved its version. On July 28, it became law.

For the formal bill signing, Lyndon Johnson made a particularly nice gesture. Instead of signing the bill in Washington, he decided at the last minute to fly to Independence, Missouri, to share the moment with ex-President Truman. Wilbur Cohen, then undersecretary of the

Department of Health, Education and Welfare, protested. He thought it would be chaotic to fly all those who planned to attend the signing to Missouri. Besides, holding the ceremony with Truman would be a reminder of his much more radical plan for national health insurance. LBJ would not be deterred. "Why, Wilbur," he is reported to have said, "don't you understand? I'm doing this for Harry Truman. He's old and he's tired and he's been left all alone down there. I want him to know that his country has not forgotten him." Then the Texan added ruefully, and perhaps clairvoyantly, "I wonder if anyone will do the same for me."[19]

Whatever future political problems denied LBJ a second term, the Medicare-Medicaid package was not among them. It was considered a magnificient achievement. It was also a watershed. For better or worse, American medical care was never to be the same again.

3 HOW WE GOT WHERE WE ARE, PART II

THE EARLY SEVENTIES

The operative word concerning health care in the 1970s was "crisis." President Richard M. Nixon set the tone six months before the decade began at a July 10, 1969, press conference, where he declared, "We face a massive crisis in this area ... Unless action is taken within the next two or three years ... we will have a breakdown in our medical system."[1] Prestigious business magazines like *Business Week* and *Fortune* published articles detailing problems in the American health care system so serious as to merit being called "on the brink of chaos" and demanding "radical change."

A poll showed that 75 percent of those interviewed agreed with the statement, "There is a crisis in health care in the United States."

What had gone wrong?

Medicare and Medicaid had been passed into law and were in operation, providing health care to millions of Americans—the aged and the poor—who had received few or no services in the past.

If some pundits complained that these government programs of unprecedented scope were "too little, too late," others wrote that they were "too much, too fast."

The single inescapable fact—the one most responsible for the sense of crisis—was that medical costs were skyrocketing. In the seven years prior to Medicare, costs had risen at an annual rate of 3.2 percent; during the next five years this rate more than doubled, to 7.9 percent. Nationally, health care expenditures of $198 per capita rose to $336 per capita. Hospitals, in particular, were victims of an explosive increase: After Medicare, their expenditures grew by 14 percent a year.

At the same time, hospitals—as Rosemary Stevens put it in her exhaustive study of American hospitals—"appeared to be gaining as much from the programs as were the elderly patients who were saving money on hospital bills."[2] The fault seemed to lie with the reimbursement procedures of the new government programs. They paid hospitals on the basis of cost. Simply put, the higher the hospital overhead costs, the more the hospital received.

Medicare also helped to spawn an entirely new development in America: investor-owned, for-profit hospital chains. By 1970 there were twenty-nine such organizations, the largest of which was American Medicorp Inc. with thirty-one hospitals. Right behind them in size was Hospital Corporation of America with twenty-three institutions. In the 1970s such organizations were among the country's major growth industries.

Another big winner because of Medicare was Blue Cross-Blue Shield. The law allowed hospitals participating in Part A to choose a "fiscal intermediary" for administration. The overwhelming majority chose Blue Cross. Indeed, at this date, the umbilical cord between the specialized insurer and the hospitals had not been cut. Blue Cross had gotten its start at Baylor University Hospital in Texas in 1929, and one of its original primary purposes had been to help hospitals fill their beds and thus survive the Great Depression. In addition, under Medicare, Part B, insurance "carriers" could be chosen to funnel government funds to physicians. Blue Cross came away with the lion's share of those contracts, too.

Physicians also did well, getting their share of the massive infusion of government dollars. "The doctors especially benefited," wrote Ed Cray in his book *In Failing Health, The Medical Crisis and the AMA*.[3] He cited the prediction-come-true of one of the AMA House of Delegates listening to anti-Medicare attacks: "The fools. It's a gold mine for most of them and they haven't realized it yet." Four years after the passage of Medicare, Dr. Edward Annis, an AMA president, admitted to Wilbur Cohen that he would not advocate its repeal.

Between 1960 and 1970, Blue Cross rates rose 202 percent. But causes of the crisis went far deeper than the extraordinary increases in costs. A fundamental change in the American health care system had taken place since the passage of Medicare-Medicaid. Like an insidious cancer, it had gone unnoticed until it burst forth in full magnitude.

Our current system, with all its built-in structural flaws—its competing special interests, its emphasis on high technology and continual innovation, its unstoppable rising costs and shrinking coverages—had taken shape by the beginning of the 1970s. So-called "health empires," built around medical schools and teaching hospitals, began to dominate the health care field. They had replaced in the public mind the comfortable image of the old-fashioned, fee-for-practice doctor and the cozy, not-for-profit hospital, both of which could usually be counted on not to turn away those unable to pay for their care. In place of these familiar institutions was a "medical-industrial complex," where giant drug companies poured millions into research, then millions more into the promotion and marketing of the high-cost medicines they had created. Medical technology companies perfected sophisticated diagnostic machines and procedures—far more efficient than older equipment, but immensely costly—and they, too, tacked sales costs onto their products. The computer revolution hit at the same time, and, burdened by mountains of paperwork, the providers bought into these innovative systems. By the time the dust of change had settled, the entire health care system had been transformed forever. While none of these players were new, they had always been subservient to the dominance of the AMA. Now they were suddenly many giants, operating sometimes in conjunction with one another, sometimes in conflict. What had happened was a "metastasis" of health care, a spreading of malignancies whose effects are being felt today.

The 1970s were a time of awakening, when we first heard the health care vocabulary used today: "crisis," "costs out of control," "number of uninsured." We commenced experiencing the despairing sense of a vital system gone haywire. Viewed from the vantage point of the 1990s, however, it appears in miniature—a scene observed as if through the wrong end of a telescope. American health care expenditures had gone from an awesome $69 billion in 1970 to an unbelievable $230 billion by the close of that decade. But even those staggering figures are dwarfed by the unthinkable $700 to 800 billion we spend today. Health care's portion of the GNP rose from 7.2 percent to 9.4 percent in the decade ending in 1980. Those jolted by such figures can barely accept that it is presently at 12 percent, and predicted to rise to 15 percent unless action is taken at once. More than twenty-four million Americans were without health insurance in the 1970s and it was a scandal. How much more disgraceful to realize that twenty years later the figure has risen to perhaps as high as forty million. If Richard Nixon could declare a "crisis" in health care at the beginning of the 1970s and attempt, conservative that he was, to bring it to the attention of the nation, surely there is an imperative to learn why matters have gotten worse—much worse—after two decades of attempting to cope with the problem.

When it came to health care, Nixon admitted, in his autobiography, to having something of a soft spot for the problem, based on his childhood experiences when his father was forced to sell off property to pay the medical expenses of his older brother, who died early of tuberculosis. The young Nixon watched the family struggle, and ever after described himself as "a strong advocate of government leadership in helping people bear health care costs and helping scientists fight dread diseases."[4]

In February of 1974, to the consternation of virtually his entire inner circle, Nixon declared that "national health insurance is an idea whose time has come in America." More shocking still, his secretary of Health, Education and Welfare, the budget-cutting Caspar Weinberger, backed the president.

In essence the administration was proposing coverage for everyone, using private insurance for those employed and a government-run program for the rest. The key was that everyone would receive the same benefits. As a deductible, everyone would have to pay 25 percent of his or her bill, up to fifteen hundred dollars.

In the beginning of the 1970s, in response to the "crisis" cited by Nixon, a flurry of old national health care proposals reappeared. The "third wave" was underway. In their muckraking 1970 book *The American Health Empire*,[5] Barbara and John Ehrenreich describe three alternate national health plans of the time: the AMA plan, the Nelson Rockefeller plan, and the Walter Reuther plan.

The AMA plan was predictable. Called "Medicredit," it depended on tax credits to provide individuals with an incentive to buy health insurance. The poor would receive government vouchers for the same purpose. Needless to say, the plan included no cost controls on providers.

The Rockefeller plan was compulsory. Employers and employees would both contribute to the cost of mandatory private health insurance. The uninsured would have their premiums paid by the government out of general tax revenues. Medicare would continue. No doubt Rockefeller intended the Federal government to be the prime source of funding since the 1969 Governor's Conference overwhelmingly endorsed the plan. It was also favorably considered by the American Hospital Association.

The Reuther plan was just what might be expected from the United Auto Workers Union leader. It required compulsory health insurance for everyone, with the government supplanting the private sector as the insurer. Two thirds of the financing would come from employer-employee contributions and the rest from general tax revenues. Medicare would be folded into the program and Medicaid eliminated.

With every part of the political spectrum represented, from GOP conservatives like Nixon and Weinberger to Republican moderates like Nelson Rockefeller and New York's Senator Jacob Javits (who teamed up with Wilbur Cohen) to Democratic conservatives like Representative Wilbur Mills and liberals like Walter Reuther and later Senator Edward Kennedy—all promoting some form of national health care—it seemed that the 1970s would inevitably witness at last the emergence of an American national health care program. Yet, once again, nothing happened.

So short is the national memory that few today remember that Nixon, Weinberger, Rockefeller, Mills, and Reuther all championed national health care. If any of the activists of those days are remembered, it is probably Senator Kennedy, still active in the pursuit of the concept.

The youngest brother of President John Kennedy has a long history of support for national health care. It began before the start of the 1970s, when he introduced legislation to implement the Reuther plan. He then teamed with Representative Martha W. Griffiths of Michigan in 1970 to produce the Health Security Bill, legislation which followed the sense of the Reuther plan and included budget restraints for providers and incentives for prepaid group practice.

Prepaid group practice was a concept also proposed by the Nixon administration. Under the heading of "health maintenance organizations" (HMOs), such practices had become acceptable—particularly to free-market exponents—because they were seen as businesses that operated outside of government purview and they blended insurance and medical care. It was obvious that the days were long past when the AMA, which had never liked the HMO concept, could tarnish them with the label of "medical soviets."

Early in 1971, acting on his perception of the need for national health insurance, Nixon chose HMOs to be the centerpiece of his strategy. He called for $45 million in planning grants and loans to encourage such group practices. The goal was to increase the thirty existing HMO's to seventeen hundred by 1976. Republicans hoped that by the turn of the century the HMO's would be serving 90 percent of Americans. It did not take long for Nixon to realize the hopelessness of such an eventuality.

Meanwhile, Ted Kennedy, facing strong opposition to the Kennedy-Griffiths bill and competition from Nixon's Comprehensive Health Insurance Act, sought a compromise. He allied himself with a new bill, the Comprehensive National Health Insurance Act, which was not dissimilar to the president's. Organized labor would not go along. It still wanted the original Reuther-type measure, still strongly backed by Martha Griffiths. With the Watergate scandal breaking and the possibility of a liberal sweep in the 1974 congressional elections, they saw no reason to compromise.

1974 was Pickett's Charge for the champions of national health care—the high-water mark of their efforts. They came heartbreakingly close to achieving their objective, only to be undone by a combination of Watergate, the scandal surrounding Congressman Wilbur Mills, political infighting, and too many false expectations.

Replacing Nixon in the White House, President Gerald Ford asked for passage of national health insurance in his first message to Congress. It was not a serious request, merely a pro forma bow to his deposed predecessor. Two years later, in his State of the Union address, Ford withdrew his support, swayed by the arguments of treasury secretary William Simon, who had convinced the president that such an act would be "an unmitigated disaster that could bankrupt the country."[6]

While the "third wave" of enthusiasm for national health care rose and fell, regulation was entering the equation. It began on the state level with "certificate of need" programs designed to limit runaway hospital construction, unnecessary acquisition of expensive equipment, and the proliferation of nursing homes. An initial impetus for such programs had actually come from the American Hospital

Association, anxious to limit competition; it was a move the AHA would come to regret bitterly. By 1972, twenty states had created bodies to give or deny permission to hospitals and nursing homes for any expansion or capital construction.

On the Federal level there were amendments to the Social Security Act in 1972 that gave the Department of Health, Education and Welfare the power to deny full Medicare reimbursement for hospital and nursing home capital improvements not approved by planning agencies.

Another new wrinkle was the emergence of PSROs. These Professional Standard Review Organizations were legally authorized groups of physicians mandated to review the work of their peers and determine whether any of their colleagues had abused the Medicaid system. Significantly, the bill creating PSROs had been fathered by the strongly conservative Utah Republican, Wallace Bennett, who saw it as a way to save money. Although modified by the AMA, the measure was denounced by right-wing doctors as an unwonted intrusion on the practice of medicine, and by liberals who perceived it as having the fox guard the henhouse.

With Congress obsessed by planning, a new system was created under the National Health Planning and Resource Development Act. A host of new acronyms cropped up on the health scene: HSAs, SHPDAs, SHCCs—all various boards that turned out to be merely advisory and toothless, but added new layers to the bureaucracy and churned out mountains of paper.

The one effective mechanism put in place during this period was the Nixon freeze on wages and prices. These controls remained on health care costs more than a year longer than on the rest of the economy until, at the end of April 1974, they were removed. During their lifetime (beginning in August 1971), they managed to hold increases in the price of medical services to 4.9 percent—actually lower than the 5.2 percent average for the rest of the economy. Once the controls were lifted, health care costs shot up at an alarming rate—12.1 percent for the remainder of 1974—a rate they maintained the following year.

True to expectations, the Watergate aftermath saw large Democratic gains in Congress and the election of a Democratic president. But a combination of economic recession and spiraling inflation—as well as infighting among the Democrats themselves—made it impossible to make any progress toward national health care. Democratic Presidential candidate Jimmy Carter pledged his support for the concept all during his 1976 campaign. In the Senate, Ted Kennedy kept trying despite the odds. But these two men were on a personal political collision course which resulted, once more, in no action being taken.

THE LATE SEVENTIES

As Ted Kennedy developed his challenge to President Carter, the issue of health care became an integral part of his appeal and he seemed always at least a step ahead of the president on the issue.

On May 14, 1979, Kennedy unveiled a new plan for comprehensive health care. It preceded the president's proposal by a month. Following up on his advantage, Kennedy (with California Congressman Henry Waxman as a co-sponsor) introduced a bill on September 6, 1979 to implement his plan. This time he anticipated Carter by almost three weeks.

The content of the Kennedy bill also gave Kennedy an edge on the president. His bill, while not as all-encompassing as his original health security measure, offered far more than Carter's. It was enough to win the senator the support of labor, African-Americans, senior citizens, and religious and farm groups.

The Kennedy-Waxman Bill, the Health Care for All Americans Act, called for establishment of a National Health Board to prepare an annual national health budget. It also called for health insurance to be marketed by five private consortia. The result would be health insurance for every American. Those not employed or otherwise eligible would be covered by a Federal Hospital Insurance Fund or a Supplementary Medical Insurance Fund. Medicare and Medicaid would be retained. Doctors' fees would be negotiated and hospital budgets set in advance every year. The result would combine cost-containment and an employer-based overall plan.

The Carter forces were led by Connecticut senator Abraham Ribicoff and Charles Rangel, a black Congressman from New York and a former Kennedy ally. The Carter bill provided comprehensive coverage for "catastrophic" illnesses with a deductible of twenty-five hundred dollars a year, included at the insistence of economists to discourage overuse of medical services. Some employers who did not cover their workers would be pressured to do so or pay additional taxes. Workers would pay 25 percent of the premiums, plus the annual deductible. The Kennedy bill had them paying 35 percent, but included no deductible.

The feuding Democrats went at one another. Kennedy attacked the president's program as unfair and potentially very expensive, since it set no controls on doctors' fees in the private sector. The deductible was also attacked. Kennedy called it regressive, since a family with a ten-thousand-dollar income would have to pay 25 percent of its income before receiving benefits, while a family earning fifty thousand would spend only 5 percent.

HEW Secretary Patricia Roberts Harris shot back with a charge that Kennedy's plan was "a potential $200 billion a year pork barrel"[7] that would fuel inflation, ration health care, and result in an 80 percent increase in employers' health care premiums.

Lost in the smoke of the battle was a Republican plan put forth by senators Robert Dole of Kansas, John Danforth of Missouri, and Pete Domenici of New Mexico, which concerned itself exclusively with catastrophic protection. Like the Carter proposal, it mandated that employers provide catastrophic coverage. It also included a mechanism for those who fell through the cracks. The deductible was five thousand dollars, and coverage would kick in after sixty days of hospitalization.

The split in the Democratic ranks assured nothing would be done in the late 1970s. A raging inflation also mitigated against the legislation and was, no doubt, one reason the president had retreated from his 1976 campaign pledge. A succession of political events in 1980 once more destroyed the thrust for national health care as Carter beat out Kennedy for the Democratic nomination only to be turned out of office by the election of Ronald Reagan. That seemingly wrote an end to any hope of national health care.

REAGAN AND BUSH:
(CATASTROPHIC)

In June of 1988, while Ronald Reagan sat in the White House, Congress passed the largest extension of health care benefits for Americans since Medicare and Medicaid. The president, an ultraconservative on the issue, not only signed the bill, but also took the occasion to announce that the new law would "remove a terrible threat from the lives of elderly and disabled Americans."[8] For a glorious moment, it seemed that the overall problem had been solved by a single dramatic stroke, which eliminated what was perceived as the real problem with the system (the threat to the elderly and disabled from the costs of lingering or chronic ailments that could wipe out all their savings.) Yet a little more than a year later, the Medicare Catastrophic Coverage Act was repealed by a panicky Congress.

Setting the stage for this incredible fiasco was Reagan's secretary of Health and Human Services, Otis Bowen. For years Republicans had argued that the cost of catastrophic illnesses, which could wipe out even the wealthiest of families, was the essential flaw in an otherwise rosy medical care picture. They pointed to the attempt of Republicans in the Senate to deal with the problem back in the 1970s. Despite a sad record on domestic initiatives, the Reagan Administration came forward with Bowen's proposal for a modest increase in Medicare benefits for extended illnesses, to be funded by a small increase in the monthly premium under Part B, an increase to be paid by Medicare recipients.

Congress enlarged the scale of the new benefits to cover hospitalization, doctor bills, and prescription drugs. To get the all-important Reagan approval, lawmakers had to agree to his plan for funding. The understanding was that payment for the increased benefits had to come from the beneficiaries. No tax money was to be involved.

The result was the infamous surtax. Bowen's increased premium was retained, and one more wrinkle was added: Those who paid over $150 in annual taxes were to be charged an additional $22.50 for every $150 in taxes, not to exceed $800 per person for the first year (a limit that would increase to $1,150 in 1993). This meant a couple could pay $1,600 a year initially and $2,100 eventually.

Congress was astonished by the reaction. The American Association of Retired Persons (AARP), the largest organization of senior citizens in the country, had lobbied hard for the bill. They were stunned as thousands of membership cards were turned in by outraged members. The elderly were apparently angry about two things: many already paid for Medigap supplementary coverage, which provided better protection than the new plan for which they had to pay; and they felt those paying (about 40 percent—those with assets above a certain level) were being penalized for having set up nest eggs for their old age. Their fury was whipped up by another group that strenuously lobbied for repeal of the bill, the Committee to Preserve Social Security.

The intensity of the reaction to the new law was exemplified during Congress' 1989 August recess. Dan Rostenkowski, chairman of the House Ways and Means Committee and a political power in Chicago, had been a strong supporter of the catastrophic coverage bill. On a visit home he was chased down the street by a mob of senior citizens infuriated by the new law. Waving signs attacking him for his position, they pursued him with catcalls and epithets, including "Rottenkowski." Other legislators reported similar reactions from the folks at home. California Democrat Pete Stark, one of the authors of the legislation, reported he had "received considerable feedback on his plan [to keep the bill alive], but most of it's unprintable."[9] Oklahoma Representative Mike Synar reported, "It's the only issue out there. Nobody wants to talk about the flag or abortion."[10] Trips home soon came to be known as "catastrophic tours."

House members got the message. A bipartisan repeal effort was accepted overwhelmingly, 390–36. Of those who had supported the legislation a year earlier, most recanted.

The Senate was not as precipitous. A move to save the bill in the upper house was led by Republican freshman John McCain of Arizona. A Vietnam war hero and former POW, McCain bucked his own leadership and the Bush administration in his attempt to eliminate the hated surtax while retaining some of the benefits. Nevertheless, a conference committee finally took the path of least resistance and repealed the entire bill.

Once the dust had settled, many perceived Congress as having caved in to pressure by the wealthy elderly who were too selfish to share the burden of their less fortunate fellow seniors. Others defended the bitterness of the elderly, who were outraged that Congress had refused to act responsibly and leave some benefits intact, as McCain had wished. Still other observers saw a broader picture, and pointed out that the ills of the American health care system could not be solved by forcing one group to pay for another. In their view, comprehensive reform was needed. Hints of this view had perhaps been foreseen when, in one part of the original catastrophic coverage bill, there had been provisions for the creation of a commission to study the financing of long-term care and the health care system as a whole.

The result of all the furor was the creation of the Pepper Commission, named for its senior member, Florida congressman Claude Pepper. When he died three months into the committee's work, his place as chair was taken by Senator Jay Rockefeller.

Two veterans of the debacle delivered epitaphs on what they considered the lesson of the bill's failure. John Rother, legislative director of AARP, said, "The old strategy of piecemeal, incremental reform may be coming to an end." And Massachusetts congressman Brian Donnelly added, "It's an idiotic and indefensible health care system."[11] One implication was clear—once more, the nation had begun to think seriously about the need for a national health care program.

Before long, plans were springing up like mushrooms after a rain. Even the Bush administration, originally determined not to do anything meaningful, finally came forth with a proposal, a dusted-off version of an idea advanced in the 1970s by the AMA—tax credits for buying private insurance.

But this latest "wave" deserves a chapter of its own, and later on we will examine what is currently happening on the political front in Washington and around the nation.

IN RETROSPECT

Almost a century of intense political activity designed to better the American health care system has produced a remarkable paucity of results. The clear lesson of this long history of failure is that half-measures and tentative solutions simply do not work. It also raises the question of why we have been content with half-measures. Is it because we view health care as a "commodity to be bought and sold in the marketplace?"[12]

To the latter question we have answered *yes*. Yet when asked whether health care is a right to which people are morally entitled, we have also replied *yes*. But then we seem to have added the caveat that such care is applied only to certain segments of the population.

The United States has never set a public policy concerning health care, as it did in the nineteenth century when the nation decided to provide public education for all children at the public expense. No means tests or need to be at a certain percentage of the poverty level in income is required before children may enter their community schools. It is understood that if parents elect to pay extra so that, in theory, their children will receive a better education, they are free to enter them in private schools. But the basic need for universal education has been met and the system has stood despite all attempts to dismantle it.

Whether the American failure to make the same policy decision concerning health care is the result of a uniqueness of the American character, as some have suggested, is open to argument. Uwe Reinhardt, a Princeton economist who often speaks on health care issues, attributes our ambivalence to the fear of big government that has become so large a part of political ideology. Yet Social Security, certainly a big government program, remains an untouchable part of the American landscape.

In a Washington, D.C., restaurant, I recently overheard a diner at a nearby table comment to his companions: "I hear the Canadian health care system has some good points. But we're an impatient people. We would never stand for not receiving care right away when we need it."

Perhaps. But there are now close to 40 million Americans who are forced to be patient. Are they less American than those who have the ability to pay for their care?

This short history has been intended to cast light on the reasons why our nation has not chosen to join the rest of the industrialized world in providing minimum basic health care for all. It does not flow from geographic or historic foundations. It is, rather, the result of deliberate actions by individuals and groups, many of whom had personal economic interests to protect. They have made effective use of political realities. Their long history of successful resistance to a meaningful revision of our health care system has become a strong and valid force against change. Yet history shows, over and over again, that nothing on the American political scene is immutable if there is enough public pressure.

Attitudes do change. Minorities become majorities. Not too long ago in this nation, slaves were considered inviolate personal property. Eventually, after several hundred years, that idea changed, and became one with the concept of a flat earth—consigned to the limbo of one-time historical "truths."

The ideas that health care is a "commodity to be bought and sold in the marketplace," or offered to the poor as an act of charity, are concepts that have retained a powerful hold on the American mind. The agonized political contortions of our elected representatives, which have led time and again to failed programs and runaway costs, may well continue to reap their harvest of bewildering initials— DRG, PSRO, PPO, HMO, ET, MVPS, RBRVS—until a satisfactory public policy decision is finally reached.

The wheel of history has turned. Events have led us to the point where the need to make such a public policy decision is necessary. Given the forces at work on the American health care system, the question becomes whether or not we have the courage and the political will to make that decision. It is now time to take a closer look at those forces.

4. THE FORCES I
The Providers

DOCTORS

Doctors have always been fair game. The razor wit of Voltaire noted that the prime task of physicians was to amuse their patients until nature took its course and they either died of natural causes or cured themselves. Perhaps the ironic *philosophe*'s attitude was at the root of the steps taken a few years later by French revolutionaries who eliminated the licensing of doctors so that all citizens could practice the healing arts in the egalitarian new France. It was a situation that was not changed until Napoleon stormed onto the scene—and then only partially. From an equally acid pen, that of George Bernard Shaw, came this biting observation of a phenomenon that is, to this very day, not uncommon, and a cause for concern within the medical profession.

> That any sane nation, having observed that you could provide for the supply of bread by giving bakers a pecuniary interest in baking for you, should go on to give a surgeon a pecuniary interest in cutting off your leg, is enough to make one despair of political humanity. But that is precisely what we have done. And the more appalling the mutilation, the more the mutilator is paid. He who corrects the in-growing toenail receives a few shillings: he who cuts your inside out receives hundreds of guineas, except when he does it to a poor person for practice.[1]

An article of faith, therefore, in any discussion of the economics of health care is that the provider (in this case the doctor), not the consumer, is the decision-maker. It is an argument sometimes conveniently forgotten by economists who wish to promote the use of co-payments and deductibles as a method of reducing medical utilization. But nothing has changed the basic problem Shaw fulminated against in those days before the 1911 Lloyd George Insurance Act, when England's medical system was not unlike our own of today. Doctors still prescribe what elements of the system the consumers will use. And it is always a temptation to believe that some of them will be guided—if not openly, then at least subliminally—by their own self-interest.

A case in point is the action taken in July 1991 by the Federal Health and Human Services Department. The agency issued new rules to curb what the *New York Times* described as "the widespread practice of doctors' referring Medicare and Medicaid patients to clinics and other health-care businesses in which the doctors have invested."[2]

That opens a king-sized can of worms with ramifications for the entire practice of medicine in the United States. For one concomitant of the spate of regulatory efforts by the Federal government—together with equally stringent supplementary state legislation—has been unwittingly to promote the "entrepreneurial doctor," and private investments in expensive new technology kept out of hospitals by certificate of need rules.

For example, in Maine, global capital costs for hospitals are controlled by a state agency, the Maine Health Care Finance Commission, while another agency, the Department of Human Services, must approve specific projects under the money cap. But doctors' offices and clinics do not operate under these limitations. Predictably, facilities have been created outside the hospital system to provide MRIs, lithotripsies, CAT scans, and other high-cost procedures. Naturally, attempts have been made to bring these facilities under the regulatory umbrella. The 1991 legislature enacted a measure to do just that, but the governor vetoed the bill.

Government studies allege that 10 percent of American doctors nationwide have invested in businesses to which they refer patients. The profits can be spectacular. Returns of up to fifteen times the original investment within a few years are not uncommon.

Understandably, many doctors have had a negative reaction to Federal interference with their money machines. Dr. Howard B. Krone, an Atlanta orthopedist with shares in two imaging centers, is quoted as fuming that if the Feds don't want doctors to invest, "let the government build these facilities or let the patients do it."

As a further illustration of questionable money-making opportunities under our present system, consider the United Communications Group of Rockville, Maryland. This company specializes in advising physicians on investments, and it plans a seminar which it advertises will teach doctors and lawyers how to "structure profitable joint ventures without worry of heat from aggressive H.H.S anti-kickback enforcers."[3] Such specialists, along with the "practice consultants" who steer physicians in directions that can maximize their incomes under the present regulatory system, constitute yet another force with a hefty financial stake in the present health care structure.

It is, therefore, understandable that when a Federal agency cracks down on such practices, the trend for doctors to pull out of Medicare and Medicaid is accelerated. Stories abound of Medicare and Medicaid recipients who are unable to find doctors willing to accept them as patients. It is not only that these programs pay the doctors less than prevailing rates; in addition, the bureaucratic requirements are so daunting and expensive, and even risky, that eventually many providers simply opt out of the system. Under Federal law, anyone who pays or receives a kickback to influence the referral of Medicaid or Medicare business is liable to a twenty-five-thousand-dollar fine and five years in prison. And all of this is happening at a time when the profession, through the AMA, is arguing that the salvation of the system is not through national health care, but through an expansion of Medicaid to cover all the nation's uninsured.

The title of the AMA's sixteen-point plan is *Health Access America.* Ideologically, the proposal is light years removed from the days when the organization was fiercely fighting the "radical" idea of granting Federal funds to states for child and maternal health care projects. In a remarkable turnaround, the doctors' organization is now calling for billions of dollars in Federal expenditures.

Also, from the ideological point of view, the laissez-faire attitude of the past toward those who lack access to the system has also been abandoned. The AMA has joined forces with three other powerful health care special interest groups—the American Hospital Association, the Blue Cross-Blue Shield Association, and the Health Insurance Association of America—to issue a joint statement endorsing "universal access to health care services for all Americans."[4]

This action, by the groups most opposed to an American national health care system, was characterized by a former Reagan White House official as "a fundamental shift...These groups are no longer fighting reform. They are supporting it...I think they want George Bush to get moving."[5]

It is most certainly a shift. Whether it is fundamental is another question. What seems evident is that events have caught up with the AMA and its allies. They are finally recognizing the firestorm of discontent that has led many Americans to look to a Canadian-style single-payer system as the answer. To the AMA and its friends, it is thus imperative that something be done about what they perceive to be the problems most bothersome to the public—high costs and the fact that so many millions are without health insurance.

Government, according to the AMA's sudden change of attitude, now has a critical role to play. Not surprisingly, that role relies on the deep pockets of Uncle Sam and the states. They can save the existing system by huge infusions of taxpayer dollars to supply health insurance to those who either cannot afford it or whom the insurers do not wish to cover. Government can do even more. It can spend more taxpayer money by forcing all businesses, large and small, to provide coverage for their workers, those costs to be softened by tax credits. Government can also ease the pressure of the high cost of insurance premiums by wiping out existing state mandated benefits required in commercial policies. Finally, government can change Medicare to a system of vouchers exchangeable for commercial insurance.

These are all self-serving elements of the sixteen-point AMA plan. While the Panglossian habit of endlessly repeating that "all's for the best" has been dropped from the rhetoric, the AMA plan states that 87 percent of all Americans "have access to the highest quality of health care services in the world." Then it goes on to say: "Yet a significant number are not happy with the cost of health care services, nor are they satisfied with a system that allows so many to go without health insurance. It is clear that the system requires improvement. However, efforts to improve the system should not place at risk the access to quality care currently enjoyed by the vast majority of Americans."

It is clear that the debate has taken on a new and different tone. No longer do we hear thundering diatribes against the specter of "socialized medicine." Now it is admitted that the imperiled system must be saved by those very efforts which the AMA has long condemned as "socialistic." The doctors' lobbyists also take a hard gulp when they finally honestly admit, "This beneficial goal cannot be achieved without substantial cost."[6]

Among the highlights of the AMA plan are Medicaid reform, requiring that a single standard be set for the entire country instead of allowing states to set their own standards, that all employers be forced to cover their employees by providing tax credits, that a cap be placed on noneconomic damages for malpractice, that state "risk pools" be established for those persons the insurance companies don't want to cover, and that Medicare be replaced with a voucher system so that seniors would have to buy commercial insurance.

Some language included in the tail end of the package has a curious ring. One exhortation is to "encourage physicians to provide voluntary care"—a phrase that evokes a Norman Rockwell illustration as it harks back to the kindly old country doctor, and a gentler era when charity care was institutionalized to take most of the stress off the system. The AMA claims American doctors already provide $11 billion a year of uncharged care. Then, with more than a hint of defensiveness, the AMA also urges, "Encourage physicians to practice in accord with the highest ethical standards."

The latter statement might be seen as a tacit admission that members of the profession have not been all that careful of their reputations. It is a touchy point, as the AMA found out when a 1980 editorial in their journal warned that some doctors had been infected by a "greed virus." The reaction of more than a few medical societies to this *JAMA* piece was apoplectic. Yet the association remains sensitive to any potential fall in public esteem.

Incidentally, when it comes to cost containment that might apply to physicians, the AMA proposal is somewhat oblique. Point 7 of their program states: "Develop professional parameters to help assure that only high quality appropriate medical services are provided, thus impacting favorably on the quality and cost of medical care. Such parameters are professionally developed to assist physicians in clinical decision making."

Now comes a new buzzword we are to hear frequently: *medical effectiveness.* Among schemes for cost containment, medical effectiveness is the latest state of the art and the methodology in which many, including the AMA, are putting their faith. Part of the genesis of the phrase was a study done by a Dartmouth professor, John Wennburg, and his associates concerning treatments of particular disease conditions in different cities over a period of time. They reported an inordinate number of surgical procedures in one community while, not far away, the same illness was treated almost exclusively by medications. The phenomenon gave rise to several questions. Was it the result of reimbursement practices? This did not seem likely. Was it, then, tied more to physician training and prejudice concerning the proper mode of treatment? In respect to one surgical procedure—prostactectomies, which remove the male prostate gland—they looked at ten years of records and found a far higher rate of death, permanent impotence, permanent incontinence, and a need to repeat the operation than doctors had suspected. The transmittal of these findings soon led to a 15 percent drop in such operations across the state that was studied.

The interest stirred led George Mitchell, the U.S. Senate majority leader, to help provide significant funding for an arm of the Federal government devoted to research on "the quality, delivery, and costs of health services." The group, now called the Agency for Health Care Policy and Research (AHCPR), operates under the Department of Health and Human Services. Senator Mitchell, in his own national health insurance bill, gives a prominent role to *medical effectiveness* as a tool of cost containment, and the agency is now requesting proposals for more such studies labeled PORTs (Patient Outcome Research Teams). Some of the most recent of these are for chronic obstructive pulmonary disease, the secondary and tertiary prevention of stroke, and congestive heart failure.[7]

The concept is not without its critics. Beneath the aseptic language used by AHCPR to describe that PORTs' mission is to "develop clinical recommendations regarding each condition"[8] lies the suspicion that this will lead to "cookbook medicine"—practicing according to standard recipes. Even so, the research is considered so promising as a potential money-saver that the agency has been granted $50 million to pursue its work. It is interesting to note that the problem of different practice methods in neighboring areas is not restricted to our own "free-enterprise" health care system. Similar studies done in Canada, Denmark, and England have shown the same results.

The AMA today is still a powerful organization of 250,000 members. In the 1988 Congressional elections, it spent $5.3 million, including $2.3 million in direct contributions to House and Senate candidates. By March 1990, it had already given money to 348 members of Congress, among them eight of the twelve Congressional members of the Pepper Commission. It was also, by that date, second among the top fifty PACs in receipts and spending, not counting state medical societies, which were handing out another $4 million, and individual doctors, who pumped $7.48 million into Congressional races from 1981 to 1990.

But the organization is no longer the nine-hundred-pound gorilla it used to be. Its power has waned. Only about 40 percent of America's doctors now are members, down from 70 percent in the 1960s. The College of Surgeons, which has been quite independent of late, claims fifty thousand members. An even larger group, the sixty-eight thousand–member College of Physicians, has actually had the temerity to challenge the AMA by suggesting the whole structure of American health care needs to be changed. This suggestion has been timid and tentative, but it has been made. *The Health Policy Report* of the Roche drug company for the spring of 1990 quotes the group as declaring in April, "We have concluded that nothing short of universal access to a level of basic health care will be fair in the long run."[9]

Another group of physicians, the American Academy of Pediatrics, has come forward with a specifically designed strategy. Quite understandably, their program is aimed at children and pregnant women. The pediatricians want all of them covered, just as Medicare covers the elderly. Preventive care would also be included in their proposed government entitlement program.

Finally there is the Physicians for a National Health Program. As the name implies, these are doctors who openly call for universal health coverage. They are also outspoken proponents of a Canadian-style single-payer system. While still representing a minority of American physicians, with only four thousand members, the group has attracted a great deal of attention, especially through the writings and lectures of two of their leaders, the husband and wife team from Cambridge, Massachusetts, of Dr. David Himmelstein and Dr. Steffi Woolhandler.

The failings of the American health care system have become a consuming problem for most physicians. Individually they are searching their souls, publicly and privately, in quest of an answer. In a speech delivered in April 1991 before the annual session of the American College of Physicians, Dr. Samuel Thier, then president of the National Academy of Science's Institute of Medicine and himself an internist, asked, "Health care reform: who will lead?" He answered his own question by telling his audience that physicians should be the leaders. After expressing the thought that neither the business sector nor labor nor insurance companies nor the Federal or state governments would take charge of changing our health care system, he said, "That leaves only the physicians." His reasoning held that physicians still have public credibility, that reforming the system "requires the ability to change the behavior of physicians," and that they have a professional responsibility to place the interests of their patients ahead of their own by setting and enforcing their own standards of performance. "They must get back to their roots and heritage as professionals, protecting their patients and putting their own interests second ... Barbara Tuchman described folly as knowing what to do in the face of all the circumstances and in your own self-interest, and then failing to take that action. Physicians are very close to committing folly in the health care system".[10]

Another thoughtful doctor is not so sure physicians can take such a lead. Dr. Howard H. Hiatt, a distinguished Massachusetts physician and professor at Harvard Medical School, writes, in his 1989 book *America's Health in the Balance,* about the dilemma an idealistic medical student faced with his first patient, an octogenarian woman who had been left paralyzed and unconscious by a stroke. The student had earlier railed against the expenditure of huge sums of money to sustain elderly patients with no favorable prognoses. Now, face-to-face with reality, he was astounded that he instinctively chose to resolve the conflict in favor of his patient. Dr. Hiatt's point focused on the fact that physicians, acting as doctors, "would have been influenced only by what was best for their patient,"[11] not by what was best for the system as a whole. The wistful implication is that physicians would prefer such public policy decisions to be made by others.

A third, unexpressed implication of Dr. Thier's diagnosis holds that physicians won't want to lead a way out of the present mess. It was contained in a letter from a neurosurgeon (nameless for reasons that will be obvious). This particular socially conscious doctor, who has done work for the Veterans Administration as well as maintaining a private practice, was appalled by some of the things he saw happening in contemporary medicine. He cited several examples.

He wrote of a patient charged forty-five hundred dollars for a cervical spine operation to relieve muscle weakness who was taken to court when he couldn't pay the entire amount. The patient lost his car, his only means of getting to work. The forty-five hundred-dollar fee, according to the writer, was "more than twice a reasonable fee in today's market." Then he cited another surgeon who billed seventy-five hundred dollars for essentially the same procedure.

His indignation extended to the case of a "poor old man," told he had an emergency need for a similar operation and that his bills for hospital and surgery would come to eighty thousand dollars. It turned out the patient did not need surgery at all, and is doing well without it. Also documented were other instances of needless surgery being ordered after diagnostic tests conducted on machines in which the surgeon had a financial interest. Finally, the communicant expressed amazement at hospital waste of materials that could easily be sterilized and reused. He cited a hundred-dollar "compression bag" that is regularly thrown away after a single use. He also marveled at the prices paid to medical supply houses and drug companies. "For example, our new anesthesia machine cost some $160,000, and it is a relatively simple piece of machinery—standard components—much less complex than the four Saab automobiles one could buy with that money."

Obviously the physicians in the medical community are split in numerous directions. But whether they speak with one voice or many, whether they are active, reactionary, or passive, the doctors will be key players in whatever changes are made to a system that no longer serves them as it once did, a system that now makes it difficult for them to do what they have been trained to do—ethically care for their patients.

HOSPITALS

In my small community of nine thousand souls, the largest single employer in town is the local hospital. That should be no surprise. It perhaps should be no more of a surprise that in Philadelphia, a city of over 2 million, "hospitals are the largest category of employer, with the largest annual payroll," according to Rosemary Stevens in her latest book, *In Sickness and in Wealth: American Hospitals in the Twentieth Century.*[12]

The bad news for Philadelphians is that the biggest business in the City of Brotherly Love is losing money at an alarming rate. At the end of 1990, it was reported that of the ten hospitals in Pennsylvania losing the most money during the year, nine were in Philadelphia.[13] Total gross operating losses for all Philadelphia hospitals were $85 million.

The situation in Philadelphia is no more than one example of the intensity of the fiscal crisis facing America's inner-city hospitals. And, unfortunately, institutions in rural areas fare no better. Across the nation, hospitals—major businesses, often with more employees than all but the biggest factories—are closing or curtailing their activities. According to the 1988 edition of the American Hospital Association's *Hospital Statistics*, there were 5,881 community hospitals in the United States in 1977. Ten years later there were only 5,611, a drop of almost 5 percent.[14] This despite the fact that Americans spent more than 38 percent of the $604 billion they expended on health care in hospitals.

The sad situation in Philadelphia graphically illustrates the sicknesses of America's hospitals. Chief among them is the problem of uncompensated care. Voluntary hospitals, non-profit institutions with tax-exempt status, "pay back" that status by providing free charitable care to the community—a time-honored arrangement turned into a nightmare by today's heavy concentrations of the poor and uninsured in the inner cities. For example, the biggest money-loser in Philadelphia, the Hospital of the University of Pennsylvania, spent $37 million in uncompensated or undercompensated care. Mount Sinai Hospital, another major Philadelphia money-loser, reacted by closing its emergency room and shifting emphasis to more profitable specializations. Yet emergency rooms are frequently the only place where the medically indigent—those without health insurance or eligibility for government programs like Medicare and Medicaid—can find help. Another aspect of the problem accompanying uncompensated care was described bluntly by the president of the Delaware Valley Hospital Council: "Government payers are not paying their fair share. The worst payer of all is Medicaid. Until that system gets in line, many of our members will have financial problems."[15]

The underfinancing of Medicare and Medicaid, resulting in payments that fail to meet real hospital costs, represents what is probably the industry's biggest complaint. It is certainly the prime target of its considerable political efforts. The American Hospital Association does not appear, like the AMA, to have its own plan for "universal access." But its publications are filled with pleas for members to lobby against spending reductions in Medicare and for increases in the prospective payments to hospitals from the government, which it claims have fallen below the "marketbasket" of expenses hospitals must incur.

For instance, elaborate instructions on such lobbying were the centerpiece of *Key Hospital Issues*, a booklet distributed at the 1990 annual membership meeting of the American Hospital Association in Washington, D.C. The tone was consistent throughout, no matter what the issue: The solution to every problem was, "give us more government funds." And how did the hospitals expect the government to get those funds? Prominently mentioned was the idea of mandating employer coverage of all employees in all businesses. Oblique support was also given to what was then the Kennedy-Waxman Bill, now revised into the Senate Leadership Bill, sponsored by Majority Leader George Mitchell. The hospitals also took care not to rule out an increase in broad-based taxes, including a boost in the income tax.

No matter how successful hospitals are in persuading governments to help them with large infusions of cash, they still face daunting struggles. The problem is illustrated by recent events in New Jersey. That state had established an "Uncompensated Care Trust Fund." When the fund legally expired at the end of 1990, New Jersey hospitals had to sue the state for more than $22 million they claimed was due them, which the state refused to pay on grounds that the program had terminated. In the legislative action taken to extend the fund, two new provisions were added that were vigorously opposed by the hospitals: First, hospitals would be reimbursed only for 90 percent of uncompensated care (hospitals claimed that would add $72 million in red ink), and second, an overall cap of $200 million would be imposed for all hospital capital improvements. Another legislative proposal would tax the hospitals one-half of one percent of their revenues to provide a variety of "cost reduction" programs the legislators did not want the state to fund.

There is no end to the seemingly insurmountable problems facing hospital administrators. Both state and Federal governments have reversed previous open-handed policies, while at the same time their demands, particularly in the area of regulation, appear endless. The Sequoia Hospital, a 430-bed not-for-profit institution in the San Francisco Bay area, estimated that it cost them $7.8 million every year just to comply with bureaucratic regulations. Providing records to outside "peer review" agencies mandated by Federal law required twenty new staff people. With the same number of inpatients it had in 1966, when the Medicare-generated explosion of activity began, the hospital has been forced to increase staff from 448 to 734. The nursing staff alone has increased by 159 because paperwork takes up so much of their time. The attitude of those who work in hospitals is caustically reflected in the comments of Dr. Sidney Marchasin, Vice President of the Sequoia Hospital Board of Directors: "The best way to start solving the health care cost crisis is to suggest that many of the government's regulators resign en masse, and then accept those resignations so fast they don't have time to hit the table."[16]

Not-for-profit hospitals like Sequoia make up by far the majority of American hospitals. Once known as voluntary hospitals, in part because they were run by "volunteer" trustees (and possibly, too, because of the large numbers of citizens who volunteered to work in them), the terminology used to describe them was changed to *not-for-profit* or *non-profit* after the passage of Medicare and the growth of what were formerly called proprietary hospitals, now known as *for-profit* institutions.

The non-profits, in today's environment, have been forced to change their traditional role as they are caught between the Scylla and Charybdis of competing with for-profit institutions while still fulfilling their moral responsibility to provide charitable care as a trade-off for their exemption from taxation. In fact, it is more than a moral obligation, since government is constantly breathing down their necks. Federal, state and local tax exemptions to hospitals are calculated to run about $8 billion annually.[17] A 1990 Government Accounting Office study of hospitals in five states (California, Florida, Iowa, Michigan, and New York) found that 57 percent of their hospitals provided free care of less value than their tax exemptions. That triggered congressional action mandating that not-for-profit hospitals provide specified levels of charity care in order to maintain their exemptions. Now Congressman Brian Donnelly of Massachusetts wants to establish a direct link in tax laws between the value of exemptions and the amount of charitable care delivered.

This problem becomes particularly exacerbating for non-profits when for-profits are nearby. The for-profits can turn away all nonpaying patients. In El Paso, Texas, when the for-profit Columbia chain took over a local hospital, the Providence Memorial, a not-for-profit, saw its Medicaid load jump from 9 percent to 17 percent.[18] For-profits often make no bones about their desire to put their competition out of business. They are strictly business and practice "creaming," a term describing efforts to attract those with the ability to pay for their care and exclude all others. Richard Rainwater, a Texas financier with a controlling interest in Hospital Corporation of America, has also been extremely successful with this and other hospital chains he controls by openly soliciting doctors as investors, "on the assumption that they will steer patients to the hospitals in which they have personal stakes and consider financial matters when making medical decisions."[19]

A bill to prohibit referrals to doctor-owned facilities, introduced in Congress in 1989 by California's Pete Stark, was defeated after intense lobbying by the AMA. Stark plans a new bill that would expand the 1976 anti-rebate laws, which pertain mostly to clinical labs. The new provisions may well be in line with the recently issued Department of Health and Human Services regulations against kickbacks.

The third tier in this configuration of providers is the publicly run hospitals. These are the last resort for the poor and uninsured, shunned by the for-profits and unable to get treatment at not-for-profits, which have a limited capacity (or an unwillingness to serve them). The crowded waiting rooms and decaying facilities of such institutions form an image in the public mind that is used by opponents of a national health care system when they rail against the horrors of "socialized medicine." This, they insist, is what it will look like. Yet these sad conditions are the result of the structure of our present hospital category system in the United States.

A key moment in defining the place of public hospitals in the U.S. came in 1932 in California. The state's not-for-profit hospitals sued the county hospitals because several of the latter had begun to accept paying patients of local doctors. This, claimed the not-for-profits, was "unfair competition." The test case came to court in Bakersfield (Kern County), where the county hospital was admitting local farmers able to pay for their care. After the case wended its way through the system to the California Supreme Court, a 1936 ruling held that county hospitals could basically accept only indigents. It was a ruling whose impact lasted until the advent of Medicaid in the 1960s. The import of the decision, as pointed out by Rosemary Stevens,[20] was its affirmation that "tax-supported hospitals had a different, lesser mission than voluntary institutions." The pejorative term "lesser" should be underscored. It was as if under law—and in the design of American health care—medical care under government auspices was, ipso facto, required to be second-class—or, in this instance, even third-class.

It is ironic that hospitals now see their salvation in a gigantic government bailout that will pour billions of taxpayer dollars into their operations and leave them with total freedom to spend those dollars. That is their political fantasy and it may well remain so, since the Reagan and Bush administrations, dedicated to "free enterprise" and "competition," have indicated no disposition to come up with the kind of funding hospitals need. Indeed, as indicated by hospital complaints, they have consistently come up with far, far less, and have elected to shift the health care financial burden onto the shoulders of providers.

In *In Sickness and In Wealth,* Rosemary Stevens writes:

A major conclusion of this book is that the United States has a de facto national health system, expressed through its hospitals, although Americans are unwilling to recognize the fact and will indeed go to enormous lengths to deny it. As a result, we have high costs without concomitant social benefits. Without the commitment to a consistent national health policy and the will to implement it, the hospital system will not work equitably. The complaints of hospital critics fifty or sixty years ago will still ring true; American hospitals constitute a production system with an inadequate distribution and financing system.[21]

Whether a national health care system that serves everyone equitably can be grafted onto the present three-tiered hospital system will probably depend on how bad conditions become for the largest component—the not-for-profits. With no safety net to keep more and more of such hospitals from closing their doors, and little prospect of a government fiscal bailout or relief from regulation, a search may begin for another way.

5 THE FORCES II
The Payers

COMMERCIAL INSURERS

In 1973, one of the most conservative publishers in America, the Henry Regnery Company of Chicago, published the sort of muckraking book that might have been expected to come from the pen of Ralph Nader. It hardly seemed the sort of thing to expect from a fire-breathing, anti-Communist, midwestern champion of the status quo. Entitled *The Health Insurance Racket and How To Beat It*, it was written by John E. Gregg, described as a lawyer, former FBI agent, one-time health insurance salesman, and national chairman of an organization called the Policy Holders Protective Association International, a consumer group with headquarters in Georgia. The book roasted the practices of the industry, particularly its devotion to substantial profits at the expense of policyholders, and concluded that "insurance is a very poor method of health care financing."[1]

In one way, the book was an indication that health insurance in America had become an American institution and, as such, worthy of skepticism. These days we accept without question that fifteen hundred health insurance companies constitute a powerful political entity, a force—perhaps even a more powerful force than all other providers, including the AMA—in opposition to the idea of national health care. Even though the country has been debating "national insurance" since before World War I, private insurance companies were not a factor until much later, and did not blossom into big business until well after World War I.

The birth of the American health insurance industry took place in

60

1847, when the Massachusetts Health Insurance Company offered a restricted sickness policy. By the turn of the century there were forty-seven companies hawking *accident* insurance, but staying clear of illness. By 1910 some limited group policies were being sold combining accident and sickness insurance. And by 1928 a few companies started offering group hospitalization and surgical plans. (Most notable among these was Metropolitan Life's contract with General Motors to cover 180,000 workers for health care).

The big breakthrough in health insurance came in 1929. At the request of a group of Dallas schoolteachers, Dr. Justin Ford Kimball, the executive vice-president of Baylor University Hospital, enrolled 1,250 of them at fifty cents a month for a policy that provided twenty-one days of semiprivate care in his hospital. Part of his motivation was the large number of unpaid bills from teachers that came with the onset of the Great Depression.

The importance of this Texas innovation was seen only in retrospect, for it is now considered to mark the beginning of Blue Cross. And from Blue Cross, like Eve from Adam's rib, came Blue Shield, a separate type of prepaid service—insurance that provided payment for doctors' care. The split was made necessary by the initial strong opposition of the AMA. The doctors' organization, which only grudgingly accepted group insurance for hospital costs, fought tenaciously to keep their members on a fee-for-payment schedule within the hospitals, billing patients directly and using the hospital as a "workshop" whose expenses were none of their concern.

The technical term *service-benefits* insurance is often used to distinguish this form of coverage from an *indemnity* policy, where a subscriber incurs a medical expense and then submits a claim. Under service-benefits, it is the physician or hospital that seeks payment from the insurer. Such distinctions are less clear today than they were when the industry was in its infancy.

The Baylor University Hospital plan was so successful that it was quickly extended to several thousand other people in the Dallas area. It was copied by the Dallas Methodist Hospital and soon institutions in California, New Jersey, Minnesota, Washington, D.C., and Ohio organized variations on the hospital service contract theme. It made sense at a time when the hospitals were in deep financial trouble. Their average per capita receipts had dropped at the onset of the depression from $236.12 to $59.26, and deficits had soared from

15.2 percent to 20.6 percent of disbursements. Only 62 percent of their beds were filled. In 1932, Michael Davis and C. Rufus Rorem, in their book *The Crisis in Hospital Finance*, warned that patients could no longer support hospitals through out-of-pocket payments; they had to have insurance.[2]

That co-author, with the intriguing name of C. Rufus Rorem, is credited with organizing Blue Cross. An original member of Calvin Coolidge's Committee on the Cost of Health Care, he was hired in 1933 by the American Hospital Association as a consultant on group hospitalization, and asked how it might be expanded. A 1934 bill passed in New York State, giving such "free-choice" plans premium tax exemption, became the model. By 1945 it had been copied in thirty-five states, by 1947 in forty-seven, and in twenty of those states the Blues *were* tax-exempt. Another milestone on the road to Blue Cross expansion was a grant to the AHA from the Julius Rosenwald Fund for a special committee to encourage community health. Rorem became its executive director, and used the post to continue to promote Blue Cross plans, each within a defined territory.

Strangely enough, Blue Cross was begun against the advice of industry professionals who thought the concept too risky. Rorem was told by a panel of insurance executives that hospitals could never solve their financial woes in that manner. But as the idea caught on, major insurance companies began to take notice and hesitantly went along. In 1934 the commercials began to offer indemnity coverage to groups for hospital expenses. Four years later they broadened their plans to include surgical bills.

It was the beginning of a hare and tortoise race. Blue Cross, with a running head start, as well as tax exemption, was far in front at the outset. By 1938 the Blues had 1.4 million customers, while the commercials had a mere 100,000. In 1945 Blue Cross had 61 percent of the hospital insurance market and the private companies 33 percent. But by 1951 the lead had changed hands: the commercial companies had 40 million policyholders and Blue Cross 37.4 million. The gap continued to widen, and by 1969, after the introduction of Medicare, with only those under sixty-five counted, commercial carriers were insuring 100 million people (57 percent) to Blue Cross's 70.6 million (35 percent).[3]

Competition stimulated Blue Cross to assist in the creation of Blue Shield. And it was the AMA's fear of compulsory national health insurance that made it, however grudgingly, drop its opposition. In 1939 one of AMA's most distinguished members, Dr. Ray Lyman Wilbur, the president of Stanford University and former chairman of Coolidge's Committee on the Cost of Health Care, played a leadership role in establishing the California Physicians Service, a plan offering coverage for doctors' home, office, and hospital visits. It was sponsored by the California Medical Society, which had once flirted with compulsory insurance and was currently contending with a governor pushing for health insurance for all workers with incomes under three thousand dollars a year (then 90 percent of the population). Other medical societies followed the California example, and these programs eventually became Blue Shield.

Blue Shield trailed far behind Blue Cross in subscribers at first, but by 1945 they had a respectable 2 million members (Blue Cross had 19 million). The AMA had given its approval two years earlier with the caveat that doctors control the plans.

The phenomenal growth of all major forms of voluntary insurance—Blue Cross, Blue Shield, and private hospital and medical plans—was in part an outcome of the government's World War II wage-stabilization program. With raises restricted, fringe benefits took on a new importance, and health insurance became a key item in collective bargaining.

The unions had made impressive gains by the war's end: Some 600,000 workers were covered by health insurance plans. But that was just the start. In 1946, led by the Congress of Industrial Organizations, and spurred by the realization that Truman's national health insurance initiative would not get through Congress and by the Supreme Court ruling holding benefit plans to be a "condition of employment" in which unions had a legitimate say, the trend became a tidal wave. Within two years, 1948 to 1950, workers covered increased from 2.7 million to over 7 million. After the next four years the number of covered union members had risen to 12 million plus 17 million dependents—one quarter of all the health insurance in the nation.

The dizzying growth of health insurance is illustrated even more dramatically in the progression of statistics for the entire country regarding hospitalization insurance.

1940: 9 percent of Americans covered.
1950: 51 percent of Americans covered.
1966: 81 percent of Americans covered.

In another of her books, *American Medicine and the Public Interest*, Rosemary Stevens neatly sums up the phenomenon. "The health insurance industry [including the non-profit Blue Cross and Blue Shield] could congratulate itself on one of the most spectacular selling achievements of modern times."[4]

There was a down side however, also noted by Stevens.

> Health insurance, as it evolved, only paid part of the medical bills and was dedicated primarily toward hospital and surgical care, was applicable only when the person was sick (it was not a mechanism to keep him well) and was dependent on existing facilities and services. Even today [1971] private health insurance covers less than one-fourth of expenditures for medical care. Moreover, as a predominantly middle-class phenomenon, voluntary health insurance did not meet the expenses of those in direst medical need.[5]

The obvious inadequacies of voluntary insurance—that it failed to cover all expenses and that it excluded segments of the population—were glaring impediments to the argument of its proponents—i.e., that there was no need for national health insurance because the existing private (and private non-profit) system met the need. Attempts were therefore made during the Eisenhower administration to shore up the weaknesses of commercial (and Blue Cross-Blue Shield) insurance through the resources of the Federal government.

Harold Stassen, one-time boy wonder governor of Minnesota and perennial GOP presidential candidate, had come up with the notion of creating a Federal "reinsurance" fund to protect health insurance companies against losses. Eisenhower, in whose administration Stassen served, adopted the idea. Both for-profit and non-profit insurance companies would have been reimbursed for average losses on reinsured contracts, the idea (and hope) being that they would then extend coverage to higher-risk customers.

The concept evoked opposition from everyone. The AMA saw it as a step toward socialized medicine and Federal control of private insurance. Those favoring a national insurance program saw it as just the opposite—a raid on the treasury to bolster the existing system. Even the insurance companies were opposed, fearing long-run government domination. Through the middle 1950s, Ike persisted: HEW

Secretary Marion B. Folsom several times sent versions of the scheme to Congress. Nothing happened.

There has been little change in the health insurance configuration to this day: A large number of Americans (about 87 percent) are covered, they receive inadequate benefits, and there is no coverage at all for most of the highest risks and for growing numbers of the working poor. The stability of this arrangement is coming under increasing question.

The dropping of 100,000 people in small group associations by New York's Empire State Blue Cross-Blue Shield has been matched in the private sector. Consider this California headline:[6]

GREAT REPUBLIC CANCELING 14,000 POLICIES

Great Republic, a Santa Barbara company, simply notified a mass of customers, many ill with cancer, AIDS, and other diseases, that they were no longer covered—a step permitted by state law. The company explained that it was responding to pressure from the state Department of Insurance, which claimed they had sold too many new policies in the second half of 1989 and did not have the cash reserves to cover possible claims. Therefore it was dropping its oldest and most costly plan, developed in the mid-1980s and sold to individuals and small businesses. A company spokesman acknowledged that this $25 million block of business, "unlike the company's other health plans, is not producing a profit."

Criticism was not new to Great Republic; a few months before the company had been fined fifty-five thousand dollars for delaying claim payments and assessed a judgment of eighty-thousand dollars for discriminating against gays. The company was immediately attacked by advocates of national health care. Maryann O'Sullivan, executive director of Health Access, a San Francisco–based group promoting California universal health insurance said, "What this demonstrates is that the moment you're going to need your health insurance the most that it's most likely not to be there for you."

O'Sullivan's argument goes to the heart of the problem. Is insurance, a product sold with the educated guess (informed by actuarial figures) and hope and expectation that it won't be used, an appropriate vehicle for financing health care? Cynical ex–health insurance salesman John E. Gregg describes the psychological implications of this structural reality on those in the profession. "Once policyholders file claims, the companies cast them in the role of adversaries who must be outwitted whenever possible. If administrative checks disclose any basis for non-payment, denial letters are sent to test what fight claimants will put up."[7]

The American health insurance safety net is full of holes. The obvious ones are where there is no coverage for financial reasons, inadequate coverage, discrimination against the sick, and harassment of the insured by entrenched bureaucracies. The mutual good deal made by unions and management in the postwar years (business has always loved the tax write-offs, worth $36.3 billion in 1991[8]) has deteriorated considerably. One indication, certainly, is the high percentage of strikes (73 percent in the last three years) based on disputes over health care benefits.

A survey of workers in private industry, conducted by Northwestern National Life Insurance of Minneapolis in February 1990, showed an overwhelming belief that health benefits are considered entitlements—"a right for themselves, their dependents and to a large part their retiree benefits."[9] Union members, in particular, believe they have bargained away pay increases for health care benefits. Demands that they now pick up part of the cost of those benefits are, in reality, pay cuts. Yet a Northwestern National survey of four hundred employers found that nine out of ten said they would soon have to ask their workers to assume some part of those costs. In that survey, 48 percent of all workers had all health care paid for by their companies. But the tide is running in the other direction. A study by the Employee Benefit Research Institute found that between 1982 and 1988, annual contributions by workers to job-related insurance plans grew four times as fast as did the contributions of their employers.[10] Deductibles went up steeply, too. 1988 figures from the Health Care Financing Administration show Americans are paying 24 percent of the nation's health care bill out of their own pockets.

The health insurance industry and the hospitals have tangled frequently in recent years due to the insurance industry's strong support for restrictions on hospital usage and reimbursement. Although they publicly beat the free-enterprise drum, the industry has been an advocate of state control of hospital rates—as blatant a case of government interference with the private sector as can be imagined. The exasperation of insurance executives with hospital attempts to recover costs from them has the tone of moral outrage usually reserved for policyholders who do not fill out their forms with enough candor so they may be denied coverage on the basis of pre-existing conditions. The rare times payers and providers agree is when they jointly ask government for tax dollars to bail them out of their latest problem.

The insurers' conflict with doctors is more serious. It impinges on medical judgment, and involves a relatively new player on the health care scene: "review companies." It is amazing to contemplate the hirelings of a billion-dollar business—made up of over four hundred companies—reviewing doctors' procedures in order to authorize or deny payment of insurance bills. They are the creation of the insurers. One such is U.S. Behavioral Health, a California unit of the giant Travelers Insurance Company. Doctors have complained bitterly that some employees in these companies have no medical qualifications on which to base their judgments—some are social workers or nurses. The doctors point out that even qualified reviewers hardly understand the subtleties of cases unless they have access to the patients. They certainly cannot get enough information over the phone.

A California appeals court will soon hear a damage suit against a review company and two insurers brought by the parents of Harold Wilson, Jr., a twenty-five-year-old who died after his premature release from a drug addiction program. The review company, Western Medical Review, Inc., told the hospital after Wilson had been a patient for eleven days that Blue Cross of Southern California would no longer pay for his care even though his policy covered thirty days of hospitalization.

"Managed care" is the euphemism for the types of review organizations that have so riled the doctors. These health care management firms are the fastest growing part of the health care industry, expected to zoom to $7 billion, in gross earnings annually in the next few years. Whether they will save as much as they cost is an open question.

The medical profession, not content with appeals and litigation, is pushing for state laws to control the review practice. They want assurance that reviewers are properly qualified and have the credentials to question physicians' recommendations. Such laws, which also deal with patient confidentiality, have been enacted in fifteen states and are being proposed in twenty more. Not all have been successful. In Georgia, the politically powerful Georgia Pacific Paper Company persuaded Governor Joe Frank Harris to veto such legislation. Gregor

Scandlen, director of the Blue Cross-Blue Shield Association, said that employers regard the review process as "their last chance to get a handle on health care costs," and that if it fails, "there's a good chance that employers will throw up their hands and support proposals for a government run health system."[11]

A single-payer system akin to the Canadian plan is the recurring nightmare haunting the health insurance industry. It is a lucrative industry, now bringing in about $175 billion a year, and a single-payer system would put it out of business. There would be a marginal role for the health insurers (Canadians use such private insurance for extras like a private room in a hospital or cosmetic plastic surgery), but insurance as the money cow mainstay of this system would be, as it is in Canada, a thing of the past.

It is no wonder that the Health Insurance Association of America, the prime spokesman for the totally private side of the industry, is considered to be the leading opponent of any plan calling for a single payer.

The HIAA was started in 1891 as the International Association of Accident Underwriters, and following the industry metamorphosis from accident into health insurance became the Bureau of Health and Accident Underwriters before assuming its present name. Like the AMA, the HIAA has its own plan for dealing with the health care crisis. The Committee for National Health Care Insurance that it organized proposes to "solve the access problem through reforms which preserve private insurance. These are to end state mandates, develop low-cost plans for basic coverage, extend tax preferences, establish risk pools, extend Medicaid, etc."[12] A bill incorporating many of these features has been introduced in Congress by Maine's Senator William Cohen and Wisconsin's Robert Kasten.

The HIAA proposals were critiqued in a special issue of *Consumer Reports* on health care in September 1990. The magazine quoted Carl Schramm, HIAA president, as frankly characterizing his opposition to any Canadian approach to health care financing as "a life or death struggle."

It has long been the goal of the industry to do away with pesky mandated state benefits. There are reportedly some seven hundred such mandates from the fifty states. This is because state legislatures, always under pressure to increase access and open the system to providers left out of third-party reimbursement (chiropractors, podia-trists, psychologists, etc.) have passed laws requiring policies sold in their states to include coverage for them and for items (including mammography, mental health, alcohol and drug treatment) that insurers don't want to cover. They have also forbidden companies to exclude people on the basis of pre-existing conditions. Insurers claim this is why policies are so expensive. They hold that without these mandates they could offer "no frills" insurance to more people. While they've never estimated their savings, the argument has gained ground in some states. Virginia, Washington, and Florida, for example, exempt no frills policies sold to small groups from state mandates. In Virginia the premium is expected to be $80 a month per person as opposed to the normal $130.[13]

The same *Consumer Reports* critique warned against the shortcomings of such policies. In Oklahoma, a no frills policy sold by Pyramid, which the magazine ranked at the absolute bottom of its list, would have left a person whose heart attack cost fifty thousand dollars with a personal bill of ten thousand dollars. *Consumer Reports* didn't either care for the idea of state risk pools, which provide "last resort" coverage for the uninsurable. "Such pools are yet another way for the industry to shed a group of policyholders that are not profitable. The HIAA further proposes that the states pick up the tab for pools' losses." A survey of risk pools in nineteen states showed only 55,500 people covered, all pools losing money, and more than 4 million people waiting to get in them.

Expanding Medicaid, another HIAA proposal, would require everyone below the Federal poverty line ($12,675 for a family of four, $8,075 for a couple) to be covered. Presently, only about 38 percent are. For insurers this might not mean more money in their pockets (save for the possible wrinkle that would give vouchers to recipients so they could buy private insurance at taxpayer expense), but it would relieve the pressure of having so many uninsured—a growing pressure that just might lead to national health care.

Overlooking no angle, the industry has also dusted off the old Eisenhower "reinsurance" ploy discussed earlier. This would cover any losses for them incurred by doing away with the practice of excluding coverage for various health conditions and forcing those with pre-existing conditions to wait for coverage when they change jobs or when their employers change carriers.

The HIAA is not passive in its resistance to universal health care.

It lobbies incessantly against the very idea and has, in recent years, taken aim at the Canadian system in a series of scathing attacks. Carl Schramm told *Consumers Reports* that "we produce lots of research bulletins that are classy little numbers." One such, issued in January 1991, was entitled *Canadian Health Care: The Implications of Public Health Insurance.* It was written by Edward Neuschler, whose credentials are not listed. It is no surprise the author concludes that public insurance on the Canadian model does not seem to be an approach that would work well in the United States." Furthermore, he adds defensively, "Canada spends a smaller percentage of GNP on health care than the U.S. primarily because its economy grew faster than ours over the past 20 years." Carl Schramm states in the preface to his report that he believes "privately managed-care plans are the best hope."

Allied with the HIAA (and the AMA, etc.) in the attack on Canadian health care is a right-wing Dallas think tank, the National Center for Policy Analysis. Its director, John Goodman, is frequently quoted when anything negative occurs in Canada. They, too, issue "classy little research bulletins," one of the most recent (February 1990) entitled *What A Canadian State Health Care System Would Cost U.S. Employers and Employees.* Their conclusion: $339 billion in taxes—without, quite obviously, any reference to what would no longer have to be paid in out-of-pocket health care costs and insurance premiums (about $380 billion). The NCPA, which has been sniping at the idea of national health care since at least 1983, also has other conservative fish to fry, as evidenced by the titles it publishes: *Paying People Not to Work: The Unemployment Compensation System, Private Alternatives to Social Security in Other Countries, Why Worry About Global Warming?* and *Crime Pays, But So Does Imprisonment.*

The HIAA and the health insurance industry do not restrict themselves to cranking out classy little bulletins. As one might expect, they are active players in political campaigns. The Travelers, Metropolitan, and Prudential Life Insurance Companies, who collect over $1 billion annually in health insurance premiums, are among the top fifty corporate contributors to Congressional campaigns. American Family Corporation, the fifth largest marketer of health insurance, ranks eighth as a contributor, ahead of Boeing, Citicorp, and Ford Motor. Their work pays off, and Carl Schramm was delighted when the Pepper Commission more or less adopted the HIAA's recommendations for the small-group market.

One final cloud continues to hang over the powerful, if beleaguered industry. It will not go away even if they weather the current storm swirling about national health care. It is something called the "human genome project." A $3 billion effort, it will in time be able to map an individual's genetic susceptibility to future illness. The implications for the present insurance system are enormous, and Roger J. Bulger, an internist and president of the Association of Academic Health Centers, argues that "the genome project, therefore, raises the specter of differentiating our insurance groupings according to an assessment of genetic risk, a specter so unpalatable and unjust that our society could not tolerate it." Or put more simply, as a line in his article from the *Washington Post* put it, "Mapping genes that cause disease will destroy our health insurance system."[14]

BLUE CROSS-BLUE SHIELD

Eight days after New York's Empire Blue Cross-Blue Shield announced it was dropping 100,000 small group subscribers, the giant insurer ran a full page ad in the *New York Times*.[15] It featured three large portraits of chairman and CEO Albert A. Cardone looking alternately earnest, excited, and benign. The accompanying text extolled the virtues of the company's new program aimed at groups of over 250 people—Empire Blue Choice. "Bet you didn't know we had plans to save your company 20 percent on health care costs," the ad ballyhooed in large type. It then ended, after a spate of detail, by saying, in even larger type, "Now you know."

The ad copy was full of all the modern buzzwords: managed care, preferred provider, comprehensive utilization review—all intended to reassure the reader that costs were being squeezed and that "unexcelled savings" would be available to those who bought into the new plan—as, they boasted, AT&T and its unions already had on behalf of fifty thousand employees.

Not long after, Empire took another ad in the same publication. This time there were no photos of the jowly Cardone—nor was it a full page ad. Instead, it was a small-print public notice for a rate change "applicable to the downstate New York region of Empire Blue

Cross and Blue Shield," and for a public hearing to be held at the NYU Medical Center.

The so-called rate adjustments would affect the contracts of 350,000 people in small groups with major medical or extended medical coverage. The company was seeking rate increases of 21 percent for hospital only, 31 percent for basic medical or hospital and basic medical, and 50 percent for major medical.

The hearing was held on August 5, 1991 and drew a "restive audience of about 200,"[16] which immediately criticized Cardone for having raised his own salary from $540,000 to $600,000 a year after an earlier rate increase of 19.5 percent.

The Blue Cross-Blue Shield executives blamed the increases on commercial insurers who, they claimed, had stolen away 400,000 of their customers through lower-cost plans that covered only people with good health records. It was estimated that some of these affected subscribers would see their costs raised to $4,402 a year, while for certain families with major medical the increase would be to $11,239. As one Brooklyn mother put it, "That 50 percent increase will mean that is the last time we will be insured." An advocate from a social service agency handling cancer cases asked, "What will happen to Bob F. who has colon cancer and would have to give up his monthly chemotherapy?" The individual had a job, and was thus not eligible for Medicaid. A number of group representatives at the hearing told Cardone that if the increases were rescinded they would join Empire and lobby the state legislature for laws to prevent commercial insurers from refusing to cover people with expensive illnesses like cancer and AIDS.

The ambiguous nature of the Blue Cross-Blue Shield configuration is perfectly illustrated by this event. Called the nation's largest health insurer because it covers 73 million people, Blue Cross-Blue Shield is not really a single company, but a composite of thirty-seven local plans loosely coordinated for national purposes like lobbying. It is not strictly a commercial operation, either, for the separate plans are nominally non-profit, and in certain states still enjoy tax-exempt status (their Federal tax exemption was ended in 1986).

Germane to this discussion are two technical insurance terms of great importance in the debate about health care: "community rating" and "experience rating." The former is a means of pricing premiums based on the overall statistical health care pattern of a community at large. It provides the cheapest price to the consumer, and was the original method by which Blue Cross costed its products. It is still apparently required or practiced in some states under particular circumstances.

The more precise experience rating is based on actual usage. In this case, small groups, in particular, are devastated when one member of the group contracts an expensive illness. Then premiums for the group soar. And that is what seems to be at issue in the Empire rate increase request.

As long ago as World War II, Blue Cross plans began to drop community rating on the grounds that it was too costly for them. One of the few plans left with it was in New Jersey, and that Blue Cross plan, in danger of losing its designation due to a continuing deficit, went to court to appeal the denial of an almost 25 percent requested rate hike. In turning them down, the appellate court drew a distinction between their form of health insurance and that of the for-profit companies. "Blue Cross is not a commercial carrier," the court ruled. "It is a non-profit tax-exempt corporation invested with the public interest. What may be good business practice for commercial insurers in not necessarily an option compatible with its unique statutorily mandated public role and may in fact be an option antithetical to that role."[17]

So Blue Cross-Blue Shield struggles on. It is neither fish nor fowl in the public eye. Clearly the organization offers insurance plans that must follow the nature of the industry, which is to narrow risks and to gamble that their services will not be needed by the majority. Those most prone to use the services should be excluded whenever possible. In her book *Blue Cross, What Went Wrong?*, Sylvia Law answers her own question in one way by stating, "The practice of controlling utilization of services [by Blue Cross-Blue Shield] through ex-post-facto denial of claims has been an administrative and human disaster." (18) Yet how else can an insurance company be expected to act?

In 1987, Blue Cross-Blue Shield of Maine lost $36 million. In 1988 it lost another $26 million, and also lost nearly 25 percent of its subscribers. That caused the Commonwealth Fund to hire Lewin/ICF of Washington, D.C., to conduct a study to determine the factors most at fault. Another element contributing to the study was the effect of the losses: premium rates in Maine rose 40 to 50 percent, far above the national average of 20 to 30 percent.

Lewin/ICF concluded three elements were the major contributors to the problem.

1. A sharp rise in administrative costs. They soared from 5.5 percent of total underwriting costs in 1983 to 10.2 percent in 1989, and cost each subscriber $34.
2. Cost shifting. Under Maine law, hospital costs not picked up by the Federal government due to Medicare and Medicaid shortfalls can be transferred to third party payers. This caused an increase of $45 per member.
3. The growth in outpatient claims. This was by far the biggest factor, accounting for a cost per member of $149.

Important to note is the fact that mandated benefits, the *bête noire* of the industry and the usual whipping boy when it comes to explaining rate hikes, played only a minor role. They were estimated to cost no more than seventeen dollars per member. Despite hard evidence, the insurance industry and its AMA allies insist that removing mandated benefits is the panacea that will put a control lid on costs.

Sylvia Law, writing in 1970, was clairvoyant about the role of Blue Cross-Blue Shield vis-à-vis any national health care plan. "No doubt there are individuals within Blue Cross who would welcome Federal pressure to orient the organization toward consumer and public control. But if, as is likely, those in control of this powerful organization are determined to resist fundamental change, then the efforts to enact and enforce requirements to reform Blue Cross might be more difficult than the effort required to create a new public administrative agency."

In the battles to come in the 1990s, this huge insurance complex, hybrid though it may be, will no doubt stand firm for the status quo.

THE GOVERNMENT, MEDICARE, AND MEDICAID

In 1965, Congress passed the elaborate compromise that created three separate major health programs: Medicare, Part A; Medicare, Part B; and Medicaid. By that act they put both Federal and state governments into the insurance business. Prior to Congress' action, governments had been involved primarily as direct or indirect providers: direct providers to the military, the veterans' hospitals, and certain public health activities when the government hired and paid the doctors, and indirect providers in the form of grants sustaining services furnished by others. The only exception was the Civilian Health and Medical Program for the Uniformed Services program (CHAMPUS), where the Federal government assured insurance services to military retirees and dependents of military personnel. It was really only with the advent of Medicare and Medicaid that the major governing bodies of the country became insurers on a scale hitherto unimaginable—"third-party payers," like Blue Cross-Blue Shield or the commercial companies.

It must be understood at the outset that governments behave like any other insurer, and will do everything they can to avoid paying a claim. For example, it has been revealed recently that Medicare is refusing to pay for the use of certain cancer drugs in the treatment of eligible patients, because although the treatment is effective—even lifesaving—the drugs in question are not designated by the Food and Drug Administration as the approved medication for their particular type of cancer. One such case involves carboplatin, a drug which costs patients one thousand dollars a month. It has been found to be very effective against lung cancer, but is listed by the FDA only as a treatment for cancer of the ovary. Another is erythropoetin, found to help sufferers from a prostate cancer that has spread to bone marrow—not the drug's original target. The Medicare funding for its use, four hundred dollars a week, was refused, and the drug was not made available to the patient in question, whose only source of funding was Medicare.

Government administrators (or those administering for them) can be as creative as any private insurer when it comes to finding reasons to deny payment of a claim. They can delay, as other insurers do, and often do so in spectacular fashion. Witness the problem of a deficit-ridden small hospital on the Massachusetts island of Martha's Vineyard. In the summer of 1991, the hospital was able, primarily though the intervention of a state senator, to collect half a million dollars owed it by Medicaid for the years 1985, 1986, and 1987—and still sought payment of another half-million owed it for the subsequent three years. The government also has a power not available to its fellow insurers: It can refuse adequate funding. Thus, while all insurers (and providers) play the game of cost-shifting—getting the other guy to pick up the tab—the government plays with a loaded deck.

BUDGET OFFICE PROPOSES
$8 BILLION MEDICARE CUT

This headline appeared November 30, 1989, in the *New York Times*, with a story describing the Bush administration's plan for the Medicare budget in Federal fiscal year 1991 (October 1990 through September 1991). For fiscal 1990, Medicare spending was slated to reach $114 billion. At the same rate of increase, the projection for the following year would be $130 billion. Yet the administration planned to spend only $122 billion.

What the Office of Management and Budget proposed was cutting funds for medical education and capital improvements in urban hospitals, plus—and this was the killer blow—instituting a lower reimbursement rate than under existing law (a 4 percent increase in place of the stipulated 5.5 percent). Instead of the increase of $3 billion sought by the Department of Health and Human Services, the budget would result in an $8 billion shortfall. AIDS funding would be reduced by $7 million in place of the $225 million increase sought by HHS.

The reaction was predictable. Hospital representatives, in particular, swarmed over Capitol Hill. The Medicare shortfall was declared to be the leading cause of increasing health insurance costs. "A Resolution to Protect Medicare" was filed in Congress, and at least a third of the Senate and half the House signed on in the first week. Even conservatives Republicans like Congressman Bill Archer of Texas and Senator Nancy Kassebaum of Kansas spoke out, saying hospitals could not withstand another year of cuts and low reimbursements.

Feeding the hospitals' sense of outrage was the fact that enough money was already in the Medicare trust fund to meet their needs, but under the provisions of the Gramm-Rudman deficit reduction law, was being used to make the Federal deficit appear smaller. Health insurance customers, they argued, were being forced to pay an indirect Medicare tax to help balance the Federal budget.

Medicare is a huge program, providing benefits to 30 million elderly and 3 million nonelderly disabled people. Its complicated financing arrangement is worth examining as background to the continuing debate over how much funding it should get. Part A—the hospital portion, sometimes known as HI (hospital insurance)—is paid for through a payroll tax on current wage earners. That brings in 58 percent of Medicare's total revenue. Workers and employers share the tax evenly to a specified level, and this provides enough to fund Part A. Part B—also called SMI (Supplementary Medical Insurance)—pays the doctor bills. That requires a combination of revenue sources. A quarter of the cost is met by the premiums recipients pay, and the rest by appropriations from the Federal government's general fund.

In fiscal 1989, Medicare had risen to 7.6 percent of all Federal expenditures, or 1.8 percent of the nation's GNP. Benefit payments grew at the rate of 12.2 percent annually between 1980 and 1989. About 32.6 million people were covered by Part A, and 32.5 million by Part B. As with many Federal programs, responsibility for administration lies in several different governmental entities. Treasury collects the taxes and disburses payments, Social Security takes enrollment applications from the public, and the Health Care Financing Administration (HCFA), under the Department of Health and Human Services, operates the claims processing and program management through eighty-eight contracts with Blue Cross and other private insurers.

In the words of a research report to Congress, "Medicare represents a blend of insurance and social welfare features. As such it is called social insurance. The Government is the insurer, underwritten by its power to tax. The Nation's workers are a 'mandatorily' insured group, but for protection that is deferred until retirement or disability occurs and the current elderly and disabled populations are the immediate risk group."[20]

Not only does the president manipulate Medicare by withholding funds, but Congress also tinkers—usually in the opposite direction, in reaction to public pressure, by expanding benefits. Sometimes these congressional actions do not require actual expenditures, but if they are not cost-shifting they are burden-shifting. A recent change in the law, for example, stated that Medicare patients will no longer be required (or even permitted) to fill out claim forms. This paperwork will now be done by providers—a burden shifted to doctors, who are forbidden to charge for the service. Congress acted in this case because many elderly found the paperwork confusing and intimidating and never filed at all.

An important Medicare addition by Congress is coverage for all kidney dialysis patients of any age, and for kidney transplants, plus a year of "immunosuppressive" drugs following such surgery. Also recently added were Part B coverage for mammography screening every other year for women over sixty-five, intravenous medication therapy treatments provided at home, and eighty hours of respite care to relieve those giving free care to patients, usually relatives, at home.

But what Congress giveth, it also taketh away. Generous as it has been, it has also worked hard to constrain costs. By slapping on the prospective payment system of DRGs, it clamped down on the open-ended "retrospective cost basis" financing that had been such a bonanza for hospitals. Since 1984, the squeeze has been put on doctors as well. Congress has limited the size of increases in something called the Medicare Economic Index (MEI), which reflects yearly changes in the operating expenses and earning levels of physicians. As a result, doctors believe they are considerably underpaid by Medicare, and this belief has added to the growing number of doctors who refuse to accept Medicare patients. The new imposition of Relative Value Scales in weighing physician fees under Medicare can only add to the problem.

Congressional restrictions have had other unintended results. While the number of enrollees using Part A has dropped slightly, many suspect this may be due to an increased usage of out-patient services, which fall under Part B. The steep climb in Part B costs (15.5 percent per year) is also attributed to payments to independent laboratories and to increased payments to HMOs. Such statistics have led to calls for the expansion of the DRG concept to cover laboratory procedures, and for the setting of flat rates for outpatient care.

There is no reason to believe that this one-step-forward, one-step-backward approach to Medicare, and the somewhat schizophrenic handling of the program, will not continue.

On the one hand, the charge of "back door rationing" is leveled at HCFA and at Secretary of Health and Human Services Louis Sullivan for promulgating rules that require cost-effectiveness to be considered when deciding whether or not Medicare will pay for new medical procedures, devices, and drugs. AARP, speaking on behalf of the elderly, protested the action not only as rationing, but as cost-shifting from the government to individuals.

On the other hand, pressures continue to mount for more services. Since Medicare coverage, for all its expense, is still inadequate, most of America's elderly have to buy supplementary "Medigap" insurance, which is also rising precipitously in cost. The poorer elderly cannot afford these extra policies, nor are they able to afford the Medicare deductibles.

All of these complications make Medicare seem convoluted, bureaucratic, ineffective, and often schizophrenic. Yet Medicare stands as a paragon of simplicity and success when compared with Medicaid.

MEDICAID

Like any program that has to be means-tested, Medicaid requires an army of bureaucrats—first to determine eligibility, and then to monitor recipients to make sure they do not hide any earnings that may end eligibility. Scandals in which providers rip off the program for huge amounts of money are constantly being uncovered. One was the scam of Dr. Giovanni del Gizzo, a physician who wrote out $3.9 million in unneeded prescriptions. But public imagination, frequently stimulated by conservative rhetoric, is usually focused on those cases where someone has earned a few dollars more than the legal limit and continues to receive services.

The complexity of the program is magnified by the fact that all fifty states are involved, and each determines its own poverty level and its own range of benefits. Furthermore, since the states pay part of the program cost (there is an elaborate formula for determining how much the Feds pay, starting at a minimum of 50 percent), the program sometimes works like a fulcrum: Lawmakers in Washington are tempted to add requirements, secure in the knowledge they can pass on a large part of the cost to the states.

In recent congressional testimony, a Colorado state representative, Carol Taylor-Little, pleaded with the Federal lawmakers not to pile any more mandates on financially strapped state governments. She pointed out that Medicaid expenditures from fiscal years 1990 to 1991 had increased by 25 percent, and that Medicaid already accounted for more than 10 percent of the states' general fund expenditures.

But Congress cannot seem to resist expanding the system. An example is California congressman Henry Waxman's $25 billion expansion proposal ($14 billion Federal, $11 billion state) to mandate eligibility for all women, infants, and children up to 185 percent of the Federal poverty level. Former vice-presidential candidate Lloyd Bentsen of Texas has a similar plan in the Senate to cover all pregnant women, infants and children. Senator John Chaffee of Rhode Island was equally generous, and drew strong support from his colleagues, when he proposed adding the developmentally disabled and mentally retarded to the program.

The National Council of State Legislatures, alerting its members to these congressional moves, offered sage if resigned advice: "States must make [the] case as [to] how affordable or unaffordable expanded coverage is... Arguing against all *mandates* will not work since Congress and the Administration are intent on achieving some broadening of Medicaid coverage."[21]

Coping with such burdens is a nearly intolerable burden for the states. The New York state legislature has toyed with the idea of putting one million people—half its Medicaid recipients—into HMOs and other "managed care" plans within five years. Participation would be voluntary at first but, if necessary, would be mandated. Savings would reach $10 million in the first year—still a far cry from the $1 billion that reputedly needs to be cut from Medicaid and other social services in the state budget.

More pressure is being exerted on the states from another direction by hospitals suing for higher rates. In one such 1990 suit in the state of Washington, a Federal judge ruled in favor of the hospitals. This followed on the heels of a decision by the U.S. Supreme Court in a Virginia Hospital Association case to allow the states and Federal government to be litigated for higher rates. The Supreme Court set no rate standards; it ruled (5–4) only that providers could sue. As a result, lawsuits like the one in Washington have surfaced in at least a dozen states.

A significant discrepancy between Medicaid and Medicare payments was revealed in a survey done for Congress's Physician Payment Review Commission. The survey showed that Medicaid reimbursements averaged about two-thirds of Medicare payments— which are, in themselves, admittedly inadequate. The National Governors Conference, polling its members as part of the study, found that in forty-three states it was difficult getting doctors to accept Medicaid patients, primarily because of low fees. Payment levels, set by states, vary widely. New York pays $240 for a total hysterectomy, while California pays $810 and Georgia $1,337. The thirteen-member commission recommended that Medicaid fees across the country be raised to Medicare levels, and Congressman Pete Stark of California introduced a bill to do just that.

Medicaid cost $72 billion in fiscal 1990—$41 billion Federal and the rest from the states—and covered twenty-seven million Americans, including thirteen million children. Its inadequacies notwithstanding, Medicaid expansion has become a political goal on which differing groups agree. An advisory group appointed by the Bush administration has called upon the president to have Medicaid cover doctors' services and hospital care for all 10 million Americans below the poverty level who have no health insurance. Heading the group was Deborah Steelman, an assistant director of the Reagan budget office and a top official in the Bush election campaign.

The group did split on the all-important question of whether coverage of all those below the poverty level would solve the problems of America's health care crisis. Some thought it would be useful only as part of a comprehensive effort to solve the financing problems of those above the poverty line through national health care. Not surprisingly, in a group dominated by Bush appointees, this view was in the minority.

A final word about Medicaid: It has become the payer of last resort for the elderly in nursing homes. When "private pay" patients exhaust their life savings, Medicaid picks up their costs. Such expenditures, if those for the mentally retarded are also included, now account for 40 percent of all Medicaid funding. Because of the burden on the states, a fifteen-member bipartisan subcommittee of the National Governors Conference proposed that the Feds pick up all costs of long-term care on the model of Medicare and Social Security. These fifteen governors maintained that if this were to happen, they could then use the state money they saved for expanding Medicaid eligibility.

Recently, in a self-defensive action, the states turned the tables on the Feds with a nifty arrangement whereby they impose a special "tax" on hospitals, or convince them to "donate" to the program; these funds are then used to gain Federal matching funds on a two-to-one or three-to-one basis. The hospitals eventually get their money back. Not to be outsmarted, the Federal Department of Health and Human Services riposted with regulations ending what they called a "scam," thus leaving the states without millions of dollars they had already programmed into their budgets.

"Clearly, the nation's health care system is in trouble," the governors said, after taking a swipe at private insurance for its discrimination against small businesses and people with serious medical conditions, and condemning the lack of prenatal care, the breakdown of immunization for children, and the high infant mortality rates under America's present arrangement.[22]

6 THE FORCES III
The Consumers

On August 30, 1989, President George Bush, vacationing at his summer home in Kennebunkport, Maine, had scheduled a luncheon with his guest, Canadian Prime Minister Brian Mulroney. They chose to eat at a local upscale restaurant, the Shawmut Inn. Nearby, a coalition of health activists staged a rally, and were permitted to present the presidential party with a huge, poster-sized "letter."

The oversized document had two columns. One was headed, "Is It True That Canada," and the other, "Is It True That The U.S." The columns listed the advantages of the Canadian health care system and the disadvantages of the U.S. system. The letter ended with a plea to the President: "Please make *National Health Care* an agenda item with Prime Minister Mulroney." It was signed, "Sincerely, *Concerned Maine Citizens.*"[1]

There were ten groups participating in the carefully staged media event. Some, like the Maine People's Alliance, the Maine Lesbian/Gay Political Alliance, the Maine Project on South Africa, United Seniors in Action, and Bangor's Local 2327 of the International Brotherhood of Electrical Workers, were local. Others were national groups: Consumers for Affordable Health Care, the Rainbow Coalition, Veterans for Peace, the National Health Care Campaign, and Jobs with Justice.

The point is that agitation for national health care has brought together many diverse groups. The above collection is a random example that can and has been duplicated in many parts of the nation. Back in the 1930s, or the 1970s, similar "liberal-minded" groups engaged in the same sort of united action. And, with the exception of Gomper's AFL, pre–World War I supporters of universal health might not have been a great deal different. Since then, organized labor—or at least a significant portion of it—has joined and even led the fight to create a national health care program. In the Kennebunkport rally and the march that followed, the electrical workers had a particular motivation for their participation. They were on strike against NYNEX, and the key issue was the telephone company's intent to cut back on their health benefits.

Some six months laters, eyebrows were raised when the formation of yet another coalition for health care was announced in Washington, D.C. The surprise was the appearance of new players in the game. The National Leadership Coalition for Health Care Reform included not only NYNEX and the IBEW, but also an extensive representation from the Fortune 500 list, as well as a number of powerful labor unions. Coming together to "develop an American plan for health care" were corporate powerhouses including AT&T, Bethlehem Steel, DuPont, Ford, Kodak, Lockheed, the Marriott Corporation, Minnesota Mining, and W.R. Grace & Company. Some had always been nonunion if not aggressively anti-union, but now they were making common cause with the American Federation of Teachers, the Communications Workers of America, the Service Employees International Union, and the United Steelworkers. Also joining this unlikely collection were AARP, the American College of Physicians, the Association of Health Centers, and the Families USA Foundation. It was an odd—and potent—alliance.

What caused these diverse organizations to coalesce was the common belief that the American health system was in an ever-worsening crisis. Big business was feeling the pinch of rising health insurance costs for its workers and retirees and appeared willing, if the action at the coalition's first meeting was any indication, to abandon long-cherished ideological positions. By a vote of 17–6, the group agreed to go beyond simply exploring private market approaches and investigate the possibility of governmental intervention as a possible solution to the problem.

The emergence of large industrial companies as consumers, with consumer interests, may turn out to be an important new element in the drive to achieve national health care. The careful use of the word "may" should be noted, because it remains to be seen whether, for these companies, "governmental intervention" means more than just another bailout. It could be significant, or it could be just a coincidence, that Chrysler, a company that has shown itself to be sympathetic to a Canadian-style single-payer system, was not among those organizing the National Leadership Coalition for Health Care—nor, officially, was the AFL-CIO. In fact, among the participating labor unions were those known to be lukewarm to the single-payer system (like the SEIU).

Experience in Maine has taught that the Business Roundtable, a collection of large companies and insurers, would band together to pressure government into imposing regulations on providers—often extraordinarily intrusive ones—if they thought such action might save them money. The Maine Chamber of Commerce, for all of its hoary preaching about "keeping government off the backs of the people," had no reservations about leading the fight to place government on the backs of doctors and hospitals and keeping it firmly planted there.

The Business Roundtable in Maine went a step further, allying itself with what it had always considered the "left wing." Of course, there was profit in it for them when they backed the Maine Health Program, a legislative initiative that included something for everyone. The unifying ingredients were that state taxpayers would pick up the cost of health care coverage for a portion of the uninsured and of some of the hospitals' uncompensated care and bad debts. It was a win-win situation for everyone. Insurance companies benefited because, under state law, they were required to absorb some part of the expenses of uncompensated care and bad debts. For businesses the plan meant an easing of the pressure for higher premiums. And for consumer groups it was a case of getting more access to health care for more people. The groans of the taxpayers were muted since the new taxes to pay for the program were mostly "sin" taxes on cigarettes and liquor, with a sales tax on used boats thrown in to complete the package.

It was a case of the lion laying down with the lamb when the Chamber of Commerce made common front with the Maine Peoples Alliance. But when the march on the Shawmut Inn took place in Kennebunkport, the Chamber of Commerce was nowhere in sight. Leadership had devolved onto the activist groups.

The Maine Peoples Alliance is itself something of a phenomenon.

It is part of a nationwide network of grassroots organizations devoted to social issues and loosely banded together under the rubric of Citizen Action in Washington, D.C. The strength of the Maine Peoples Alliance is in its method of operation, depending heavily on door-to-door canvassing to back up its legislative agenda. It has worked for various causes in the past, but lately has put emphasis on universal health care. To that end it has formed a coalition with other groups under the umbrella name of Citizens for Affordable Health Care. Similar multitiered operations now exist throughout the United States.

"GIVE 'EM HEALTH" printed in large letters on a poster is one of the first sights to greet a visitor to the offices of Health Access on San Francisco's Mission Street. Another Citizen Action spinoff, Health Access shares offices with one of its creators, an older organization known as Public Advocates. Health Access's creed is simply expressed: "Current health spending, once intelligently rearranged, is enough to cover all Californians with comprehensive benefits, including long-term care." The group publishes reports, including one in 1988 entitled *The California Dream, The California Nightmare: 5.2 Million People With No Health Insurance.* It also has a foundation for collecting tax-deductible contributions, and a non–tax-deductible organization for lobbying purposes. And lobby it does, especially on behalf of the Health Access Plan, a single-payer concept introduced by an Oakland state senator. Health Access is made up of 120 organizations, including "religious, civil rights and local grass-roots organizations, unions, seniors, health care workers and consumer advocates."[2] In addition, this statewide conglomeration works closely with local coalitions in Alameda, Contra Costa, Los Angeles, Yolo, San Diego and Orange Counties. A possible strategy the group is considering is to conduct a statewide referendum on the issue of universal health care, in the fashion of the famous Proposition 13. It is generally agreed among proponents of national health care that action by California, the nation's most populous state, would have a tremendous impact on the nation as a whole.

Maine and California are not unique. Many other states have similar groups. In Louisiana there is the Louisiana Health Care Campaign. As it explains in its brochure, this organization, too, has brought together "a coalition of citizen groups; health, education and social service agencies; unions, religious and community organizations, and others who are concerned about ACCESS TO AFFORD-ABLE HEALTH CARE."[3] Among the twenty-eight groups cited as members are the United Methodist Church, Catholic Community Services, the Louisiana AFL-CIO, the St. Tammany Health Care Coalition, the West Feliciana Council on Aging, and the Oil, Chemical and Atomic Workers Union. During the 1991 session of the state legislature, the Louisiana Health Care Campaign joined forces with two other major groups, the Louisiana Consumers League and the Coalition for Realistic Insurance, to conduct "day-in, day-out" lobbying against "a well-financed industry with a history of heavy political contributions to legislators." Their goal was to achieve a series of salient insurance reforms, including protection for consumers when an insurer goes out of business.[4]

Health Care Campaign executive director Marcus Carson explained the consumers' concerns: "It's no longer just the poor who don't get care...Failed companies and canceled insurance coverage are experiences that cross all boundaries. What we saw this year was men and women, black and white, Democrat and Republican, all pulling together, finally figuring out that we have more in common than differences."[5]

Minnesota COACT (Citizens Organization Acting Together) also canvasses and lobbies, but goes beyond health care measures, particularly to help farmers in this northern agricultural state. It claims its health care coalition, the Minnesota Health Care Campaign, is the "largest health care coalition in the state's history."[6] Its victories include helping to stop doctors from overcharging senior citizens and pushing for legislation to create the Minnesota Healthcare Access Commission. Currently it is supporting universal health care legislation in the state legislature, and not long ago it issued a report showing that commercial insurers in the state spent $190 million a year more in administrative costs to deliver the same benefits as Medicare.

Efforts in Montana are being spearheaded by the Montana Senior Citizens Association. It is a state affiliate of the National Council of Senior Citizens and the National Health Care Campaign, two of the more prominent national groups promoting universal health care. Organized in 1973 to address a wide range of issues, it has forty-five chapters in twelve districts. Priority issues include "a comprehensive National Health Care Program to replace the ineffective patchwork of programs which currently leave millions with no health care or without adequate health care coverage,"[7] as well as improved transportation for rural communities and opposition to a state sales tax.

Whether in Maine, California, Louisiana, Minnesota, or Montana, grassroots organizing for better health care is a constant force. It is stronger in some places than others, but it seems to be picking up strength as a movement. As the Louisiana experience demonstrates, when more than the "poor" are affected—as happened when the Champion Insurance Company collapsed, or when the costs of medical insurance and care began biting too deeply into middle-class pocketbooks—local action is inevitable.

In Washington, D.C., there are innumerable consumer groups applying constant pressure. None of them, with the possible exception of organized labor and the advocates for the elderly, have resources to match those of the provider and payer groups like the AMA or the HIAA. As for the involvement of business on the side of the consumer, that is as yet questionable—even suspicious—as evidenced by an article in a Labor Research Association publication headlined, "Is Iaccoca for Real? Labor Should Not Depend on It."[8]

The reference was to Lee Iaccoca, chairman of the board of Chrysler Corporation. Iaccoca gained national attention when he openly supported a national health insurance program, reputedly after discovering he was paying five hundred dollars more in health care costs to produce a car at his Michigan plants than he was just across the border in Ontario. Iaccoca is quoted in the LRA article as saying: "American industry cannot compete effectively with the rest of the world unless something is done about the great imbalance between health care costs in the U.S. and national health care systems in virtually every other country ... Other countries put those costs in their taxes, but we put them in the price of our products." Also quoted is the former chair of Goodyear Tire and Rubber, Robert Mercer: "I never thought I would be in favor of a government health policy, but there are things that government must do." Even the chairman of the ultraconservative National Association of Manufacturers, Richard Heckert, is reported to have conceded that the structure of American health care must be changed "if we want to be internationally competitive." After mentioning agreements between labor and management to lobby for change, the LRA expresses the skepticism implied in its headline: "As employers continue to push cost-shifting and benefit-cutting, it is appropriate to question whether in fact they are solid allies in the fight for national health care. Recognizing the distinct possibility that they are not, it is necessary for labor to develop its own program and seek allies in the broader community."

Fueling labor's cynicism is the fact that insurance companies are major investors in large corporations. In 1988, the top fifty insurance companies poured $58 billion into stocks and bonds. As the LRA article concluded, a real question of self-interest arises: "Will corporate heads like Lee Iaccoca be willing to cut off a hand that feeds them with enormous sums of capital?"

Organized labor recognizes that it must "develop its own program." Yet the same LRA publication, in announcing that the AFL-CIO had formally established a committee, under the leadership of SEIU president John Sweeney, to promote national health care, admitted that "the committee has not yet determined, however, the kind of new system of national health care it will attempt to win." The debate had begun within the ranks of labor.

That was 1989, and apparently the debate is still going on. The split can be seen in the lineups of labor organizations in Washington in support of competing measures offered in the 1991 Congress. One such measure is the Senate Leadership Bill, whose prime sponsor is Senate Majority Leader George Mitchell of Maine, which builds on the present system and has received the blessing of the AFL-CIO leadership. Another is the "single-payer" bill of Congressman Marty Russo of Illinois. The roster of unions that have signed onto that bill is impressive, particularly in light of the opposite action of the AFL-CIO Executive Council. Russo Bill supporters include auto workers, textile workers, postal workers, mine workers, machinists, and longshoremen.

Another union giving strong support to the single-payer approach is the Oil, Chemical and Atomic Workers Union (OCAW), which, in March 1989, endorsed the proposal for a Canadian-style health care system devised by the then–newly organized Physicians for a National Health Care Program.

Having made their decision, the OCAW leadership had to sell the idea to its rank and file. To many union members, comfortable with the insurance provided by employers (sometimes covering 100 percent), a change—and certainly a change that might involve a tax increase—is not an easy sell. But labor can see the handwriting on the wall. They face downward pressure on wages and, most visible to the rank and file, the increasing bites coming out of their own paychecks. OCAW showed its members that in 1980 less than 50 percent of American companies made their workers pay for family coverage, but six years later this figure had jumped to 69 percent. One-third of all companies negotiating in 1987, the union told its membership, were trying to eliminate or cut health insurance coverage.[9] Thus unions are on the defensive, their goal the maintenance of benefits rather than any expansion of either benefits or wages. A strategy adopted by the OCAW was to try and induce companies to work jointly with them for the long term solution of a national health care program, and write such cooperation into the contracts they signed.

An active consumer group with close ties to labor and an uncompromising position on universal health care is the National Council for Senior Citizens, composed mainly of retired union members. Founded in 1961, primarily to push for Medicare, the organization calls enactment of Medicare legislation "NCSC's first major legislative victory." That heritage, it goes on to say, "will serve us well in the coming years as we join with other concerned groups to realize yet another dream—a national health care program for all Americans."[10]

Claiming 5 million seniors in its 605 clubs, NCSC has thrown its support behind the Russo Bill since, in its view, it incorporates the ten principles necessary in any health plan. These include universal access, comprehensive benefits, downplaying of co-payments and deductibles, cost-containment, protection of patient rights, long-term care, and a single payer. Their current activities are focused around a nationwide petition drive under the heading "Grandparents Care." The idea behind using grandparents as a theme is to counteract any negative residue from the catastrophic illness fiasco—the sense that senior citizens were being selfish in objecting to a method of financing that would have fallen on their shoulders. Grandparents who care, the argument holds, want to see everyone, young and old, fully covered.

The NCSC lobbies aggressively, and in 1990 worked successfully for a bill to impose Federal regulations on Medigap policies being sold to make up for the inadequacies of Medicare. This represented a significant breakthrough, since insurance companies had long fought to keep the Feds from regulating any part of their business, leaving it instead to state regulators who were notoriously prone to be from the industry and thus sympathetic to the industry point of view. Controversy over abuses in Medigap insurance had raged for some time before Congress mandated changes. The 1990 bill required that at least sixty-five cents of every dollar be paid out in benefits, and that Medigap policies not overlap—i.e., one policy can only replace another, not supplement it. The latter restriction ended a situation in which many seniors were convinced by salesmen to buy unneeded coverages. Other recent actions of the NCSC have included protests over Medicare cuts, a picket of the AMA's headquarters by a thousand delegates to the NCSC convention in Chicago, and a well-publicized trip to view Canadian health care.

Adding to the income of seniors is a feature of the nation's largest organization of senior citizens, the 30 million-member American Association of Retired Persons. AARP does not just represent the consumer interests of its members; it is also an insurer, or, more properly, an agent for a very large group policy. In the announced interest of offering its members a break as consumers, AARP works with Prudential to offer members a range of supplementary policies. AARP also has its own "pharmacy service," which dispenses prescription drugs by mail.

These activities are not without their critics. The Public Citizen Health Research Group, an offshoot of Ralph Nader's organization, has called AARP "a well-paid lackey of the health insurance industry."[11] The group charged that because AARP took in $348 million from its health insurance business, it failed to come out strongly for universal health care (although some state affiliates have strongly backed single-payer legislation). AARP has also been faulted for not offering insurance plans to all members. That AARP cannot, or will not, do this is made evident by the disclaimer in one of the ads in its publication, *Modern Maturity*. The ad states, "Long Term Care Plans available only to AARP members ages 50-79 *who meet certain eligibility requirements.*" (Italics added). Insurance is, after all, a business, even when conducted by a consumer organization. Ergo, another AARP disclaimer, this time appearing on the enrollment form of any AARP Group Hospital Plan: "DO YOU UNDERSTAND THAT THE PLAN WILL NOT PAY BENEFITS FOR STAYS

WHICH START OR CARE RECEIVED DURING THE FIRST 3 MONTHS OF COVERAGE IF CAUSED BY OR RESULTING FROM CONDITIONS FOR WHICH THE INSURED HAS RECEIVED MEDICAL ADVICE OR TREATMENT DURING THE 6 MONTHS PRIOR TO THE INSURANCE EFFECTIVE DATE?"

It is not hard to see the ambivalence of AARP toward the ultimate shape of a national health care system. You have only to look at their publications. While access to health care is set as a priority issue for its National Legislative Council, the language setting that priority is so vague as to be open to any sort of interpretation: "Health care coverage should be extended to the millions of currently uninsured Americans. Health care costs should be controlled through a restructuring of reimbursement without further increasing the burden of already high out-of-pocket costs."[12]

Highlights, the AARP volunteers' newsletter, published a favorable article about the Canadian health care system in the spring of 1989. It received some flattering mail, which it published in the next issue. "I am immensely cheered by the report in Highlights ... that AARP is impressed with the universal health care system in Canada," wrote Russell Simmons of Raton, New Mexico. "It was very good to see the article about Health Care in Canada and I hope AARP will push vigorously for us to have the same coverage in the USA," said Gladys Goddard of Asbury, New Jersey. "Some new medicines and technologies are available in Canada long before they are available to doctors here ... One wishes we had a comparable system here," volunteered M. Vesta Papafagos of Houston, Texas, who had undergone emergency treatment in Canada.[13]

Despite this, there is no strong sense that AARP is, or intends to be, out front for a Canadian-style system. The organization's executive director, Horace B. Deets, emphasizes his support for the "Medical Treatment Effectiveness Program" of the Agency for Health Care Policy and Research. AARP's president, Robert Maxwell, in attacking the Bush administration's Medicare cuts, called for "comprehensive reform" of the American health care system, and suggested Congress pave the way by holding public hearings around the country to "focus attention on the tough choices that must be part of the solution."[14] Finally, AARP's legislative director gives qualified praise to the Senate Democratic Leadership Bill by noting that it advances the debate to a higher stage.

It is unclear whether the tentativeness of AARP's leadership is, as muckrakers allege, based on the organization's vested interest in selling private insurance and cut-rate drugs, or whether it is the result of the brutal beating it took when it rushed out front to support the catastrophic illness measure only to find out after passage that the law was detested by many of its members. Or can it be that a combination of self-interest and caution is acting as a brake on this huge and powerful organization?

Physicians for a National Health Program (PNHP) is a small group, but one that has made an impact on the debate far out of proportion to its size. In contrast to the 30 million member AARP, the four-thousand-member PNHP seems to know exactly what it wants. It argues and lobbies for a Canadian-style single-payer health care system. It has articulately set forth its views in medical journal articles and has drawn increasingly respectful attention in the national media. The reason this small organization has captured so much attention is that for the very first time, doctors themselves are proposing a radical change in the health care delivery system.

The PNHP proposal was put forward initially in an article in the prestigious *New England Journal of Medicine* in January 1989. It was written by Dr. David Himmelstein and Dr. Steffi Woolhandler, who are husband and wife. Also credited with authorship was the "Writing Committee of the Working Group on Program Design."

This writing committee was made up of thirty members who, after drafting the program, submitted it to 412 other physicians "representing virtually every state and medical specialty."[15] The document opened with a litany of complaints about the present system from the physicians' point of view. It railed against the "countless hours" they wasted on billing and bureaucracy, the lack of attention they could give the uninsured, their dilemma when caught between "administrators demanding early discharge and elderly patients with no one to help at home—all the while glancing over our shoulders at the peer-review organizations," penny-pinching in HMOs that has an adverse effect on medical outcomes, and the frustrations they faced when dealing with public health, where even such basic services as prenatal care and immunization cannot be assured in this richest health care system in the world.

Then the document went into the desired changes. The writers started by explaining that "our plan borrows many features from the

93

Canadian national health care program and adapts them to the unique circumstances of the United States." They then discussed the impact of the switch to a system featuring universal access, "lump-sum" payments from a single source to hospitals, and similarly nego-tiated "lump-sum" fees or salaries for doctors. It is interesting to note their perception of how physicians would be affected. Since HMOs would be permitted, physicians could either work for them on salary (as many now do), work on salary for the government (currently the case in the VA, the military, the Indian Health Service, and other government agencies), or accept fee-for-service (the custom of the bulk of American doctors). The difference in fee-for-service pay-ments would be that they would come from a single payer and be subject to a cap.

In the eyes of the PNHP, such a system would have important advantages for physicians:

- Physicians could concentrate on medicine...
- Billing would involve imprinting the patient's national health pro-gram card on a charge slip, checking a box to indicate the complexi-ty of the procedure or service, and sending the slip (or a computer record) to the physician-payment board. This simplification of billing would save thousands of dollars per practitioner in annual office expenses.
- Bureaucratic interference in clinical decision making would sharply diminish ...

This last point is heavily emphasized: "Indeed, there is much less administrative intrusion in day-to-day clinical practice in Canada (and most other countries with national health programs) than in the United States."[16]

The PNHP proselytizes actively. Its newsletters report on attempts to convert other groups. The 125,000-member National Association of Social Workers was mentioned in the November 1990 newsletter as issuing "a plan closely resembling PNHP's." On the state level, the PNHP has been particularly active in helping form health care coali-tions (Virginia and Florida are recent examples) and working on state health care legislative initiatives. The chapter in California's ultra-conservative Orange County has a busy speaker's bureau, out talking to groups such as the League of Women Voters, the American

Association of University Women, and the Screen Actors Guild. At conventions of the American College of Physicians, the American Psychiatric Association, and Physicians for Social Responsibility, PNHP has manned informational booths and signed up new members. It has coordinated closely with the Oil, Chemical and Atomic Workers Union, which adopted the PNHP plan and is promoting it, and for the past year has shared offices in Washington, D.C., and worked closely with the Public Citizen Health Research Group. These two were involved in an important joint action on May 13, 1991. They scheduled an issues background conference for the media the day before the appearance of the AMA's special issue of its journal dealing with the question of what to do about the uninsured and underinsured in America. In other words, they scheduled an expert rebuttal before the fact. Ralph Nader was the lead speaker. His subject was "National Health Care Program: The Issue For The 90s."

The Public Citizen Health Research Group was founded in 1971 by Nader and Dr. Sidney Wolfe, the latter still editor of its publication, *Health Letter.* Wolfe likewise serves on the board of directors of Public Citizen, also founded in 1971 by Nader. It describes itself as a non-profit citizen research, lobbying, and litigation organization. Health, together with the law and energy policy, are among its prime concerns. *Questionable Doctors,* a report released by the group in June 1990, listed seven thousand doctors who had been disciplined by state or Federal government agencies, as well as reporting that a hundred thousand people are injured or killed in hospitals every year as a result of physicians' negligence. The report also noted that state medical boards have actually decreased disciplinary actions against doctors, even as the number of practitioners has grown by 6 percent.

Public Citizen uses both the Health Research Group and the Litigation Group in its attempt to end false health advertising—as in the case of potentially harmful silicone breast implants promoted in a commercial on a Denver radio station—or to have drugs approved by the Federal Food and Drug Administration (FDA) removed as useless. While working on these bread-and-butter consumer product safety issues, Public Citizen and its Health Research Group also promote a change in the entire system.

The Consumers Union, publisher of *Consumer Reports,* seems to operate in the same fashion. Their two-part series in the summer of

1990, comparing the American health care system unfavorably with Canada's, attracted much attention. One article was accompanied by one of the chart-style ratings for which the publication is well known. Being judged were medical health insurance policies (Minnesota Blue Cross-Blue Shield's Aware Gold PPO Plan was deemed the best; Aid Association for Lutherans Total Med II Plan the worst). While lining up firmly in favor of national health care, the Consumers Union, like Public Citizen, continues to try to lead the buying public through the minefield of present-day health care realities.

The range and diversity of consumer groups with a stake in the national health care issue is immense. However, two more important groups deserve mention.

Families USA Foundation has been a pioneer and a prime mover in the latest thrust for national health care. Its original name, National Health Care Campaign, speaks for its commitment. What the group describes as its "major grassroots event for 1991" was an "Emergency Drive," involving ambulances driving through the country and converging on Washington, D.C., with petitions for a national health care program. Within various states, rallies were staged where intrastate ambulances would meet with the interstate ones. The goal was to collect a million signatures of people who had "voted" for a new health care system in the nation. In this complicated, attention-getting media event, the principal aim was to inject the issue into the 1992 presidential and congressional elections. Families USA works closely with Citizen Action's grassroots network and Jobs With Justice, the latter a coalition of labor unions.

Finally there is the American Public Health Association, reputedly the largest organization of health professionals in the country. They, too, produce a number of publications. The *American Journal of Public Health* is their professional organ, devoted to scholarly articles on public health subjects. For the most part, policy matters are left to *Nation's Health*, the publication the organization calls its official newspaper.

The American Public Health Association has declared itself in favor of a national health program. It has not selected a specific approach, but has devised a set of thirteen criteria against which it intends to judge proposals. These include coverage for everyone in the U.S., comprehensive benefits, elimination of financial barriers to care, fair payment to providers, non-discrimination in delivery of services, consumer education, and—perhaps of greatest interest from the viewpoint of public health workers—disease prevention and health promotion programs. The APHA, as a private organization, lobbies government. Although it has not yet chosen an exact legislative vehicle, its aims are clear—it wants a program where every child will be able to get regular checkups and care when ill, where no doctor or hospital will turn away anyone who can't pay, and where no one will be surprised by financially ruinous medical bills. The APHA instructs its members to tell their congressmen that "you want some of your tax money to be spent on a national health program for everyone."[17]

OTHER PLAYERS

The search for the ideal system of health care for the United States is reminiscent of the fable of the blind men trying to describe an elephant after each touched it once. The first insisted the beast was snakelike, the second that the creature was built like a wall, and so forth, all dependent on which part of the elephant had been touched. A similar problem exists among all the other players whose interests or concerns have caused them to involve themselves in the national health care debate. Few are neutral. It seems everyone has an opinion.

Many of the groups fall into those categories already discussed: providers, payers, or consumers. Others do not fit into such neat pigeonholes. Yet all seem intent on playing a role. They include law firms that specialize in health matters or serve as lobbyists for health care interests; technical organizations like Santa Monica's Value Health Services, a company that markets state-of-the-art computer software to help providers determine the appropriateness of given medical treatments; high-powered think tanks like the U.S. Department of Health and Human Services' Agency for Health Care Policy and Research; the Institute of Medicine, a more independent yet still governmentally connected branch of the National Academy of Sciences; the many other private health policy consultant groups; drug companies; medical technology producers; medical goods suppliers; a gaggle of foundations, including giants like the Robert Wood Johnson Foundation, which pours millions into health care policy experiments, HMO-sponsored foundations like FHP in California, and those like New Hampshire's Seacoast Foundation for Health, established after the sale of a hospital; organizations of health care self-insurers like the California-based Self-Insurance Institute of America; various governmental operations including the VA, the Food and Drug Administration, the National Institutes of Health, which spend billions for basic research that will be turned over to private industry for exploitation after the breakthroughs are made, and the beleaguered Inspector General of the Department of Health and Human Services, who has incurred the wrath of the AMA by coming down hard on doctors for abuses and fraud in government programs. As if that weren't enough to cloud the debate, consider also other groups concerned about medical education, still others concerned with the fight against AIDS or other specific diseases, and service clubs that have adopted medical missions, like the Lions with their concern for eye care or the Shriners with their devotion to helping burn victims. Then, too, there are advocates for injured workers wrestling with the workers' compensation system, nurses, nonmedical health personnel, malpractice trial lawyers, holistic healers and other nontraditional providers, chemical dependency counselors and....but by now the idea is clear. Almost no organization or individual in the nation is untouched by the subject of health care. Few are not concerned with its future.

Obviously, all their opinions cannot be discussed. Yet a few of these other players have points of view well worth considering.

The Veterans Administration. This health care system is "the single largest health care system in the United States (and possibly in the world). It is a politicized anomaly in that it is a highly socialized health care system that resides in a nation that is highly committed to capitalism."[18] Arguing that it should play an important role in any national health care scheme, the VA cites the high quality of health care it now delivers despite what is called the "socialistic nature of the VA health care system."[19] It claims to have led the country in the development of modern care techniques and rehabilitation for the elderly. Admitting that its care was mediocre until 1946, it says that care subsequently improved vastly to become comparable to the very best, due to its ties to medical schools and to superior research. It points to research accomplishments on tuberculosis, hypertension, psychoses, coronary heart disease, and drug and alcohol addiction, outstanding enough to have resulted in two Nobel Prizes.

Operating on a budget of $11.2 billion in 1989-90, the VA treated 3 million individuals despite new Federal restrictions limiting eligibility to "service-connected" veterans and the financially needy. This volume of care is one reason it claims it can play a key role in guiding any national health care system—it has had to increase efficiency in the face of shrinking budgets, operate with fewer people, cut administrative costs well below those of the private sector, and still produce, in its opinion, "a level of quality of care that is comparable to that of the private sector.[20] The VA has cited a number of ways it could be helpful in a health care system expanded to cover everyone. It admits there would be political opposition from veterans' organizations to the extension of service to nonveterans, but suggests it could remain a viable entity within the system by expanding its services to care for veterans with non–service-connected ailments, and for the families of veterans. In this way some thirty thousand currently unused VA hospital beds would be utilized. In discussions of this alternative, particularly with regard to those over sixty-five, it has been admitted that there is a "total lack of dialogue between the VA and HCFA [Health Care Finance Administration] regarding the development of efficient methods of sharing resources and responsibilities for caring for the aged."[21]

The VA's ties to the other large government provider of health care, the military, have also been less than satisfactory. The Defense Department's outlay for medical care is actually even bigger than the VA's—$14 billion a year—and has been attacked by some who believe it is "riddled with waste, consistently exceeds its budget and doesn't even have a clearly identified manager in charge."[22]

Attempts by VA secretary Edward Derwinski to establish closer ties with the Pentagon health system—particularly an arrangement by which the VA, with unused bed space, would care for certain categories of military patients—have yet to result in a signed agreement. Along the same lines of turf defense, the military health establishment, until recently, has resisted congressional pressure to merge the really separate fiefdoms of the Army, Navy, and Air Force Surgeons General. The Military Health Services System not only tends directly to the health needs of active members of the armed services, but also administers the insurance program popularly known as CHAMPUS. Its relationship to Medicare and to private insurance is a constant matter of congressional concern.

The VA, given its support by powerful veterans' groups, will clearly have to be assigned a role in the evolution of any American national health care system.

Another player of potential importance is a previously obscure Federal body now called the **Agency for Health Care Policy and Research.** As mentioned earlier, Congress has funded this agency generously to continue what is considered promising work on "medical effectiveness." This appears to some to be the new panacea, a cost-saving wonder cure, relatively painless and nonintrusive, that will save the present system from radical surgery. The thinking holds that if these studies can show the way to standardize means of eliminating unnecessary and unjustified medical intervention, the benefits of the current system can be maintained while the spiral of cost increases, the engine driving the push for drastic reform, will be diminished.

How realistic this notion is remains to be seen. Meanwhile the agency, while concentrating on "medical treatment effectiveness research," will continue funding and promoting research in many areas. A few of their studies are *Patterns of Hospital Utilization Among Privately Insured Patients, 1980–1986, Choices of Health Insurance and the Two-Worker Household,* and *Delivering Essential Health Care Services in Rural Areas: An Analysis of Alternative Models.* In most cases the agency contracts with private researchers to conduct their investigations. One recent "medical effectiveness" study involved a look at the removal of wisdom teeth. Led by an expert from Harvard, a team of researchers found that removing wisdom teeth before they become impacted or diseased produces more disability and cost than is justified—$278 million and 3 million days of discomfort versus $51.5 million and 776,000 days of discomfort for not taking them out early.[23]

The AHCPR, through its "User Liaison Program," distributes important findings to policymakers on state and local levels, often through seminars held around the country. One such seminar, held in the fall of 1990, was entitled "Medical Effectiveness Research: Implications for State Government." It was held because "state officials have expressed concern and some confusion over newspaper reports (as well as articles in scholarly journals) which indicate that a significant number of major medical interventions were judged by research to be 'unnecessary' or even 'unjustified.'[24] In sponsoring such workshops, the agency uses private contractors, in this case Washington-based Health Systems Research Inc., one of the number of small consultant groups that are also players on the health care scene.

The **Institute of Medicine**, a scholarly institution with direct ties to the Federal government, advertises itself with the slogan "Twenty Years of Making a Difference In The Nation's Health." It was chartered in 1970 by the National Academy of Sciences to examine problems in human health through a body of diverse, unbiased experts.

Often called upon by Congress and the administration to conduct specific studies, the IOM prides itself on changes in laws and regulations that reflect its recommendations. In addition to publishing reports, IOM brings together experts from universities, industry, government, medicine, etc., for "workshops, forums, roundtable sessions, symposia and other gatherings."[25]

The IOM's work is often wedded to particular government action. Its 382-page report on Medicare-Medicaid reimbursement policies became a report of the House Ways and Means Committee on Health. A three-volume study called *Contrasts in Health Status* was the basis for an amendment offered by Congressmen Edward Roybal and Sylvio Conte, one that added $31 million to maternal and child health appropriations. At the request of the National Cancer Institute, the IOM evaluated the initial plan for a "war on cancer," and was a strong factor in shaping that plan's final design. An IOM report on the medical effects of abortion created a storm of protest from anti-abortionists. That controversial report, it should be noted, was privately financed. Another important study, requested by the White House Office of Management and Budget, examined the National Institutes of Health. Its purpose was to determine whether major structural changes were needed to attract and retain scientists needed by the NIH. Congressional action was taken on some of the suggestions, including creation of endowed chairs for distinguished scientists, the Senior Biomedical Research Service, and a scholars program for young researchers. In the Omnibus Budget Reconciliation Act of 1986, the IOM was mandated to conduct a two-year study of the quality of health care under Medicare.

National health care is obviously a question of great interest to the IOM. In 1989 and 1990, it used a five-year lecture series established by the Richard and Hinda Rosenthal Foundation as a vehicle to explore the subject. The proceedings were published under the title *Providing Universal and Affordable Health Care*. Speakers included political leaders like Senate Majority Leader George Mitchell, Utah governor Scott Matheson, and San Antonio mayor Henry Cisneros. Participating health care scholars included Harvard's Robert Blendon and Rashi Fein, author Karen Davis, and consultant Lawrence Lewin.

The **National Institutes of Health** are a multibillion-dollar operation mainly involved with biomedical research and development. They are not specifically concerned with policy as such. In 1991, they spent $7.5 billion on studies designed to eventually provide new weapons against illness. Occasionally, however, their actions do impinge on areas of public policy.

President Ronald Reagan's executive order forbidding the NIH to fund work on fetal cell transplants, which showed promising results in treating several disorders, particularly Parkinson's disease, has stirred continual controversy. According to *Time* magazine, "frustrated U.S. researchers watched helplessly as their European counterparts moved ahead on medical applications of fetal tissue."[26] A poignant open letter to President George Bush from a self-described staunch Republican activist in Florida, pleading with him to rescind Reagan's action, further brought home the implications for average Americans. Mrs. Judy Culpepper of Fort Pierce was pleading for her thirty-nine-year-old husband, who had just developed Parkinson's disease. "Please, please, don't send my husband and millions like him into his lonely battle without the funds he needs, without the equipment he may well need to win the war against the disease of the living … Don't tie his hands behind his back. Please lift the ban on federally funded fetal research transplantation at NIH."[27]

Another controversy recently erupted over steps taken by the NIH's newly appointed director, Dr. Bernardine Healy. After three months in office, she sharply criticized the operation of the Institutes' Office of Scientific Integrity, and forced the resignation of its chief investigator. That incurred the wrath of Michigan congressman John Dingell, who charged she was dismantling the Office of Scientific Integrity, which looks into charges of incompetency and fakery by research scientists. Dingell charged she had sabotaged two important investigations—charges denied by Dr. Healy.

The whole question of biomedical research and its role in a national health care system arises frequently. Opponents charge that a change to a single-payer system will end America's preponderant lead in medical research. Proponents react and say that is "preposterous." They point out that research like that of the NIH is funded separately, and they point to research breakthroughs in countries that have universal health care programs—breakthroughs like the discovery of the AIDS virus in France.

The question has validity, however, when seen from the point of view of the **drug industry**. The Pharmaceutical Manufacturers Association boasts that its spending on biomedical research, $9.2 billion in 1991, surpasses the NIH as the "world's principal source of biomedical R&D funds."[28]

Drug companies are enormously profitable. *Fortune* magazine says that "no American industry has ever defied the laws of economic gravity like the pharmaceuticals."[29] Their returns on equity to shareholders have been 50 percent higher than the median for the Fortune 500 industrial companies; in 1990, returns climbed 26 percent, double the Fortune 500 median. American companies now produce 42 percent of the major drugs marketed worldwide. In 1990, Americans paid $50 billion for prescription medications.

American drug companies defend their high prices by citing their investments in research. *Fortune* quotes John R. Stafford, CEO of American Home Products, a leading drug company, as saying, "We don't want to see a gem of U.S. industrial prowess hampered by limits on prices."

But their argument isn't bought that easily, even under present conditions. Senator David Pryor of Arkansas has been a relentless antagonist of high drug prices, which rose 152 percent in the 1980s. Legislation he sponsored, which became law in 1990, required drug companies to sell to Medicaid at the lowest price they offered to any other purchaser. Furthermore, Pryor has consistently questioned the drug companies' assertions, claiming that they spent more on marketing and advertising in 1991 ($10 billion) than they did on development of new medicines ($9 billion). He also cited companies with large increases in prices that have brought no new drugs to market in years.

More work for drug company lobbyists lies in Pryor's latest bill in

Congress. It would reduce the Federal tax credits a drug company now receives for producing in Puerto Rico if its prices rose faster than general inflation. It would also initiate a study, presumably for eventual application to the U.S., of Canada's drug price review board, which can restrain excessive price increases for pharmaceuticals.

A whole panoply of consumer groups of the types mentioned earlier have supported Pryor's bill. Further illustrating the interconnections among many of the different players on the health care scene are several other measures currently under consideration in Washington. Senator Edward Kennedy wants drug price breaks, similar to the Pryor ones for Medicaid, to be applied to the Public Health Service and other government health care provider agencies. At the same time, the House Veterans Affairs Committee is trying to restore discounts for veterans' hospitals, discontinued by some drug companies in an attempt to evade the provisions of the 1990 Pryor bill.

The impact of high drug prices on the current U.S. health care crisis was aptly illustrated by a study of the disbursement of two drugs for treating heart attacks. One, called T.P.A., costs $2,200 a dose. The other, streptokinase, costs $76 to $300 a dose. Although two studies have shown both equally effective in dissolving blood clots, American doctors generally choose the high-priced brand, unlike most doctors in other countries. Had streptokinase been used instead of T.P.A., the U.S. health care system would have saved about $200 million in 1990 alone.

A number of reasons have been given to explain why American doctors so frequently prescribe T.P.A. Genentech, its producer, did such aggressive marketing to herald its beneficial effects that some cardiologists were afraid they would be sued for malpractice if they didn't order it. Genentech has been just as aggressive in casting doubt on the studies that show the two drugs have equal efficiency. A touch of conflict-of-interest also entered Genentech's operations when it was revealed that eleven cardiologists involved in clinical trials of the two drugs had bought Genentech stock.[30] Genentech detail men (i.e., salesmen) have been accused not only of preying on doctors' fears of malpractice, but also of trying to discourage them from entering their patients into clinical trials, plus recruiting them for seminars held at posh resorts. In addition, the company apparently pays hospital nurses to train others in the use of T.P.A., thereby putting "a paid advocate ... right into the emergency room."[31] Under increased pressure to provide proof of its drug's superiority, Genentech has now launched a huge new clinical trial involving thirty-seven thousand patients. This trial, it has been charged, has allowed many doctors not to switch to streptokinase until the results are available.

With enormous financial stakes in maintaining the status quo, drug companies can be expected to be strong opponents of any major change in the so-called free-enterprise American health care system.

The same undoubtedly holds true for the **service companies** in the system. One such giant in the medical supply field is Baxter International, reputedly the field leader. In 1985, it acquired American Hospital Supply and took a dominant position in the provision of diagnostic procedures, blood therapy, and medical specialty devices. It markets 120,000 health care products, 70 percent of which it manufactures itself. The company's annual profit growth was estimated to be 20 percent in 1992, and its penetration of the diagnostics market is expected to increase with the introduction of a new product for treating hemophilia patients and new items for the cardiovascular market. Investment counselors (perhaps yet another "player") see Baxter as an outstanding stock buy.

Until now, **private foundations** have entered the health care policy arena only with cautious steps, fearful of the political world and charges of "lobbying" that could affect their tax-exempt status. The largest of the foundations showing a consistent interest in health care is the New Jersey–based Robert Wood Johnson Foundation, an independent offshoot of the Johnson and Johnson medical supply and pharmaceutical company. Its assets have increased considerably in the past five years, and now stand at $3.5 billion. In 1991, it will give out $165 million, an increase of $33 million over the previous year. In the spring of 1991, the foundation indicated that it would change the direction of its grants from the past, when it spent a lot of its money researching the control of health care costs. Now a prime focus will be "assuring access to basic health care for all Americans."[32] Two other key goals will be delivery of care to the chronically ill and reducing substance abuse. Particularly by tackling the access question, the Robert Wood Johnson Foundation has entered the area of health policy. And so has California's Henry J. Kaiser Foundation, which declared it would spend $100 million over five years on projects to help make Medicare and Medicaid work better. As summed up by Daniel Fox, the president of the venerable Milbank Memorial Fund, these new developments show that foundations are "rethinking the relationship between philanthropy and the goals of private and public health policies."[33] A whole new group of players is thereby added to the national health care debate.

Since the health care industry, with all its ramifications, is one of the major economic forces in the nation, the forces that compose it are endlessly varied. In the political struggle to come they will make their voices heard and their influence felt.

7 HOW SOME OTHER COUNTRIES DO IT

Let us first leave out consideration of Canada and its system of national health care. Interest in that operation is so intense and has been the subject of so much discussion and misinformation that it will be the subject of a subsequent chapter.

Meanwhile, since the United States is the only major nation on earth without a system of national health care, it seems instructive to take a look at how several other nations accomplish this feat.

Those opposed to any significant change harp on a belief that we Americans are somehow different, and that our uniqueness of character and system makes it impossible for us to join the rest of the industrialized world lest we somehow betray our birthright. The fact that almost every other country does have some form of national health care—and manages to run it at a lesser cost and with better health results for its people than we do—is dismissed out of hand as being somehow irrelevant. The fact that these countries have prosperous economies, in many cases outstripping our own, still doesn't silence the hysterical objections that national health care for this country is not affordable, that such a thing will ruin us financially, destroy our economy, etc.

The nations we will examine in detail are all part of the "free world." They have been selected in the hope of silencing the right-wing argument that a national health care system would put us in the "socialist" (read "Communist") camp. The governments of these nations range ideologically from ultraconservative, free-market (Great Britain) to left-wing, statist (France), with the others falling

107

somewhere between the two. In most of these countries the dynamics and politics of health care have not been stagnant. They have problems, and their disputes over possible solutions have engendered strong controversies. Perhaps the only thing all have in common is the underlying philosophy: *Everyone is included in the system.* No matter how these countries wrestle with the difficulties of their systems, that philosophy is never challenged.

GERMANY

There are those who think the German health care system is best suited to American needs, and may be the model to emulate. The chief executive of the AMA, Dr. James S. Todd, concedes that the German arrangement has "more relevance to the need for reform in this country than any nation we've looked at yet."[1]

Like the United States, Germany has a federal system, under which some powers reside in the national government and others are reserved for the states, which have their own elected bodies. The Germans call their states *"lander,"* and before the merger with East Germany, there were eleven of them. On the national level, their two legislative chambers resemble those of our Congress. The Bundestag is their House of Representatives, elected proportionately on the basis of population, and the Bundesrat represents the *lander* in the way our own Senate represents the states. Also as in the United States, most people in Germany are covered by health insurance through their employers. Government in Germany, both national and state, plays even less of a direct role in health care delivery than our own government. There are no programs comparable to Medicare or Medicaid, and spending by the government is only 14 percent of the total health bill (as compared to 41 percent in the U.S.).

Health care is much less costly in Germany. The per capita expenditure is only $1200, about half that of the American rate of $2354 (1989). The results: Life expectancy statistics are slightly better, and in infant mortality the Germans have the tenth lowest percentage in the world, while the U.S. has the twenty-second. Even the AMA's Dr. Todd admits the quality of German health care and the availability of high technology, while not quite on the U.S. level, leaves little to be desired.

The questions ask themselves: How do the Germans do it? What are the differences between our two systems?

The first thing to understand is that the health insurance enjoyed by all but a hundred thousand of the 61 million Germans (more like 80 million since unification) does not come, for the most part, from private companies. The bulk of it (90.9 percent) comes from approximately twelve hundred "sickness funds." These are non-profit organizations into which employers and employees contribute on a 50-50 basis. They are the principle payers in the German system, and they negotiate with the providers—doctors and hospitals—as to what will be paid.

The sickness funds have long been a staple in Germany. They existed even in the Middle Ages among the professional guilds. When Bismarck decided to provide health care for German workers in the 1880s, he made use of this basic element in building his system.

There are several different kinds of sickness funds: local ones that operate on a geographical basis, company funds used where a business may have branches across the country, craft-based funds that cover entire professions, special funds for farmers, miners, and sailors, and nationwide "substitute funds" for those who do not fit any of the above categories. Governance of each fund is by an elected assembly, half employer and half employee. For purposes of negotiating with providers, they are organized into state and national associations (the Germans call them "peak associations" and there are seven of them).

On the other side are national associations of physicians who agree upon a set amount for their services. Since 1977, the physicians have also agreed to an overall expenditure cap, that cap determined by a public body composed of representatives of government, payers, and providers. This is known as the "Concerted Action" (Konzertierte Aktion).

Despite the seeming complexity of the process, it all works very much like the single-payer system used in countries like Canada. The doctors accept a "global sum available for distribution among individual doctors. The doctors' associations then distribute this sum on a fee-for-service basis."[2]

Hospitals operate similarly. A "global sum" is negotiated with each individual hospital. Overall limits on hospital spending are suggested, as well, by the Konzertierte Aktion, and in 1985 hospitals were switched to prospective payment procedures. In contrast, capi-

109

tal costs—new equipment, buildings, etc.—are paid for by public funds. For twelve years (1972 to 1984) the national government contributed to them, as well as the *lander*, but now the state governments, alone, finance capital items out of general tax revenues.

Every German who earns less than (the equivalent of) thirty-eight thousand dollars a year must join a sickness fund. Many who are not required to do so also join. The premium for the average German worker in 1991 will be 12.5 percent of gross income, down slightly from 12.6 percent in 1990. This is about the same percentage paid by American workers, except some Americans pay nothing and others pay considerably more. Coverages, too, also vary widely among Americans.

For their money, Germans receive a minimum benefit package required by law. It includes the following:

- Hospital care and physician services.
- Dental care.
- Prescription drugs.
- Medical supplies and devices.
- Recuperative stays at health spas.
- Six weeks of employer-paid disability pay and 80 percent of salary for up to seventy-eight weeks afterwards.
- Fourteen weeks of employer-paid maternity leave.

Out-of-pocket costs for Germans include some co-payments for prescription drugs and for eyeglasses of better quality than supplied by the program, a minimal charge of $2.50 a day for the first two weeks of hospitalization, and about 40 percent of dental charges.

There is also private insurance in Germany. About 8.7 percent of the people buy it, and its coverage is more generous than that of the sickness funds. Some members of sickness funds also buy supplemental private insurance for amenities like private hospital rooms. Most people stay with their sickness funds for life, since once you leave one, you may never return.

The tiny percentage of Germans without health insurance consists of either the extremely wealthy content to pay their own bills, or vagabonds who do not remain in any one place long enough to be enrolled in a sickness fund.

A peculiarity of the German health care system is that it maintains a strict separation between doctors who practice in hospitals and those who do not. Doctors who work for hospitals are salaried and cannot see patients outside of the institution. Ambulatory doctors, the term for those who have practices not in a fixed setting, are forbidden to attend hospital patients and are paid on a fee-for-service basis. The exception is the hospital chiefs-of-staff. These powerful individuals may attend both hospital and ambulatory patients. In cases where an ambulatory physician is not available in a particular area, the rule is waived and a patient can see a hospital doctor.

Physicians in private practice—those outside hospitals—must accept everyone in a given sickness fund if they see a single member. They are forbidden to discriminate. Most of the ambulatory physicians in Germany practice alone—groups are rare.

Half of the German hospitals are publicly owned; the rest are private, about 37 percent non-profit and the remainder for-profit.

Politically, the German health care system has lately been in a situation analogous to that of Great Britain and, to a lesser extent, that of the United States. In the first two nations, fully developed, universal health care systems, with high levels of government support, have been subjected to what Professor Marian Dohler of the Max Planck Institute of Cologne calls "neo-conservative reform strategies in health policy."[3] The United States has seen the same phenomenon since the start of the Reagan administration, but superimposed on a system that is not universal.

In 1982, a coalition of middle-of-the-road and right-of-center political parties took power in Germany under Chancellor Helmut Kohl. They were swept into office on a wave of anti–welfare-state rhetoric. Yet, as Dohler notes, "only two concrete health measures were announced: an increase of co-payments in the statutory health insurance [sickness funds] and a reform of hospital finances. The implementation of these programmatic intentions hardly amounted to 'significant structural changes' as they were envisaged by leading neo-conservatives."[4]

In other words, the newly empowered conservatives were able to do little more than tinker with a system solidly in place. Out-of-pocket costs for Germans beyond their premiums for sickness fund insurance are still remarkably low (about 7 percent). The use of private insurance has grown somewhat, but is still less than 10 percent. In fact, the most salient of the conservative reforms has been to curtail

111

the pharmaceutical industry's control of the health care market and give people added incentive to use generic drugs since they now have to pay any price differential out of their own pockets.

There are problems in the German system, one of the most serious being the ever-present need to rein in rising costs. Another is the variation in payroll tax rates among the different sickness funds. A high rate is 13.5 percent of gross income, while others are as low as 11.5 percent. This has led to calls for a single national fund with one payroll tax level and one benefit package—certainly the opposite of what the pro-free-market conservatives would advocate. Some of the latter want to see Germany adopt an American-type system of private insurance, where high-risk coverage can be rejected.

Having multiple sickness funds does increase administrative costs. Still, Germany's administrative costs, some 5 percent of total health expenditures, though higher than Canada's, do not even begin to approach the astronomical U.S. figure of 13.4 percent.

The separation of patients into ambulatory and hospital categories also causes problems for those who feel they are being passed back and forth. Also, many think there are too many doctors in Germany. One estimate reckons there will be fifty thousand unemployed physicians in the country by 1995. Perhaps that is why, as the *Boston Globe* puts it, "All Germans, no matter what their income or station in life, are entitled to home visits from the doctor, even in the middle of the night."[6]

Could a German-style system, with its advantages of quality, relatively low-cost and high-tech medicine, and universal coverage, be adopted in the U.S.? The key is to find an American equivalent of the sickness funds. Some have suggested that Blue Cross-Blue Shield plans might fill such a role. As presently constituted—and with the high salary levels represented by Albert Cardone's annual six hundred thousand dollars in New York—that seems unlikely. If given a virtual monopoly, compulsory participation by those under a salary cap, and a mandate to cover everyone, could they do it? Possibly. But as one of Germany's health care policy experts, Dr. Michael Arnold, argues, "nobody today would consciously design and implement such a [complex sickness fund] system in its entirety."[7] And since it really is a single-payer system for more than 90 percent of the population, would it be necessary to duplicate its built-in and historically structured complications?

GREAT BRITAIN

The Fabian socialist George Bernard Shaw was a master of satirical humor. He particularly enjoyed pillorying the United Kingdom's medical profession in the days before the nation became the second in the world, after Germany, to institute national health insurance:

Nothing is more dangerous than a poor doctor: not even a poor employer or a poor landlord.

Of all the anti-social vested interests the worst is the vested interest in ill-health.

Treat persons who profess to be able to cure disease as you treat fortune tellers.[8]

In the same Shavian vein, in a 1991 letter to the editor of a Scottish newspaper, is the veiled sarcasm of a general practitioner, Dr. John S. Chalmers of Fife. The doctor was venting his anger at the ruling Conservative party government that has, to his mind, replaced the original intent of Britain's National Health Service with an ever-growing drift to commercialism:

For six years I was never seen in accountancy lectures and I could not see then the pivotal place of marketing in modern general practice. I just did not put in the hours.

I think I am going to kick the habit. I am practicing less and less medicine these days. I fill my day with writing and counting and rewriting and counting again.

In fact, practicing medicine has increasingly become something of a nuisance since it does so get in the way of my work.[9]

Shaw's dream of a government-operated health program with salaried doctors was achieved by the Labor Party in 1948. However, pure Fabian socialism bowed to reality, and compromises were made by Health Minister Aneurin Bevan in order to secure the cooperation of the medical establishment, particularly the politically powerful consultants, akin to specialists in the U.S. Consequently, the plan permitted private beds in National Health Service hospitals where

113

doctors could treat private patients. There was also a continuing place in the system for private fee-for-services practice in private offices. It has been said that Bevan made the deal with the consultants to break the resistance of the more numerous general practitioners to the creation of the NHS.[10]

General practitioners form the base of the NHS structure. Patients see them first, and if the GP thinks it necessary, are sent on to the more specialized consultant physicians or for hospital care. The NHS pays for all services and is funded through general taxation. The amounts people pay out-of-pocket are still marginal (less than 1 percent of the total) even after years under the free-market–oriented Tories, and there are mechanisms to help low-income persons afford items for which there are now charges: prescriptions, dental treatment, eye tests and glasses, hospital travel costs, wigs, and surgical supports.

Great Britain's NHS is "the biggest employer in Europe with almost 1.1 million people working for it."[11] Despite decades of laments that such "socialized medicine" is terribly expensive, the country has the lowest per capita expenditure on health care of any major industrialized nation—about one-third that of the U.S.—and devotes to it only about 6 percent of GNP, half the American share. The infant mortality rate, while not as low as those of Canada, France, Germany or Japan, is lower than that of the U.S.

Ironically, while the huge American expenditure on health care is viewed as a condemnation of our own system, Britain's low expenditure also receives poor marks. Underfunding is cited again and again by NHS defenders as the primary cause of its defects—including, most notably, long waiting lists for certain services.

When Margaret Thatcher's Conservative government took power in 1979, it might have been expected that of all the right-wing political leaders inveighing against "welfare states"—Kohl in Germany, Reagan in the U.S., and herself—Britain's "Iron Lady" was in the best position to cause an ideological turnabout in health care delivery. After all, Kohl was faced with a diffused system inherited from Bismarck, one not the least bit socialistic. Reagan not only had to cope with the checks and balances of Congress, but also had little to target. Mrs. Thatcher, firmly in control of a large parliamentary majority and constantly trumpeting the benefits of "privatization," might have been expected to jettison the entire state-run structure.

She did nothing of the kind. The reason for this lack of action is best expressed by Norman Johnson in his chapter on health care in *Reconstructing the Welfare State.* He begins by observing that "the greatest strength of NHS ... is the breadth of its support among the general population," and then quotes a writer in *The Guardian* who declared, "The NHS ... rides high in people's affections ... The perception is that its faults are caused not by the doctors, nurses or even the hospital administrators but the government. People believe that the health service is not being given enough money."[12]

It is small wonder that the Conservatives, instead of dismantling NHS, protest over and over again that "the health service is safe with us." Even Mrs. Thatcher herself, while making no bones about her personal use of a private physician, did concede that she would use the public system if she were to require complicated and expensive surgery.

Initially, all the Conservatives could accomplish was to put an end to attempts to phase out the private beds in NHS hospitals. The Labor government had wanted to do away with all forty-four hundred of them, but in a compromise with doctors had agreed to eliminate only one thousand, and to set up a Health Services Board to rule on the others. After disposing of another 981 beds, the Board itself was deposed by the Thatcher government through a legislative act that also reauthorized such beds.

In following years, the Conservative opposition became subtler. Those who oppose government programs always enjoy a built-in advantage when they take charge of government: They can starve programs financially. While Mrs. Thatcher openly did this with many social programs, Tories maintain they substantially increased NHS funding. They claim that between 1978-79 and 1989-90 they actually increased funding by 37 percent in real terms. Critics charge their calculations repeatedly underestimate increases in costs within the system, and have failed to keep pace with inflation.

The current Conservative initiative is focused on a reorganization of NHS as outlined in a 1989 government White Paper entitled *Working For Patients.* It relied heavily on the ideas of an American health economist, Alain Enthoven of Stanford University, and his concept of internal markets. The essence of the plan seems to be the creation of the equivalent of U.S.-style HMOs within the NHS. To that end, hospitals now run by the NHS are permitted to become self-governing "trusts," and certain general practitioners with large practices may apply for their own budgets from which they can shop for needed services (presumably on the basis of price). In the first round of these "reforms," which began officially in April 1991, a target of 57 hospitals and 306 "fund-holding" GP practices was set.

The process touched off a raging controversy. A Welsh physician who writes on health care, Dr. Julian Tudor Hart, has described the turmoil that occurred at what he calls "the government's chosen flagship for independent trust status," Guy's Hospital in London. Voting among those affected showed the hospital staff opposed to the plan by a nine to one margin, the local GPs opposed by a fourteen to one ratio, and the public opposed three to one. Undeterred, the government went ahead. Within weeks, management had fired six hundred employees—20 percent of staff. When challenged in Parliament's "question time," the health minister denied any governmental responsibility since Guy's was now a self-managing trust.

In Scotland, the "flagship" was the Royal Scottish National Hospital, an institution for the mentally ill. There, 95 percent of the staff opposed the move and the medical manager, Dr. George Dodds, a consultant psychiatrist, quit his post in protest and issued a stinging rebuke: "It became clear to me that it would be an exercise that would be of more benefit to managers in terms of status and pay, and could not clearly be demonstrated to be an advantage to patients. I saw it as a blind alley."[14]

Leading the attack on the Conservative program was the British Medical Association, a surprising enough phenomenon to Americans accustomed to the right-wing predilections of the AMA. Dr. Jeremy Lee-Potter, chairman of the BMA, complained that "a new, massive bureaucracy is being cranked into operation and will consume even more of the scarce resources doctors need to treat patients."[15]

A major complaint of British physicians, cited by Lee-Potter, was that they no longer knew where to send their patients. "Some hospitals," he said, "have not even issued their price lists for operations and those that have show huge variations in costs, often a difference of several thousand pounds for the same procedure." The charge was also made that reforms did nothing about "the real problems facing the NHS ... continued and chronic underfunding."

Another BMA official, John Chawner, chairman of their consultants committee, spoke to the concern that the move to more free-market, competitive health care would increase administrative costs: "The changes are going to make the service more expensive to administer, so there is every reason to think that the financial situation will continue to deteriorate."[16] Administrative costs in the British system have been (prior to any changes) estimated to be 4 to 6 percent of total costs, as opposed to the 13.4 percent in the U.S.

The Conservative government, aware that it may well be handing its opponents a hot political issue, has tried to tread softly. Although it made use of three neoconservative think tanks, including the appropriately named Adam Smith Institute, to help devise its plan, it has kept intact the NHS and its underlying principle of universal access. An especially outspoken and combative health minister, Kenneth Clarke, was replaced by the more tactful William Waldegrave. The latter has tried to mend fences with the medical community and has stressed the government's commitment to the NHS as a state-funded service. A public relations campaign has been launched and funded at £2.5 million. Glossy booklets entitled *The NHS Reforms And You* are distributed in post offices and other public places. They contain a number of soothing reassurances:

> As now, the NHS will continue to be open to all, regardless of income, and paid for mainly out of general taxation. NHS services will continue to be largely free at the point of use.

> If my doctor has a practice fund, will I still get the treatment I need? Yes.

> Will hospitals which become self-governing NHS Trusts stay completely within the NHS? Yes.

> Will I still have a choice about where I have my baby? Yes.

> Can I still have treatment at a local hospital? Yes.

> Will my doctor be able to spend as much time with me? Yes.

The Conservatives have cause for caution. In a by-election in Wales for a Parliament seat previously held by the Conservative party, Labor won an easy victory by turning the election into a referendum on the NHS changes. A 1989 Gallup poll showed that only 15 percent of the electorate supported the changes, and only 23 percent felt the NHS to be safe in the hands of the Tories.

There has been an increase in health privatization in Britain since 1979. About 10 percent of the population—5.7 million people—is now covered by private insurance. That's about double the number when Mrs. Thatcher took office. But the rate of increase slowed to a minimal 5 percent in 1986. This is not encouraging to a government that had hoped to have a least a quarter of the population privately insured by 1990.

Simultaneously, the number of private patients being treated in NHS hospitals has steadily declined—in-patients, that is. Partly this is because the number of private hospitals has increased—there are fifty-two new ones with 3577 beds. The most notable trend within this expansion is what some British health experts call the "American invasion," akin to the impact of McDonald's on the international fast-food business. The American for-profit hospital chains have come to the British Isles: American Medical International Healthcare (AMI) has thirteen hospitals with 1200 beds, Hospital Corporation of America (HCA) has nine with 452 beds, and Humana has a single large complex with 265 beds. In addition, Americans have developed some specialty services like mental health, chemical dependency, and diagnostic procedures. Some of these new hospitals, plus a leading British chain, Nuffields, have begun selling their own health insurance packages in an HMO-type arrangement.

The privates benefit from the British system since the NHS is obligated to accept all patients, leaving the field open for the private sector to concentrate on those willing and able to pay. With the payers, the Health Authorities, controlled by the Conservative party, money can be funneled to private operations in the guise of reducing waiting lists in NHS facilities. In 1987, this amounted to £25 million, and in 1989, £33 million. In one instance, work was contracted out by a NHS institution to a private hospital in which some of the consultants owned shares. And "contracting out" for nonmedical services—laundry, food, cleaning, etc.—has likewise been pushed hard by the Tories.

The applicability of the British system as a model for the U.S. is remote. For decades, in fact, it served as the bogeyman with which the AMA frightened the American public. The image projected in the U.S. of this "socialized medicine" was of a drab, overcrowded, under-staffed, second-class type of medical care. The British people do not agree—a Harris poll reveals that only 5 percent would ever want a U.S.-style system. But the American impression is hard to overcome.

To an extent, the NHS does just what American conservatives would like our system to do—it picks up, at taxpayer expense, everyone the private sector does not want to cover. What's more, since NHS covers the costs of medical education, it also has taxpayers providing the system with trained personnel. But once more, no matter how the free-marketers manipulate the elements, the provision of universal access remains the untouchable, sacred cornerstone of British health care, impervious to any assault.

FRANCE

In order to understand the French system of medical care it is first necessary to understand a term that invariably crops up in any discussion of the subject. In French it is *la médecine libérale*. For americans, the word "liberal" has a meaning completely opposite to its sense in France, and in most of Europe. To the French a "liberal" is not a free-spending, permissive politician who relies on government to solve problems. To the contrary, *libérale* refers to a believer in the free market, who wants as little government intervention as possible. Ronald Reagan, in the eyes of the French, is the quintessential liberal. Therefore, in medical matters, *la médecine libérale* refers to the practice of medicine by doctors who are as unfettered by restraint as could be wished by any AMA pooh-bah.

The French political health care debate is the exact opposite of that in Great Britain. A Socialist government rules France. With one major interruption, the Socialist party has held control since 1981. While the British have sought greater privatization of a system controlled by the public sector, the French have endeavored to root out the private elements in its system that have existed historically or been introduced during periods of conservative control.

According to a French medical journalist, Philippe Rollandin, in France "the State and the doctors have waged continual warfare for two centuries." The struggle has always been over the question of who will control the distribution of care in a nation with a long history of centralized government. Rollandin considers the French Revolution to be the starting point of the confrontation. "In 1792, medical licenses were suppressed: every citizen had the right to care for his neighbors. Without knowing it, the *sans-culottes* invented Reaganism in carrying out a measure of deregulation."[17] After 1803, Napoleon reintroduced the doctors' monopoly, but also established a new class of "health officers" who did not receive the formal training of the profession, yet were allowed to practice general medicine. Napoleon's action reflected his concern about access and distribution of care. It took the doctors nearly a full century—until 1892—to abolish these competing "health officers."

The present system is known, with some affection, as the *"Secu,"* because the payer who reimburses medical expenses is the social security *(Securité Sociale)*. Ironically, the French system has its roots in the return by Germany of Alsace and Lorraine, the two provinces lost in the Franco-Prussian War and regained after World War I. The people of those provinces had enjoyed German Bismarckian health insurance, and insisted it be retained. Since the government could not give it only to those two provinces, it decided to extend the concept of "sickness funds" to all of France.

The French system was totally revised after France's liberation from Germany following World War II, by means of the Social Security Ordinance of 1945. The structure of employers and employees contributing to third-party–payer "funds" was retained, but refined into locally controlled social security boards, which negotiated with the doctors' unions on fee schedules and then reimbursed members up to 80 percent. It has been pointed out that this tidbit of local control was a striking anomaly in the legendary centralized administration of France.[18]

The emphasis on state control has not been the monopoly of the French Left. The Gaullists were no less "statist" when they came to power in 1958. Under President de Gaulle's premier, Michel Debré, the government made it law, in May of 1960, that local negotiated fee schedules had to be approved by the central government in Paris. The doctors union, the Confédération des Syndicats Médicaux Français (CSMF), then the sole representative of the profession, vainly fought the change, and as a result, suffered a split in membership.

Another touch of irony is that Bernard Debré, son of the former premier, himself a doctor and a deputy in the French assembly, has in recent years become the most aggressive spokesman for physicians attempting to assert themselves against government controls. He has created a "Group of Ten" in the Chamber of Deputies, all rightists and medical doctors, which constitute what Rolladin calls a "veritable lobby."[19] When the Gaullist Jacques Chirac formed a short-lived government of the Right in 1986, Debré was a candidate for the post of minister of health, but was passed over for being too controversial.

In a recent interview with the magazine *Paris-Match*, Debré articulated his crusade against the "reforms" proposed by the Socialists, and railed against the condition of French medical care. The opening exchange set the tone:

Interviewer [Jean Cau]: France is said to have the best hospital system in the world.

Debré: Today it's on the verge of ruin and in the future, if things continue like this, it will be relegated to a myth.[20]

Debré then goes on to say that French hospitals have twenty-five hundred unfilled vacancies for doctors, and four hundred foreign doctors without appropriate qualifications have been hired. He complains that nurses are not paid enough, that *le budget global*, instituted for hospitals, acts as a brake on responsibility and the spirit of initiative, because if a hospital economizes, it is not rewarded but penalized the following year when it does not receive a corresponding budget increase.

The problem for Debré and those he represents centers on the role in French medicine of the most prestigious of doctors. They are those in the teaching hospitals, variously referred to as *patrons*, *chefs de service*, or with a certain Gallic sarcasm, *mandarins*. Under a system established by Debré's grandfather, Professor Robert Debré, these august physicians were originally appointed to their hospital teaching and practicing posts for life by the minister of health. This has been changed to renewable five-year terms. It was by fighting against such diminution in the positions of *chefs de service* that Debré first came to national prominence when he led a strike of doctors and interns at top-notch hospitals—a strike which included a break-in to the office of the minister of health. Now Debré, himself a *chef de service* at the noted Cochin Hospital in Paris, is concerned that a further Socialist refinement will be to have such powerful positions filled by hospital staff elections, a move he fears will lead ambitious underlings to sabotage their superiors. Or, as he puts it, "I want to be Caliph; therefore I will decapitate the one who already is."

Debré also rails against the Socialist government's moves to regulate France's private clinics. He is particularly critical of a proposed government requirement that agreements between these clinics and payers be of limited duration, insisting that such a "sword of Damocles" will prevent the clinics from attracting needed investment capital.

Where Debré really waxes eloquent is in his defense of the primary role he believes the teaching hospitals *(Centres Hospitaliers Universitaires*, or CHUs) have and should continue to have in French medicine. He says in the *Paris-Match* interview:

> It is far from me to disqualify the general hospitals, but their mission is not the same and the CHUs remain the essential foundation, since, without research, how can there be any progress and, without teaching, how can you train doctors? What does the Socialist law propose? Destroy (in the name of anti-elitism) the CHUs and the professors who are chiefs of service, the *patrons* who have been and still are the glory and shining light of French medicine ... The *mandarin*, in their eyes, is the devil. To be elite in expertise and research, that's bad ... Equalize!

The other side of this extreme expression of *la médecine libérale* is illustrated by the experiences of a large hospital (963 beds) in Chalons-sur-Marne, a city of fifty-four thousand about ninety-five miles east of Paris. The administrator, Edouard Couty, an advisor to the Socialist minister of social affairs (under which the health ministry now operates) is one of the architects of proposed hospital reform. A key element of the plan is *décloisonnement*, an almost untranslatable word that means, literally, "to take down partitions." The idea was inspired by American hospital management, wherein the hospital is divided into departments where the staff works together rather than simply responding to the orders of the *chef de service*. In 1984, the hospital in Chalons-sur-Marne attempted such a change and reorganized into a hundred departments. Councils were elected to help run them. The government-appointed *mandarins* were scandalized by the fact that some department heads were not from the ranks of the *chefs de service*. Moreover, council meetings were sometimes painful, with the formerly all-powerful *patrons* finding themselves scolded by nurses because they chose to make rounds at mealtimes, causing patients to eat cold food.

That first experiment foundered in the face of the resistance of the elite doctors. But the hospital, through its administrator and some staff, continues to push for *"démocratisation."*

Another American idea the French have considered borrowing is the notion of Diagnostic Related Groups (DRGs), the menu of prices used under Medicare to restrict hospital payments. Referred to as *groupes homogénes de malades*, (GHM), they are being fitted into a far broader context by the French ministry. As with every system of health care in the world, the overriding problem, once in fighting over turf and ideology is set aside, remains control of rising costs. French health care is still considerably less expensive than American health care, yet at 8.6 percent of GNP it is, along with Canada, the second most expensive among industrial nations.

Public hospitals in France employ 740,000 people, making them the largest employer in the nation. As a result, the direction of health care within this huge complex, and the settling of what appear to be internal political power fights, is of signal importance. Yet it is also important to recognize that while there are 1,059 public hospitals, there are an even greater number of private establishments (1,500).

Paul Godt, a professor at the American University in Paris, writes:

> The French health care system has for centuries been characterized by a shifting public and private balance ... The public role in private care has been so extensive that some authorities even question whether France's sacred *médecine libérale* ever really existed ... The public/private mix today seems, nonetheless to satisfy most French— patients and physicians alike—who find that their system is an excellent compromise between the egalitarian but financially strapped NHS and the technologically advanced but profligate American way. Consumers receive high quality care, accessible to all, at not too great a cost, while preserving a certain measure of individual choice.[21]

Is there a French lesson to be learned by the United States? Perhaps the answer lies in the objection voiced by another elected deputy of the Right, Jean-Yves Chamard, protesting that a Socialist plan to do away with fee-for-service for doctors would lead France toward a British system of health care. His point is that France has found a means to care for all its citizens' health needs and for doctors to find a way to practice on a one-to-one basis with free choice for the patient. Therefore, he holds, it is not necessary to have large proportions of the population go unserved as they do in the U.S.[22]

THE EUROPEAN COMMUNITY

In a recent conversation with a British visitor, it was interesting to learn that some in Britain, frustrated by having to wait for service from the NHS, cross the Channel to make use of the French system rather than rely on private care at home. They find the care to be of high quality, and a lot cheaper than the free-market medicine available in the United Kingdom.

This bit of information brings up the question of what will happen to health care after the twelve nations of the European Community merge even more closely in 1992. Goods and services will then circulate freely among these dozen countries. What will this portend for their health care programs?

The European, a new newspaper on the Continent, in an introduction to its "European Healthwatch" page, states: "Health regularly tops the list of priorities for most Europeans. Recent polls have rated it as more important than employment, housing and crime. Health care is now seen as an irrevocable right in Europe."

In discussing the future after 1992, the editors of *The European* confidently predict that "patients and their families will look beyond their national borders to meet their health needs and competition among health centres should help to improve European medicine."[23]

Improvements will also be coming from specific actions by the governing bodies of the European Community. Even now, prior to the official lowering of national barriers, there are fourteen hundred national teams working on "the programme coordinating medical research in the Community."[24]

AUSTRALIA

"Why don't you look into the Australian system?"

The speaker was a doctor, a specialist unhappy with the present U.S. health care system but leery of the Canadian. He had heard that

124

Australia had found the proper mix between a public system offering a bedrock of care for all, and privately paid medicine that allows freedom of choice for those with means.

Actually, the health care system in the Land Down Under is not that simple. The public-private mix that exists is not really the result of careful, rational planning, but the aftermath of years of battle between two dominant and ideologically motivated political parties, the Labor party and (remember the French definition) the Liberal party.

In a sense, the history of health care in Australia presents a microcosm of what may lie in store for the U.S. Prior to the 1970s, health care there was similar to what we have here today. It was a "free market" dominated by private health insurance companies that covered the vast majority of the population. Government programs, like our Medicare and Medicaid, took care of elderly pensioners and the poor. There was also government intervention during the long years of control by the strongly conservative Liberal party (1949 to 1972) on behalf of private insurance companies providing tax exemptions for those who bought private health insurance—a favorite proposal of American conservatives for solving our problems, and an actuality that costs American taxpayers billions when employers deduct the cost of worker insurance.

The inequities resulting from this state of affairs in Australia were similar to what we now face—many people lacked health insurance or access to health care. In Australia at that time, insurance wasn't purchased through employers, but by individual families. In 1972 the Labor party swept into power on a platform that included compulsory universal health care. They promptly implemented their plan. It was named Medibank.

Australia, which calls itself a commonwealth, has a federal form of government. Its six states (there is also a Northern Territory) all have their own elected governments. It took three years in the early 1970s, due to resistance in states controlled by the opposition, for Labor's universal health care plan to become fully operational. As in Canada, one of the prime incentives was that the federal government would share state costs on a 50-50 basis.

Shortly after the plan was in place, Labor was driven from office by the Liberals in coalition with a small group called the Country party. Since health care delivery had just gone from a private insurance-

125

dominated system to a government-controlled universal system, the next step in this yo-yo of ideological push-and-shove was the undoing of the public system in favor of the old private one. That's just what the Liberal-Country coalition did, but it was forced to do so incrementally. Medibank was replaced by Medibank II, in turn replaced by Medibank III, all moving in the direction of replacing Medibank insurance with private coverage and reintroducing markets into health care. Co-payments for patients were put in place, first 25 percent of the government-mandated fee, then 60 percent, with a twenty-dollar-per-item ceiling. Access to hospitals at government expense was restricted to pensioners and those on welfare. Government subsidies (or tax exemptions) were reserved only for those who bought private health insurance. The private companies, which under Medibank had been providing only supplementary insurance, returned as the dominant factor in Australian health care. By 1983 the old Medibank program was dead.

The situation was analogous to what might happen in the U.S. if the current system were overthrown and replaced by a single-payer system which would, in turn, be set aside and the old system (with a government assist through tax-exemptions) brought back.

But wait! The Australian story is not over. In 1983, stressing health care as an issue, Labor won the election. It promised to bring back Medibank and it did, this time under the name of Medicare.

The new Australian health care program works like this: Patients who opt for Medicare are not charged for any part of their hospital treatment but they do agree to accept a hospital assigned physician. That physician is either salaried or working under contract. If the patient wants a private hospital, or wishes to be a private patient in a public institution with a choice of physicians, he may buy supplementary insurance. That will cover the physician and hospital charges over the rates allowed by the system. Since Medicare pays only 75 percent of the "scheduling fee" for doctors in such cases, and 85 percent of the same for ambulatory care, the private insurance can pick up the difference. Yet, according to a recent American study of the Australian system, under law private insurance "may not be sold to cover extra-billing above the 'scheduled' fee. This prohibition has the effect of making any extra-billing very visible to the patient and reinforcing Australian patients' long-standing resentment of physicians who charge substantially above the schedule of benefits."[25]

Another feature of Australian private insurance that benefits the consumer is that "experience rating" is not permitted. Insurers cannot offer different premiums based on health status or claims experience. Also, health insurance as a "fringe benefit" is taxed as income, so there are few cases where companies provide it to employees. Nor do there seem to be any discounts for group purchases. Since Medicare's introduction (or reintroduction in reincarnated form) in 1984, the number of those buying standard hospital private coverage has declined from about 65 percent to 45 percent of the population. Most of the private health insurance is sold by Blue Cross-Blue Shield non-profit types of organizations, often connected with a profession. Examples are The Associated Pulp and Paper Makers Council Health Benefits Fund of Tasmania and the Commonwealth Bank Health Society of New South Wales. What seems to be a feature wholly unique to Australia is that the government markets its own supplemental health insurance plan, Medibank Private, in competition with other insurers. Some commercial for-profit plans have also been approved by the federal government as "registered medical benefits organizations."

The Australians' health care system is partly financed through a 1.25 percent federal income tax charge, called the "Medicare levy." Their public hospitals, which resemble our own not-for-profits, have their own boards of trustees and account for 75.8 percent of all bed days in acute care. They are also the major teaching institutions and research centers. Unlike the U.S., Australia has far more general practitioners than specialists. Finally, 71 percent of Australians are reported to be satisfied with Medicare and the present arrangement.

The down-under system does require a constant balancing act between public and private health care. Public hospitals come under state budgets and each hospital budget is controlled by the state. If a hospital receives additional revenue from private patients, that amount is often subtracted from state revenues, a practice that keeps hospitals from concentrating on attracting private patients at the expense of public patient care and accentuating any two-tiered health care tendencies. In contrast with the U.S., capital expenditures for buildings and equipment come directly from the state government.

The tug of war between public and private systems continues as a constant in the country's political dialogue. The Achilles' heel of the system, as it seems to be in all universal systems, is that there are noticeable waits for some kinds of service. The extent of such waits is a matter of considerable debate. A former commissioner of the Department of Community Services and Health, Neal Blewett, responded to the matter: "The much touted figure of 100,000 people on public hospital waiting lists is a myth dreamed up by Medicare's opponents, most of whom have a financial interest behind their attempts to undermine Medicare."[26]

The present commissioner, Brian Howe, gave as his assessment that Medicare "compares well with the U.K. where people can wait 80 weeks for hip replacements or the U.S. where it seems only big money can buy the most basic health care."[27] The average wait for elective surgery in Victoria, the second most populous state, has been estimated at seven weeks.

Nor has everyone been leaping to the private sector for relief. Brian Howe stated that one of the main problems facing the government in developing a national health strategy by 1993 was that there were too many empty beds in private hospitals and too many people were dropping their private insurance.

It has also been emphasized that prior to Medicare and after the demise of Medibank and the substitution of the "user-pays" program, the only choice was to buy private insurance or go without. In the state of South Australia, the largest single cause of imprisonment for debt (apparently that antiquated law remains in force down under) was failure to pay medical bills.

Australian health care, according to the latest available figures, cost the Australians 8.1 percent of their GNP, compared at the time with 6.1 percent for Great Britain, 8.6 percent for Canada, and 11.2 percent for the United States.

Unless the political balance changes soon again, Australia will have a universal health care system grafted onto a free-market private system that was grafted onto a universal system that supplemented a totally private system.

Since much current talk in the U.S. is of devising a system that maintains a public-private mix (with, no doubt, a far greater admixture of public than at present), Australian health care offers some interesting patterns. Though Australia's population is far smaller than our own, there are parallels in terms of the federal structure of government, the size of the country, and the existence in recent years of a "melting pot" population as immigrants flock to the southern continent. For the final word on reactions to Australian Medicare, here are the comments of a columnist in the *Sydney Morning Herald:*

> As a method of financing the national health scheme, Medicare is user-friendly. For workers, Medicare is a guarantee of free treatment in a public hospital, in return for the 1.25 percent medilevy ...

> You don't have the hassle of private health insurance, if you don't want it. Your boss takes the levy out of your pay before you see it. Thanks to direct billing, for 56 percent of doctors' visits, there's nothing out of pocket and no claim forms to send away; you just sign a chit.[28]

JAPAN

Most Americans today consider the Japanese our pre-eminent economic rivals. Where as in the days before World War II, "Made in Japan" was a synonym for cheap imitations of western goods, the opposite is now true; the phrase denotes high quality at an affordable price—more and more, something Americans strive to emulate. In dealing with the health care needs of its people, Japan seems once more to have hit upon a formula that blends the highest quality with affordability.

Bluntly put, the Japanese health care system statistically ranks as the world's best. The Japanese enjoy the highest life expectancy in the world, and their infant mortality rate is the lowest (half that of the U.S.). Their costs per capita for health care are only about one-third of our own, and, of course, they cover all their people, while at least one-third of Americans have either no access to health care through insurance, or very unsatisfactory access. Only Great Britain, among major nations, spends less of its GNP on health care than Japan does, and the incessant complaints of underfunding and long waits for service that are so common in the United Kingdom are apparently absent in the Land of the Rising Sun.

All of which makes it reasonable to ask if the U.S. should therefore stop looking at other models and run pell-mell to imitate the Japanese health care system just as our manufacturers are urged to adopt Japanese management techniques and our Federal government to follow the "industrial policy" so successfully pursued by the Japanese government. Or might it be suggested, with more than a little tongue-in-cheek, that since Japanese cars made in the United States are now selling like hotcakes in Japan, and some corporate types are saying that industrial nirvana is when American workers operate under Japanese management, perhaps the best thing to do would be to turn over our present messed-up health care system to the Japanese and see what they can do with it.

Before drawing any rash conclusions, let us look a little more closely at the Japanese method of handling health care. To begin with, it is a very complicated system. Modern Japan emerged only slowly from its feudal past after the Meiji Restoration of 1868. In 1889, Japan adopted its first constitution, patterned on the model of imperial Prussia. This happened only a few years after Bismarck had instituted his ground-breaking health insurance program, and the initial inspiration for Japanese health care was, not surprisingly, predicated on a German model. To this day, the Japanese system remains employment-based, its original modern structure having been created by the Health Insurance Law of 1922, and added to by increments of benefits and populations covered until the entire society came under its provisions in 1961. Lest it be thought that the health of Japan's citizenry is more a function of diet or culture and has always been exemplary, let it be noted that in 1947, the country's life expectancy for males was 50 years, and for females, 53 years; by 1986 this had risen to 75.2 years for males and 80.9 for females.

The political battles that have been so evident in most of the other health systems discussed thus far have not been a strong factor in Japan. On the national level there has been essentially one-party rule by the Liberal-Democrats, a centrist, business-oriented faction, ever since the two groups, the Liberals and Democrats, merged in 1955. The main opposition, the Socialist party, has never held power.

As conservative as the nation's rulers appear, they do not seem to have taken the road of their counterparts in Germany, Great Britain, France, and Australia and sought ways to undermine universal health care in the name of a free-market ideology. To the contrary, Japanese leaders have had to contend with the ire of the Japanese Medical Association and go through several strikes by physicians, unhappy with cost containment measures that have limited their incomes.

The core of the Japanese system lies in two principle types of health insurance plans. One is employer-based, like the German "sickness funds." It includes employees of the larger corporations, national and local government workers, seamen and private school personnel. Funding is through contributions from both employers and employees. Under this arrangement, about 75 million Japanese are covered. Another 45 million fall under community-sponsored national health insurance, the program that covers small-business employees, the self-employed, farmers, and all of the unemployed. This program is financed and administered by local governments.

This is a definite private-public division of labor—one that functions even within the employer-based sector. The larger companies (those with over seven hundred employees) have their plans handled by private insurance companies. Plans covering small and medium-sized businesses are operated by the government, as are the special community-sponsored plans for the groups mentioned above. The government also runs programs for day laborers, citizens over seventy, and bedridden individuals between sixty-five and seventy. The other funds even help support some specific groups of the needy.

Much of the system is mandatory. All citizens must participate in a health insurance plan. All businesses with five or more employees have to have a plan or pay into a public fund. And all insurance plans must provide minimum benefits that include inpatient and outpatient hospital care, transportation, physician visits, laboratory services, therapy and treatment, prescriptions, and dental care. Maternity care—prenatal, childbirth, and well-baby programs—are handled separately through other social programs.

Standard coverage is for semi-private rooms, often shared by four to six persons, although private insurance coverage can be bought to provide more luxurious accommodations. In the employer-based plans, some cash benefits are paid to workers whose condition prevents them from working; women workers, following childbirth, also receive cash payments, and, to quote one report, "women who nurse their infants are paid lump sum nursing allowances."[29]

A few other facets of the Japanese health care system are bound to raise a few American eyebrows. A custom in Japan is for people to not only pay a doctor his fee-for-service, but also present him with a cash gift. While there are no statistics on how much this adds to a doctor's income, the amount is said to be substantial. Japanese law also mandates that all health care facilities must be managed by physicians. Approximately eighty-two thousand Japanese doctors own their own clinics and hospitals. Another source of physicians' income is the sale of prescription drugs to their patients. It is little wonder under these circumstances that the Japanese use more medical drugs per capita than any other people in the world.

The Japanese consumer pays for the system in several ways. Employee contributions to health insurance premiums in the employer-based plans are rated on pay grades. The range is from 6 percent to 9 percent of the monthly salary, with a maximum, set by law, of about the equivalent of two hundred dollars per month. Rates for government plans are almost uniform—8.3 percent of monthly wages (1987 figures), with a smaller contribution required from day laborers. In addition, while there are no deductibles, there are co-payments—10 percent for the insured person and dependents, 20 percent for hospital care, and 30 percent for ambulatory care. Those covered by the government's National Health Insurance pay premiums based on complicated formulas and a co-payment of 30 percent. Insurance for the aged requires very small payments, amounting to about 1 percent.

An important feature of the Japanese system is that there is a cap on the total amount of any family's liability for health care costs. In 1986 that amounted to the equivalent of four hundred dollars a month, with lesser figures for low-income people. The Japanese government pays the administrative costs of the insurance funds.

The people of Japan tend to visit their doctors about three times more often than Americans, and the average hospital stay is more than a month, the longest in the world. Mysteriously, despite what would be viewed as expensive disadvantages in our country—frequent doctor visits, long hospital stays, high usage of prescription drugs, physicians selling drugs and owning clinics and hospitals, generous social policies that even extend to paying mothers to nurse their babies—the Japanese have fashioned a high-quality, high-tech medical care system, covering everyone on their overcrowded islands, with outcome statistics that are the best in the world—and all at an extremely reasonable cost.

Is it because the Japanese are an extremely "special people," somewhat different from all the other peoples of the world? It is an argument that must appeal to American foes of national health care who insist such a program will never work for us because we are another kind of "special people."

It is true that Japanese society is unique, if for no other reason than that it has fostered the discipline necessary to live successfully in tight quarters. A related "health problem" in Japan that again may raise eyebrows in the U.S. was recently unveiled in an appeal to Americans to support the efforts of the Japan Karoshi Foundation. The word *karoshi* literally means "worked to death," and the foundation was protesting Japan's high rate of work-related deaths in a society where people often work twelve to sixteen hours a day with no weekends, holidays, or sick days off, and there is no workers' compensation for the families of those who die on the job, often as a result of work-related exhaustion.[30]

There is enough *karoshi* in the American workplace to say that the problem is not confined exclusively to Japan. Nor can it be said that, in all probability, the Japanese success with their health care system could not provide lessons to us as we struggle to find ways to make our health care system—as well as our cars—more efficient and of higher quality.

SOME RANDOM COMPARISONS

The supply of health care systems in use across the world that could be examined is almost inexhaustible. Not only is the United States the only major industrialized country lacking universal health care for its people (the Republic of South Africa does have such a program, but only for whites); it is also outstripped in this regard by many Third World countries that provide such a service to their people.

I have personally sampled universal health care at a rural clinic in Costa Rica (no charge, not even for the antibiotics given from the clinic dispensary) and in Denmark, which has a long-established national health care system in which, although private care is allowed, the best specialists work in the public system, and everyone who needs their care has access to them regardless of their ability to pay.

The Netherlands has seen an interesting development in its health care system. Prior to 1990, its German-style arrangement of "sickness funds" covered only 70 percent of the Dutch people, the rest being served by private insurance. The problem here was that since those under private insurance were the wealthier members of society, the public system suffered from not receiving the full contribution in payroll taxes of all the employed in the country. Therefore, after 1990, the

133

public system was extended to everyone. A sidelight on this public system in Holland is that in 1980, it added home care for the elderly to the long-term care it already provided. The theory was that home care, using nurses as case managers, would be cheaper and reduce utilization of nursing homes; this has not proved to be correct.

Cuba's medical system has received a lot of attention. That the Castro regime, with its totally government-run health system, has brought Cuban longevity to where it's slightly higher than that of the U.S., and cut the island's infant mortality from 38 per thousand live births to 10.7, has raised eyebrows enough to prompt a closer look at this so-called Third World nation. The opening in 1983 of the spectacular Hermanos Amejeiras Hospital in Havana revealed a high-tech showplace, offering "36 specialties, primarily in six areas: advanced heart, brain and reconstructive surgery, gastroenterology, psychiatry and nuclear medicine."[31] But what has been labeled "the greatest innovation in Cuba's health care system"[32] is the creation of the "Family Doctor Program." It is designed to link doctors and their communities and is grafted onto the system of "polyclinics," or neighborhood health centers, that has been so much a part of medicine in Communist countries. Here, the *consultorio* is an appendage of the doctor's home, and the doctor also serves as a public health officer in the neighborhood. The Family Doctor Program now covers about 65 percent of the country. The philosophic underpinnings of Cuban medicine are demonstrated by the fact that doctors do not take the Hippocratic Oath; instead they promise to abide by a set of revolutionary principles, including a renunciation of private practice.

Another noted feature of this systems is the Cuban treatment of AIDS. Ironically, it mirrors the ideas on the issue of the most raucous of American conservatives, Senator Jesse Helms. Massive testing is carried out and those found HIV-positive are quarantined—in comfortable quarters, to be sure, with permission to visit their families and also to work, but nonetheless kept isolated.

Cuba spends a great deal on health care - probably as much as 15 percent of its GNP in 1983—and this has led even sympathizers to question the policy when food is in short supply, sewage systems break down, and houses collapse from lack of repairs. "If given a choice would Cubans rather have a doctor on every block or a chicken in every pot?"[33]

Trips by Americans to Cuba for medical treatment (and they are not uncommon) bring up the question of why Americans are so dissatisfied with health care in the U.S. that they will even go to Third World countries to seek alternatives. In this regard, a paper by Sylvia Guendelman, health care researcher at the University of California, Berkeley, titled "Health Care Users Residing on the Mexican Border," makes interesting reading.[34]

Most Americans, if they think of Mexican health care at all, are likely to think of Laetrile, a supposed cure for cancer that was banned in the U.S. but was available south of the border. Many desperate Americans crossed the border to receive the usually unavailing treatment. The impression left by this well-publicized matter was that of a medical care system with little or no quality control. What a surprise to learn, then, in Guendelman's study of how many Mexicans along the border in the Tijuana area were being attracted across the line to use our supposedly superior system, that only 7 percent of the six-hundred-plus queried went to the U.S., while 93 percent remained within the Mexican system. Of that 7 percent, half were American citizens living in Mexico. Interestingly enough, 6 percent of those relying on Mexican health care exclusively were Americans. Even among those who went to the U.S. for treatment, one-third relied on Mexican services as well. A far more startling statistic from another study of cross-border medical use done in the lower Rio Grande area of Texas revealed that 26 percent of those Americans interviewed—mostly medically indigent—crossed into Mexico for their health care.

Much is made of wealthy Canadians who come to the U.S. for services they have to wait for in Canada, but we hear little about our compatriots who cross over into Mexico because they can't get the care they need in this country.

Since the Republic of South Africa is frequently mentioned in the same breath with the United States concerning health care, a quick peek at the apartheid nation's system is only fair. For whites, it is first class. The Groote Schuur Hospital in Cape Town is where Dr. Christiaan Barnard performed the world's first heart transplant in 1967. Equipment there, and at other hospitals catering to the white population, is as sophisticated as anywhere in the U.S. They have private hospitals and public provincial hospitals. There are now even private clinics for blacks, their major stockholders black physicians.

A favorite subject for the publicists who produce a glossy PR magazine for the South African government is the Baragwanath Hospital, located southwest of Johannesburg near Soweto. Called "the largest hospital in Africa," it serves a black population of 1.2 million from all over South Africa and neighboring states. The PR flacks love to emphasize that "patients pay according to their income and only contributed R2.5 million [the South African currency is the Rand] to the hospital's R114 million budget ... The rest came from the state."[35]

In a story of how two black Siamese twins joined at the head were successfully separated into two normal little girls by means of an extremely delicate and dangerous operation, South Africa's apologists made sure to mention that the expense of the procedure and their eighteen-month hospital stay was R1.5 million, but that the mother, a tribal Tswana woman from the western Transvaal, had to pay only a mere R10.

No doubt, for those South African blacks who do not provide such dramatic grist for the government's publicity mill, health care reality is far less charitable. But, as Baragwanath Hospital shows, the South African government does accept some responsibility even for those of its citizens it has made juridically second-class.

8 CANADA

The man was Canadian, his wife American. Their home was in Connecticut. They were visiting Maine, he said, because he was nearing retirement and they were looking for a new home that would be closer to Canada. "Because of the medical," he added.

That conversation, which took place at a crafts fair in Wells, Maine, had begun spontaneously. When I mentioned I was writing a book on health care in the United States, the man, whose accent more than hinted at a *quebecois* origin, spoke with some passion. "I simply cannot understand the attitude in the States," he said. "How someone can go out and fight for his country, work hard all his life, pay taxes, be a good citizen, and then face the prospect of bankruptcy and losing everything he's built up because he gets sick and can't pay his medical bills. In Canada, yes, we have to pay more for gas to put in our cars, but we don't mind because we know that's going to health care and to the security we have of knowing we won't get wiped out if we happen to have an illness."

In the early 1970s, when the U.S. was in the "third wave" of attempts to fashion universal health insurance, Senator Edward M. Kennedy, the leader of the fight, went to inspect the national health care systems of several countries overseas. In his book, *In Critical Condition,* published in 1972, he wrote of his experiences. He described the excellent health care provided to iron workers in Kiruna, Sweden, and contrasted it to the minimal and substandard care available to coal miners in Kingwood, West Virginia. He wrote of his conversation in Copenhagen, Denmark, with a former constituent

137

of his, eighty-three-year-old Ingeborg Hinding, who had reluctantly left Massachusetts and gone back to her native land because of the available health care. Senator Kennedy also examined the health care systems in Great Britain and Israel, the two other countries he and his Senate Health Subcommittee visited. The intriguing thing is that Canada was never mentioned.

In 1972, Canada had only just begun to implement its own particular version of national health care. Twenty years later, the Canadian system is the model most often mentioned as a possibility for a system of universal health care in the United States. Its importance can be measured not only by the amount of publicity generated in its favor, but also by the barrage of criticism leveled at it by such known and vociferous opponents of national health care as the American Medical Association and the Health Insurance Association of America.

To the charge that in the final analysis, good or bad as the Canadians' system is, their ideas cannot be transferred to the United States because they are a much different people, one has to note that at the outset the Canadians started exactly where we are.

The Canadian system in the early part of this century was identical to our own—private medicine, fee-for-service, and a rapid growth of private insurance until two-thirds of Canadians were covered and a significant part of the population was left unprotected. At that time, Canada's health care statistics were actually worse than those of the U.S.

The need for some kind of national health insurance was recognized somewhat later in Canada than in the U.S. It was not until after the Great War, in 1919, that a major Canadian political party endorsed the idea. The efforts of the Liberal party in overcoming Canadian opposition during this period were no more successful than the efforts of American proponents to overcome the AMA and other foes.

A "second wave" began in Canada in 1939, at the outset of World War II. Mackenzie King's Liberal government sparked the effort. Among the earliest supporters of a national plan to cover hospital and physician costs, dental services, pharmaceuticals, etc., was the Canadian Medical Association. Their action was reminiscent of the pre–World War I support of the AMA, and was based, as it had been in the U.S., on the fact that many doctors were having a hard time attracting patients and then collecting their bills. As with the AMA, the support of the official Canadian doctors' association was short-lived.

The original Canadian constitution, the British North America Act of 1867, assigned responsibility for health care to the provinces. The federal government, if it wishes to influence health care policy to any appreciable extent, must do so through its constitutional financial powers.

In 1945, the King government took the initiative and proposed a national health care program to the provinces at a conference called for that purpose. They could not reach a satisfactory agreement about funding, and the idea foundered. King's successor, Louis St. Laurent, declared that while he was willing to entertain proposals from the provinces, he would initiate no agenda of his own.

The provincial thrust came from an unexpected quarter—the Conservative premier of Ontario, Leslie Frost. At another federal-provincial conference in 1955, Frost suggested that a system of universal coverage for hospital care be created. Two provinces, working on their own, had already instituted such programs. Saskatchewan had led the way in 1947, and was followed by British Columbia in 1949.

The opposition to Frost's idea followed lines familiar to those voiced in the U.S. today. The Canadian Medical Association agreed that medical insurance should be available to all, but only when offered by private carriers. They held that government should subsidize only those who couldn't afford the private insurance, and limit its role to applying a means test to determine eligibility for government aid.

Premier Frost, assured of the support of the opposition Liberals, faced the task of convincing his own party of the inadequacy of private insurance. His words, spoken nearly half a century ago, could be used to describe the American situation today:

> Present insurance coverage ... is simply not universally available ... It is generally limited to the best risks ... generally cancelable on illness ... I may add that in many cases cancellations take place many years later and in fact at the very time the policy is needed ... It is very simple to say Ontario has 3.5 million covered. We have 3.5 million people in this province who are partially covered, and they are partially covered only through the duration of the policy, and then because of certain things that enter into the matter they cease to be covered entirely.[1]

The legislation to establish universal *hospital* insurance was passed unanimously by the Canadian Parliament in April of 1957. By

July 1, 1958, the bill's effective date, the Liberals had lost office and the Conservatives (the party is officially called the Progressive Conservatives), led by Prime Minister John Diefenbaker, permitted the program to proceed. All ten provinces had joined by 1961, and all but Ontario paid the cost through general taxation.

The next logical step was to cover physician care. The same problems of inequality of access were now revealed even more glaringly in the ambulatory area. Chronic illness, even with hospital stays covered, still meant financial hardship, if not ruin.

The Diefenbaker government recognized the problem and in 1961 appointed a Royal Commission (despite the impressive title, a group very much like a governmental study task force in the U.S.) to assess the situation. Chairing the commission was the chief justice of Saskatchewan's highest court, Emmett Hall, a lifetime friend of the prime minister.

The Hall Commission took three years complete its work, traveling abroad and touring all Canada. That it was able to reach an almost unanimous consensus recommending a full national health care plan was all the more remarkable considering events in Saskatchewan. That western province, with a strong tradition of populism, had jumped the gun. Even as the commission deliberated, their parliament mandated universal coverage of physician services. Provincial doctors reacted with a strike. The walkout lasted three weeks before the government settled, leaving a modified version of national health care in place.

The Hall Commission's final recommendation was for a program virtually identical to the original Saskatchewan proposal. The Liberals, back in power in Ottawa, accepted the plan and began to negotiate funding with the provinces. If the provinces met certain federal criteria—including universal coverage (in this case 95 percent was defined as "universal"), no means tests, public administration, and portability from province to province—they would receive 50 percent of their funds from Ottawa. Despite the virulent opposition of the CMA and the private insurance companies, the bill passed the Federal Parliament by an overwhelming majority of 177 to 2.

Putting the program into action was a slow process. Even though the authorizing vote took place in December of 1966, it was not until January of 1977 that all ten provinces had joined.

Outwardly it appeared all was going swimmingly. Those most

140

unhappy with the new system were the doctors, and in Quebec, they staged a brief strike—set off when the provincial plan refused to let the doctors extra-bill—but the work stoppage, primarily by specialists, was swiftly quashed. As matters turned out, the majority of Canadian physicians did better financially under this universal system which, like that of Australia, was called Medicare. Not that Canadian doctors had ever been in danger of being poor. Under the old system—the same as the U.S. free-market—they had been earning 3.5 times the average industrial wage. Canada's Medicare brought that ratio up to 5.5 times. Bad debts had been eliminated and the original rates allowed the doctors were generous.

The public was delighted. "Access to medical care unimpeded by financial barriers quickly became a way of life," as Canadian physician Gordon Guyatt put it in a paper on the history of Canadian health care.[2] It was a way of life which became entrenched so quickly that years later a major political argument used unsuccessfully by the Liberal party in opposition to the U.S.-Canadian free trade Agreement was that it would somehow imperil the Canadian health care system. The pro–free trade Conservatives had to counter by quelling all fears that the people's precious Medicare would ever be touched.

If anything, polls show that the Canadian system is more popular among the people it serves than the NHS is among the British or the *Secu* among the French. Yet there were problems, and they were not long in surfacing.

Of all the systems we have examined, the Canadian is the most egalitarian. It does not allow private medicine to compete with its Medicare (although most doctors are private practitioners) and private insurance is restricted to a strictly supplementary position. Policies may be sold only to provide extras like private rooms and cosmetic plastic surgery. Much of the Canadian controversy, at least initially, was about attempts to maintain or reinforce equalization, a condition under which rich and poor received care on the basis of real need, not of their ability to pay.

From the very start, three provinces did not fund their entire share of costs from general taxation. Instead they charged insurance premiums. Complaints were made that these three—British Columbia, Alberta and Ontario—were using regressive means of financing; in other words, the poor were being made to pay proportionately the same amount as the wealthy, sums that represented a much higher percentage of their incomes and therefore were a heavier burden. Ontario has since reconsidered and switched to a wholly general tax–funded program.

A far more delicate problem was posed by physicians who wanted to charge more than had been negotiated by their medical societies with the provincial government payers. It is a problem familiar to Americans who find it increasingly difficult to find doctors who will accept Medicare and Medicaid fees. In Canada, some provinces permitted "opting out." A doctor could elect not to join the provincial plan, and charge whatever he or she wished and be paid directly by the patient. The patient, in turn, would then be reimbursed by the province for the negotiated amount. Another version of the same scheme was called "balanced billing." In this case the doctor stayed in the system, was reimbursed at the negotiated rate, but was still able to bill the patient for more. Balanced billing was preferable from the doctor's point of view because it assured payment of at least the lesser fee and saved the work of chasing the patient for full payment.

The Ontario Medical Association soon urged its members to opt out. They believed if enough did so it would increase pressure on the government to grant higher fees. But only 18 percent of the doctors followed the recommendation, and the ploy backfired. Instead of pressure creating higher fees, there was a call for the government to end the option.

Once again, the government created a commission to study the problem and once again, that commission was headed by Justice Emmett Hall. The commission's findings were as follows:

1. Premiums constituted a regressive tax and should be phased out.
2. User fees, like extra-billing and opting out, threatened the principles of universal health care and had to be eliminated.

When the provinces failed to act on the findings, the federal government stepped in and proposed that for every dollar paid in user fees by a provincial resident, the province would lose a matching dollar of federal health funding. Despite frenzied opposition from some medical associations and right-wing groups, the Canada Health Act of 1984 passed unanimously. Since then every province has implemented the law and extra-billing, in one form or another, has been ended.

The power of public opinion—in this case the Canadian people's support for the egalitarian principles of their Medicare—was nowhere better illustrated than in the passage of the Canada Health Act. As Ralph Sutherland, M.D., and M. Jane Fulton, Ph.D., wrote in their book *Health Care in Canada*, "Opinion polls, petitions and public discussion convinced even traditionally conservative MP's, who personally approved of extra-billing, that extra-billing must go."[3]

How does the Canadian system work? At first blush it all looks very simple. The federal government has established certain criteria that must be met by a provincial health care plan if that plan is to receive federal funding. All ten provinces comply (as do the two territories, Yukon and Northwest Territories). The provinces then are permitted to go beyond the basic criteria. All Canadians are covered by some plan and receive cards—similar to credit cards—which they present when applying for medical care from either a doctor or hospital. Individuals are not billed for services. Each hospital, having negotiated its annual global budget with the authorities running the provincial plan, receives a monthly payment and provides services to all. A small billing department is maintained for foreigners, like Americans, who fall ill within their jurisdiction or who, for their own reasons, seek treatment in Canada. (Many are lured by specialties where Canadians lead the world, such as in the Sick Children's Hospital in Toronto, internationally known for its treatment and research in cystic fibrosis.) Doctors are reimbursed similarly. Their fees have been negotiated by their medical societies and provincial authorities, and since extra billing is a thing of the past, the patient once more merely submits his health card and the physician, having noted its number, is paid by the province.

Funding for the program is through general taxation—income taxes on provincial and federal levels, and excise taxes on tobacco, alcohol, and gasoline. The entire Canadian tax bill is high by American standards because the Canadians fund more government programs. The percentage of the tax burden attributable to health care is about 25 percent. Americans should note that under our own present system we already pay hefty sums in taxes for the same purpose; 41 percent of our health care is currently paid for by the government.

The Canadian Federal criteria for provincial health care today are as follows:

1. Access to medical services must be provided without regard to cost, and without user fees.
2. Benefits must be comprehensive and include:
   - In-patient hospital care (room and meals at "standard ward level"), nursing, drugs, diagnostic tests, medical and surgical supplies.
   - Out-patient hospital services (emergency room, lab, radiological and other diagnostic procedures).
   - Physician services, in hospitals, clinics, or offices.
3. All residents of a province must be covered. A waiting period for new residents must not exceed three months.
4. Coverage must be provided by the home province during any waiting period or for care rendered during a visit.
5. Provincial health insurance plans must be administered and operated on a non-profit basis by a public authority.[4]

The translation of the last stipulation into public policy has led the provincial health ministries to organize "health insurance plans." In at least one province, initial authority was given to a private non-profit carrier to administer the official plan, just as in the U.S. Blue Cross-Blue Shield (and some commercial companies) administer parts of Medicare. Canadians soon found that cost to be excessive. A booklet published by the Ontario Ministry of Health describes how the Ontario Health Insurance Plan (OHIP) works. Keeping in mind that each provincial plan is slightly different in the coverage it offers beyond the federal minimum, a number of excerpts from the brochure should give a clearer sense of the Canadian system.

The Plan

Ontario Health insurance is a comprehensive government-sponsored plan of health insurance for Ontario residents. It provides a wide scope of benefits for medical and hospital services; additional benefits are also provided for the services of certain other health practitioners. Residents of Ontario—regardless of age, state of health or financial means—are entitled to participate. *Tourists, transients and visitors to Ontario are not eligible.*

Thus begins the description, followed by several pages enumerating benefits: physician services (which also include anesthetics, X-rays, prenatal and postnatal care, lab services, and clinical patholo-gy), hospital services (which may include various therapies in addition to drugs and the use of all hospital facilities), extended health care (it covers some, but not all, nursing home expenses), home care (there is full payment under the plan for persons qualified by an organized home care program in Ontario), ambulance services (with co-payments of five dollars for a twenty-five-mile trip and fif-teen cents a mile over twenty-five miles up to twenty-five dollars, and twenty-five dollars for the use of an air ambulance), dental care (90 percent of the cost of dental surgery performed in a hospital), optometrist services (90 percent of the scheduled fee), free drugs (only for the fifteen hundred prescription medicines on the Ontario Drug Benefit Formulary and only for those over sixty-five years of age), chiropractic (up to $125 per person and $25 for X-rays), osteopaths (up to $100 per person and $25 for X-rays), and podia-trists (same as for osteopaths).

A listing of services *not* covered includes: acupuncture, cosmetic surgery, private-duty nursing fees, eyeglasses, artificial limbs, crutches, private and semi-private hospital accommodations, etc. In contrast to the German and other European systems, OHIP pointedly notes that "benefits are not provided for care in health spas."

There is an extensive section on out-of-province coverage. It begins, "...The Plan pays for medical and hospital care anywhere in the world for insured services." There is a caveat, however, that such payment is at applicable Ontario rates. Some doctors may not accept such rates, and the insured Ontarian is then responsible for the dif-ference. Full hospital charges (standard ward rate) will be paid any-where in the world except for nonemergency or elective care at a U.S. hospital when such care could be given in Ontario. Then the plan will pay only 75 percent of charges for insured services. A note is added that "many hospitals in U.S.-Canada border cities and in Florida will accept the OHIP certificate just as if you were in Ontario...." OHIP will cover a person who leaves Ontario to settle elsewhere for up to four months, or until other coverage is effective, whichever comes first.

Enrollment procedures are outlined. There is group enrollment in companies where fifteen or more employees are on the payroll, and the employer itself must enroll and do the enrolling. Employers of six to fourteen persons have the option of enrolling. Professional groups, farm groups, cooperatives, associations, etc., can voluntarily enroll as groups. Individuals outside the mandatorily or voluntarily enrolled groups may enroll directly.

The booklet explains:

> Each insured individual and family is provided with an identification card bearing their Ontario Health Insurance number. This card is to be presented to the hospital, physician or other health practitioner when insured services are needed. Always have this card (or a record of your OHIP number) readily available for use in emergencies, and always quote your number when corresponding with the plan.

The address of a Complaints Officer is provided to hear instances of "professional misconduct" by physicians. Such misconduct is defined as requiring advance payments or charging excess fees.

The simplified administration of the Canadian system is considered its major asset. The U.S. General Accounting Office report on the Canadian system underlines this with dramatic statistics. The per capita administrative cost in the U.S. for both public and private insurance in 1987 (the last year for which the GAO has figures) was ninety-five dollars. In Canada, the comparable cost was eighteen dollars.

The GAO explains the lesser Canadian costs: "...Having a universal single payer system lowers the cost of insurance administration by stream-lining reimbursement and eliminating expenses associated with selling multiple policies, billing and collecting premiums and evaluating risk. Having a single payer also lowers costs for providers by eliminating the burden of completing numerous complex claim forms and meeting other administrative requirements."[5]

For 1987, overhead expenses of publicly funded health programs were about 1 percent of the total program cost in Canada and 3 percent in the U.S., compared to 11 percent and 12 percent in the two countries for overhead costs for private insurance. The GAO report says: "Real per capita expenditures for insurance administration in Canada have remained nearly constant. Since 1971, this sector of the U.S. health economy has grown at an average rate of 6.2 percent per year. By 1987, U.S. spending on insurance overhead had increased to five times that of Canada."[6]

The very simplicity of the Canadian system has led to the impression, exaggerated by its enemies, that it is highly centralized, a sort of "Big Brother," telling individuals what to do. It is a charge to which provincial governments are sensitive, and none more so than Quebec, which from inception has had the most elaborate of what are known in Canada as CHCs—Community Health Centres.

CHCs vary in organization and are found throughout the provinces—10 in British Columbia, 30 in Ontario, 11 in New Brunswick, 2 in Alberta, 4 in Saskatchewan, 5 in Manitoba, 1 in Nova Scotia and, to illustrate the point about Quebec, 157 in that province. The CHCs are somewhat similar to HMOs. An Ontario variety, called an HSO (Health Service Organization), is controlled by physicians and funded through capitation rather than fee-for-service. Some CHCs are large (although not by U.S. standards), like the Sault Ste. Marie Group Health Centre, with forty-five to fifty doctors plus other health officials who provide services to forty-five to fifty thousand people, or the Saskatoon Community Clinic, about the same size.

In Quebec CHCs are known as *Centres Locales des Services de Santé* (CLSCs); they are the only CHCs in Canada that operate within a planned regional network and under provincial laws governing structure and function. They are also the only ones that include public health duties and social services.

Ralph Sutherland and Jane Fulton, discussing CHCs in *Health Care in Canada*, ask rhetorically why they are not more widespread and answer by saying they don't receive enough government support. That, in turn, may be due to "the organized antagonism of the medical profession."[7]

The Canadian medical community's resistance is reminiscent of the AMA's fierce opposition, until quite recently, to group practice, HMOs, etc. When CHCs become a threat, say Sutherland and Fulton, fee-for-service physicians find a way to compete. They cite the case in Quebec, where some CLSCs offered easier access to care in evenings and on weekends, and *quebecois* doctors scurried to set up "polyclinics offering more services over longer hours."

Some of the problems involving CLSCs are outlined in a report entitled, in its English language version, *Improving Health and Well-Being In Quebec*, issued in April 1989 by the Ministére de la Santé et des Services Sociaux (Department of Health and Social Services) of the Government of Quebec. The report states that "the slow development of the CLSC network has led to ambiguity and tension ...

Territorial attitudes, rivalries and the ambiguity of certain department-mental guidelines sometimes fueled conflicts between establishments ... It is now necessary to clearly define the roles and functions of each category of establishment." The 137-page report is full of recommendations for changes and improvements in the province's health care system, many specifically concerning the CLSCs. They are supposed to reduce pressure on hospitals, but the report claims that they have not diverted enough of those with minor ills or social (as opposed to health) problems, and that they do not have enough physicians or long enough office hours. The department's recommendations in this regard include increasing the time for appointments to thirty-five hours a week; providing walk-in services fourteen hours a day, seven days a week, and medic-alert services around the clock for CLSC's located more than half an hour from a hospital; and performing electro-cardiograms and specimen-taking to help reduce the need for those services in hospitals.

In the same specific vein, concerning services needed in greater quantity, the Quebec health department's action plan also zeroes in on the lack of high-tech equipment in certain areas. It calls for a four-year investment program in radiotherapy equipment (linear accelerators) and facilities for cancer patients, an increase in the number of beds in neo-natology units in the greater Montreal region over a two-year period, the opening of three new cardiac catheterization rooms by 1993, promotion of kidney dialysis services both inside and outside of hospitals, and increasing the capacity for kidney transplants and improving the availability of kidneys.

The question of high-tech availability ultimately becomes a central theme in any discussion of the Canadian health care system. Opponents of transferring the single-payer mechanism to this country dote lovingly on the disparity in numbers of highly sophisticated instruments in the two countries. Whereas the U.S. had 3.26 units of open heart surgery per million persons in 1987, Canada had only 1.23 in 1989, 5.06 American cardiac catheterization units versus 1.50 Canadian, 1.3 organ transplant units versus 1.08, 3.97 radiotherapy units versus 0.54, 0.94 lithotripsies versus 0.16, 3.69 magnetic resonance imaging machines (MRIs) versus 0.46. Ratios for the availability of URTs was 8 to 1, and for organ transplants, 1.2 to 1.[8] Such numbers are offered as an implicit condemnation, if not an outright scare tactic, to frighten Americans into believing that a single-payer system means their lives will be jeopardized by lack of the latest gadgetry. Although Edward Neuschler, the author who cites these numbers in a pamphlet published by the Health Insurance Association of America, adds a caveat that "the figures given here may indicate oversupply in the United States rather than undersupply in Canada (or both)," the message remains: Canada's health care is not modern enough.

Phil Pankey, the ultraconservative chairman of the Colorado House of Representatives' Committee on Health, Environment, Welfare and Institutions, is even blunter: "I feel that a one-payer system would be as successful in the United States as it has been in the Soviet Union...I recently visited the Communist block countries and found their government-provided health care system to be on the level of the U.S. at the end of WW I."[9]

But in regard to placement of Canadian high-tech health services, the operative principle is "rationalization," a word often heard. As illustrated by the document from Quebec, the provincial government's control of capital costs leads to a proactive attempt to spot weaknesses in both the types of equipment and their distribution, and to remedy such weaknesses by providing available resources on a rational basis. This contrasts to the reactive measures in many American states under the "Certificate of Need" process. Under this process hospitals apply for various types of expensive new equipment and are told yes or no by a government agency, or are told to modify their requests and resubmit. Often these regulatory systems will set a limit each year that may be spent on capital equipment, but outcries from hospitals lead the legislature to overturn these limits. The system is highly political and the planning not rational. Adding to the confusion is the fact that doctors and other entrepreneurs can install the same equipment outside hospitals without governmental oversight.

Some Canadian entrepreneurs have tried the same gambit. Great controversy has been stirred by the Ontario government's refusal to allow a private investor to locate a lithotripsy unit (used to treat gall and kidney stones) in the city of Hamilton. Although Ontario does have some private clinics operating outside its medicare system, the new provincial government, dominated by the leftist New Democratic Party, is drawing the line against such investments.

In New Brunswick, where there are no private clinics, high-tech operations are confined to a series of regional hospitals, and certain services are concentrated in only one. Thus, the St. John Regional Hospital in the province's largest city is the only place in the province to receive a coronary bypass. But that's an improvement: Prior to the establishment of the St. John heart center, which also includes heart catheterization and angioplasty units, all advanced cardiology patients in the maritime provinces had to travel to Halifax, Nova Scotia, or to Montreal for treatment. With two heart surgeons now on staff, St. John Regional Hospital is doing eight scheduled bypasses a week, plus emergencies, and more than a thousand procedures in its laboratories.

At the moment, St. John Regional has the only advanced oncology treatment for cancer patients in the province, but the Moncton Regional Hospital's oncology program is set to go on-line in 1993. The linear accelerators now in use in St. John Regional are soon to be replaced by the latest Toshiba machines under a "package deal" the hospital has made for new equipment with the Japanese company. The one piece of up-to-date equipment not yet available anywhere in New Brunswick is an MRI machine. Patients who need such sophisticated imaging must still go to Halifax or other urban centers until St. John Regional, which has a tentative agreement with Toshiba for an MRI, receives the necessary funding from the provincial government.

But the scope of the lack of an MRI machine from the Canadian point of view was put in perspective for me by Kenneth McGeorge, the executive director of the Dr. Edward Chalmers Hospital in Fredericton, the provincial capital. His hospital, a major regional, sends only five patients a year to Halifax for MRI diagnosis. Another twenty are sent by physicians. These are the patients whom doctors think must absolutely have an MRI scan in place of any other technique (most major New Brunswick hospitals do have CAT scans and other advanced X-ray equipment). McGeorge estimated that if there were a local MRI, its usage would rise to about fifteen patients per month. "But if you don't see it, you don't miss it," he added.[10]

Unlike U.S. hospitals, where there are frequently surplus beds that remain unfilled for days, Canadian hospitals receive constant use. A wall chart at the Chalmers Hospital illustrated the closeness of the fit. A portion of its bed availability was broken down into units and each bore two numbers beside it, the number of beds assigned to the unit and the number actually in use.

	Assigned	In Use
Medicine	89	94
Internal Medicine	20	27
General Surgery	48	43
Plastic Surgery	9	9
Orthopedics	33	29
Urology	23	9
Ear, Nose & Throat	5	6
Eye	7	6

That some units had more beds in use than assigned was a function of the trades continually going on—doctors swapping beds when they have patients who need them.

At the same time, because the hospital operates under a fixed global budget, it must sometimes close beds to save money. Often this is done during the summer when doctors, as well as many potential patients, are on vacation. Chalmers recently closed thirty-seven beds and had to lay off thirty employees.

The idea of beds being unavailable when they might be needed naturally causes concern. One suggestion, tempting to hospital administrators, was to try to fill those beds with Americans since they pay for Canadian health care (although it's far cheaper than at home) and the extra revenue is outside the fixed budget. But the political ramifications foreseen if Canadians, shut out of hospitals by budget problems, were to witness Americans being admitted, poured cold water on the idea. Another problem with providing care to Americans in Canadian hospitals was explained by Kenneth McGeorge. It does happen that visiting Americans fall sick or have accidents and end up in the Chalmers Hospital. The difficulty arises when payment is sought from American insurance companies. "It's almost impossible to satisfy American insurers," said McGeorge. "We need details right down to the syringes used. Its cost me two full man days of account work looking up the cost of every service for a single patient." The point is well taken: The Chalmers Hospital, with 487 beds, has four people doing its accounts; the Eastern Maine Medical Center, in Bangor, Maine, a similar-sized operation, has according to Mc George, a staff of twenty.

Since accommodations are so tight in New Brunswick's thirty-four hospitals, the province has embarked on an ambitious program aimed at keeping people out of hospitals. The cornerstone of the effort is the Extra-Mural Hospital. It is based on a concept developed in Auckland, New Zealand. In the words of its executive director, Dr. Gordon Ferguson, it is "a very complete home care program." The unique wrinkle is that the program is structured as a hospital would be. It has a board of directors chosen just as in any other New Brunswick hospital. It has admitting and discharging procedures, controlled by doctors. But the patients do not go anywhere; they are cared for in their own homes.

The majority of care is provided by registered nurses under the instruction of physicians. The doctors make house calls, but not frequently. They are kept current about each patient's condition through regular reports. On the staff of the Extra-Mural Hospital, in addition to nurses, are dietitians, respiratory therapists, occupational therapists, physiotherapists, and social workers, all functioning under the direction of the physicians. Other specialists are available as required. Ancillary services, such as homemakers, meals-on-wheels, and sickroom equipment, are also provided as needed. Physicians are paid via the single-payer system, as are all other doctors, and the Extra-Mural Hospital is treated exactly as a hospital with walls would be.

New Brunswick's Extra-Mural Hospital earned high praise in an otherwise scathingly critical book on the role of nurses in the Canadian health care system, written by a muckraking Toronto journalist, Sarah Jane Growe.[11] The major complaint of the book was that Canadian nurses find themselves too subordinate in a doctor-dominated system. But that does not apply to the Extra-Mural Hospital, where the nurse "as primary caregiver is the coordinator" of the patient's treatment. The cost-efficiency of the program also draws kudos. "If it weren't for the 'hospital without walls,' that care would cost $350 a day. This may cost only $35 a day."[12] The teaching aspect of the program likewise evokes admiration: The nurses teach diabetics to administer their own insulin and bladder patients to hook up a continuous bladder irrigator. Palliative care—making a suffering, even dying, patient more comfortable—is likewise part of the program. The nurses enjoy their responsibility, and their turnover is much lower than in conventional hospitals.

The Extra-Mural Hospital was started in 1981, and now covers 600,000 of the 720,000 people in New Brunswick. Some areas, like Moncton, maintain two units, one for those who speak French and one for those who speak English. Currently the program serves about three thousand people daily, many of whom would otherwise require hospitalization. The $18 million budget is in sharp contrast to the $67 million required for the fixed-base Chalmers Hospital in Fredericton.

The Extra-Mural Hospital is a partial response to the increase in Canada's aging population. Some U.S. opponents of the Canadian system charge that it will be overwhelmed by the coming "aging boom"—the arrival of the baby boomers into their latter years. Dr. Ferguson cautions against overreaction:

> The aging of the population is perhaps the factor that has caught the imagination of most politicians and caused concern in most jurisdictions ... I believe we should not allow ourselves to become overly concerned. In 1901, 5 percent of Canada's population was over the age of 65; in 1981, that figure was about 10 percent yet I would defy anyone to say that the dimension of the problem has doubled. It might not be an exaggeration to say that today a serious problem arises only with those aged over 85 and perhaps it is these people we should compare with the 65 year-olds of 1901. The corollary of this is that the period from 65 to 85 is one of opportunity ... a wonderful chance to institute preventative health maintenance and also to introduce balanced interventions from both social and health services.[13]

The Single Entry Point program is often paired with the Extra-Mural Hospital when talking of innovative health care programs in New Brunswick. While the Extra-Mural Hospital has about 40 percent of its patients under sixty-four and about 8 percent under fourteen, the Single Entry Point is geared exclusively to the elderly. It now operates on a pilot basis in two regions of New Brunswick— Fredericton and the northeastern, French-speaking area around Shippegan and Caraquet. The flyer advertising the project spells out its rationale, which is, through a case manager, to coordinate services for the elderly in need of assistance with a view to keeping them out of hospitals, and if possible, out of nursing homes as well.

> Do you want to stay in your own home but feel you are no longer able? Do you feel a nursing home is your only choice? A pilot project in the Fredericton region and Acadian peninsula may be another choice. Through the Single Entry Project, you may be eligible for longer home-

maker hours, financial assistance towards a live-in house-keeper, regular Extra-Mural nursing visits ... The Single Entry Project will assist you in exploring all options from community living to nursing home care.

Care in nursing homes in New Brunswick, as in most provinces (with Manitoba the exception), is not covered under the blanket, single-payer Medicare program. So there are out-of-pocket costs to seniors. Some fees, too, are required for homemakers, meals, day care, and respite care. The importance of the Extra-Mural Hospital in the mix is that it does fall under Medicare. The problem of the elderly taking up hospital beds when they should be in less expensive settings, frequent in the U.S., is even more critical in Canada, where pressure on available hospital beds is acute—thus the government's willingness to experiment with programs such as these.

The Canadian federal government has shown much interest in the Single Entry Point model and has instructed its national advisory committee on Medicare to develop guidelines for national implementation. This group, the Federal-Provincial Advisory Committee on Institutional and Medical Services, has recently published such guidelines under the title *Assessment and Placement for Adult Long-term Care: A Single-entry Model.* The attempt is to establish nationwide standards in an area not wholly linked to the national health care system, but strongly allied.

It is in the handling of nursing homes that the Canadians most closely approximate the American system. Some interesting figures in the area of administrative costs bear this out. In the health care system in general, insurance overhead, using the total of private and governmental insurance in the U.S., was 5.1 percent of all costs versus 1.2 percent in Canada. Yet in nursing homes the two nations are close—15.8 percent of costs in the U.S., versus 13.7 percent in Canada.[14]

Private insurance does exist in Canada. Despite the image of total governmental control of the system, the single-payer plan really picks up only 74 percent of costs (versus 41 percent governmental payment of health costs in the U.S.). What private insurance covers in Canada are those supplemental benefits medicare will not accept: private or semi-private hospital rooms, cosmetic plastic surgery, and, perhaps most importantly, prescription drugs (these are customarily covered only for those over 65). Private insurers in Canada cannot sell insurance for any of the basic medical and hospital services covered by

154

the provincial plans. Curiously, the privates sell group policies almost exclusively, primarily to companies who provide added insurance to their employees. Another important market for private insurers are the "snowbirds"—the thousands of Canadians who head south each winter. A billboard near the border town of St. Stephen, New Brunswick, reminds motorists: "LEAVING CANADA? DON'T FORGET YOUR BLUE CROSS TRAVEL INSURANCE." Canadian Medicare will pay its own rate in the U.S., but won't cover the added costs. Smart "snowbirds" also stock up on Canadian medicines before heading south.

A question frequently asked is how the Canadian system deals with abortion. The decision is a provincial one. Abortion rates were highest in British Columbia, Alberta, Ontario, and the two northern territories. Surprisingly, the lowest rates were not in Catholic Quebec, but in Prince Edward Island, Newfoundland, and New Brunswick.

Between 1975 and 1985, there was a small drop (from 274 to 250) in the number of hospitals where abortions were permitted. A Canadian law, struck down by its Supreme Court in 1988, mandated that abortions could be performed only in approved hospitals with therapeutic abortion committees of at least three doctors required to sanction the procedure. "In general, the rate of legal abortions in Canada has been lower than in most other industrialized countries," according to the publication, *Canadian Social Trends.*[15] In 1985, 2,798 Canadians crossed the border to have their abortions in the U.S.

Another question asked about the Canadian system regards the confidentiality of medical records. Again, the misconception is of Big Brother watching everything, since the government is the bill payer. But medical records are handled just as they are in the U.S.—only patients and proper medical authorities have access.

An American who falls ill in Canada, or needs to see a specialist, feels quite at home. The look and feel of Canadian health facilities is much like our own. The one difference, explained by a New Hampshire friend whose wife suffered a heart attack in Halifax, was the bill at the end of her stay. It consisted on two lines on a single sheet of paper: intensive care and nonintensive care. This was perhaps even more startling to him than the fact that the cost was about a tenth of what it would have been at home.

9 TWO TRIPS TO CANADA

Politics is frequently more a matter of perception than of fact. Such is the perception of the Canadian health care system that at its very mention its foes conjure up memories of all sorts of horror stories, while its advocates envision some sort of idyllic never-never land.

With that in mind, it occurred to me that the ability to gauge the "look and feel" of the system is as legitimate an exercise as is juggling statistics to prove a given point. I therefore undertook several trips to Canada, visiting several provinces, intending, as best I could, to expose myself to reality. After all, I thought, after twenty years of existence, there must be a palpable sense to the system that can add a new dimension to our American discussion.

Paradoxically, my voyage to understanding began not in Canada, but in the United States. Madawaska, Maine is a town of about five thousand that sits on the southern bank of the St. John River in the northernmost reaches of the continental United States. It is located directly opposite the small city of Edmundston, New Brunswick, population thirteen thousand. The inhabitants of these two communities are quite similar despite their different nationalities. Majorities in both share a common cultural background: they are descendants of refugees from the French colony of Acadia, expelled from Nova Scotia in 1755. There is also, in both places, a strong admixture of French-Canadians from Quebec and a generous sprinkling of Irish Catholics.

In Edmundston, the language is French. In Madawaska, everyone speaks that language, but the younger people are coming more and

156

more to speak among themselves in English. On both sides of the river the Acadian flag—the blue, white and red tricolor of France with the gold star of Notre Dame de Lorette—often flies.

In other parts of our nation, the debate over whether or not a Canadian model of health care can be brought across the border to the United States has been influenced by a particularly powerful image. That is of floods of Canadians, tired of waiting for elective surgery, pouring into U.S. hospitals for the treatment they are denied at home.

But what of the opposite image? Is there a coequal flow, or even a trickle, of Americans crossing over into Canada for their health care? Madawaska seemed the logical place to seek an answer. For a number of reasons, many in Madawaska do cross the border to have their health needs met. How, then, do they feel about it?

To begin, you must understand there is no hospital in Madawaska. The closest American one is in Fort Kent, about fourteen miles away. A more sophisticated facility is in Caribou, thirty-five miles to the south. On the other hand, the Edmundston Hospital is just a hop, skip, and jump away across the St. John River bridge.

Madawaska's Ed McHenry suffered a heart attack at work and was a patient in the old Edmundston Hospital. Despite his Celtic-sounding name, McHenry is very much a member of the French-speaking Acadian community. He works at the Fraser paper plant in Madawaska—a Canadian-owned company that employs people from both countries. Incidentally, Ed McHenry is also one of Maine's part-time legislators; for eighteen years he has represented his community in the state House of Representatives.

McHenry did not want to go to the Edmundston Hospital. He would have preferred Fort Kent, but it was felt that the distance was too great. Afterwards he was not impressed with his treatment. "The doctors were great," he said, but he found the room stuffy (he had a private room) and he couldn't always get the service he needed. Unhappy, McHenry signed himself out prematurely after four days in intensive care and three days in recuperation. His wife, too, was unhappy with her experience in Edmundston. She had badly banged her toe and the Canadian doctor did not feel her ripped, bleeding toenail should be touched. She did not agree. Yet both McHenry and his wife say they are impressed with what the Canadian health care system offers its people. He speaks of the unwillingness of those on the

157

American side, himself included, to visit doctors for fear that a serious condition might reveal itself and there will not be enough money to pay for treatment. Fraser Paper's new insurance plan for its American workers, which requires preadmission certification and a second opinion prior to surgery, pays only 80 percent of the bill after deductibles. "If I were a Canadian," says McHenry, "I would get checkups."

He also appreciates the reluctance of Canadian doctors not to rush to treatment. He cited the case of his brother, who was diagnosed in Edmundston as having advanced cancer. The Canadian doctors advised that an operation would be futile. McHenry's brother was then taken to Portland, Maine, operated on, and returned to Fort Kent for chemotherapy. Shortly afterward he died, having undergone considerable suffering and incurred significant expense. McHenry also made a point of mentioning the plight of his Fraser co-workers who had to retire before they were eligible for American Medicare. The company would only cover the disabled for six months following their departure.

An interesting element of the complex cross-border health care relationship was provided by Richard Marston, a personnel executive at Fraser. Asked how the company handled Canadian employees' health care (Canadians are about 10 percent of the workforce), he explained that they received health insurance benefits like their American counterparts, but these were Canadian benefits through Blue Cross-Atlantic Canada for supplementary coverage, at considerable less expense to the company than what American insurance would cost. "Have the Canadian workers ever asked the difference be paid them in cash?" "Yes," he answered, "but the company hasn't done that."

Joseph Gervais, at age sixty-four, is one of those Fraser workers Ed McHenry was talking about. He developed a heart condition that required three operations in four years. He plainly had to give up his job, but he's not yet qualified for American Medicare. And he worries that even with Medicare, it will cost him a total of $385 a month to get Medigap insurance for himself and his wife—"half my pension," he says.

Unlike Ed McHenry, Gervais was well satisfied with the treatment he received at the old Edmundston Hospital. He called it "fantastic service," and he still visits a Canadian doctor. His perception is that in Canada, "the old folks are happy ... but over here, we pay through the nose and get nothing. At sixty-two, they should give people pills to kill themselves." He just can't understand why the U.S. doesn't have a national health care system. He spoke of his cousin in Canada who had been poor all his life and was now making more money than he knew what to do with since he had government insurance and a good pension. He also spoke of the old days in Quebec province (where he was born), and the time his mother needed an operation but couldn't get one because she didn't have the money.

Gervais, like many Americans, has a sense that Canadians are different. But unlike those who think Canadians more passive than Americans, particularly toward government, he believes the opposite. He thinks Canadians are very outspoken—"when they get mad, they get mad"—and that it is Americans who don't speak up. It is this passivity to which he attributes the current plight of senior citizens in this country. "The older you get, the more worries you have."

Gervais' daughter Nancy is the community development director for Madawaska. She told me that close to a majority of local people went to Canada for health care, particularly in emergencies. She, herself, had been hospitalized for a gall bladder operation. It had cost sixty-eight hundred dollars for ten days in the hospital, and her only complaint was the inordinate amount of time it had taken her American Blue Cross-Blue Shield Major Medical Plan to pay the Canadian providers. She also told me it was very rare for Canadians to cross the border for health care in this country. According to her, half the Madawaska kids were born in Edmundston, and many locals went across the river to buy their medicines, some prescription drugs being available in Canada before they are in this country.

American use of Canadian health facilities in this area would increase, Nancy Gervais thought, because Edmundston had just opened a brand-new hospital. Crossing the border to see it, we encountered another phenomenon of border life—a traffic jam at the crossing. That is a new development, the recent result of an increase in Canadian consumer taxes. Many Canadians now shop in Madawaska, drawn by bargains like chicken at thirty-eight cents a pound. The rising taxes have been levied by the Conservative federal government. Critics of Canadian-style health care lay the blame on health care costs alone—a convenient but unwarranted scapegoat, as we shall see.

The new Edmundston Hospital, the Hôpital Régional d'Edmundston, is a handsome contemporary building on the outskirts of the city. It is a far cry from the gaunt, abandoned, yellow brick structure downtown that was the facility where Ed McHenry and the Gervaises were treated. It's as modern-looking as any new American hospital. The directional placards on the walls of the brightly lit, cheery lobby proclaimed a host of services: ambulatory care, renal disease, respiratory therapy, electrocardiography, electroencephalography, psychiatry, operating suite, day surgery, medical imaging, and many more.

How high-tech is this regional facility serving a population of thirty thousand? It has a CAT scan and expects soon to have nuclear medicine. The surgery done here includes thorassic and vascular, but no cardiac bypasses. These are done in St. John, where the wait for elective (i.e., non-emergency) surgery is about a month, or in Quebec, where the wait can be two to three months. There are fifty-three doctors on the Edmundston Hospital staff. Since most were away at a conference on the day we visited, the hospital was quieter than usual. The emergency room was actually empty of patients, and the bilingual staff had time to chat. They told us they usually see about fifty to sixty patients a day, including some Americans. Their biggest complaint about the system was that they believed some overused it by coming to the emergency room with trivial complaints like a cold, stomach ache, or cut finger. "We have our regulars, just like in a bar," said one of the nurses. Although we were told that the hospital's 227 beds were always filled, the pediatric clinic we saw had space available. It has eight adult's and twenty-six children's beds, plus a nursery and neo-natal unit. The rooms were what we would call "semi-private"—each contained two beds.

John Harrigan is a doctor who worked for thirty-four years in the old Edmundston hospital. His office and his work are in Canada, but he makes his home in Madawaska. When asked for his reaction to the Canadian health care system, he said, "I like it because I hate to send bills to people and you don't have to worry about being paid." His perspective, of course, antedates the present setup, under which he is paid regularly, twice a month, on a basis of agreed-upon units: seventy-seven units for a consultation, eighteen units for an office visit, thirty-two units for a complete physical. (Specialists get more). His office overhead, including rent and secretary, costs him thirty-five thousand dollars a year. The paperwork is minimal: on multiple forms, with eight spaces per form, the name of the patient, medicare identification number, and date of birth are entered, along with the diagnosis and service performed. Forms are submitted to the province twice a month and payment received. Dr. Harrigan added that dealing with Americans and their insurance companies has become a real problem for Canadian physicians.

At Fraser Paper, where Dr. Harrigan also acts as medical officer, Maine Blue Cross, which used to handle the company's policy, was good about paying, but things have changed. While admitting that he could make more money working full-time in the U.S., Dr. Harrigan said not only would he have to worry about getting paid promptly, but he would also have to factor in malpractice costs as another disincentive. He explained that an orthopedic surgeon in Canada pays ten thousand dollars a year for malpractice insurance; the same coverage in the U.S. is forty-five thousand dollars. His own coverage in Canada is going up, but is still far below American rates; at one time he paid only twenty dollars a year, now he pays two thousand. The question of being paid regularly also relates to the past. Dr. Harrigan spoke of how everyone in the little village of Ste. Anne, outside of Edmundston, owed him money. He told of an New Year's Eve incident when a drunk dislocated his shoulder and the doctor carried him through snowbanks to the hospital, patched him up, and brought him home. When he asked thirty-five dollars for his services, the man responded, "You don't need all that money. How much do you really want?"

Today's young doctors, he believes, have no sense of such a history, and push for more money. To this veteran doctor, their starting incomes seem enormous. (In his first month in practice, back in the 1950's, Dr. Harrigan earned a mere seventy-four dollars.) He believes there are too many doctors in Canada, and tells of the controversy at Edmundston Regional when the hospital board of trustees approved two more general surgeons to join the four already on staff. Dr. Harrigan feels that medical services are overused, that there are too many tests and, like the emergency room staff, that too many people seek help for minor ailments. The question of waits for elective procedures evoked another anecdote: the story of a woman on the waiting list for a hip replacement, although told by one surgeon it was unnecessary, who paid thirty-six hundred dollars for the operation to be done in Maine versus the six hundred she would have paid had she waited to have it done, anyway, in Canada.

Despite being located in this remote area, Dr. Harrigan keeps up with the latest developments in medicine through twice-yearly visits to friends at Harvard Medical School. At one time, he recalled, they used to bring Harvard professors to the St. John Valley to meet with local doctors by organizing vacations for them, but the practice died out when the doctor who arranged the exchange moved away.

The Edmundston Hospital draws not only American patients, but also patients from Quebec Province, a dozen or so miles away. Dr. Harrigan belongs to the Quebec Association of Internists as well as the New Brunswick one. Since a major feature of Canadian health care is its portability, Quebec simply pays New Brunswick for its citizens who receive care in Edmundston. The fees in the two provinces are similar, but a difference does exist between Quebec and Ontario, since the latter pays its physicians more generously.

From Madawaska I drove down along the St. John River to Fredericton, the provincial capital of New Brunswick. In Fredericton, a city of forty-five thousand spread out on both banks of the river that has been called "the Rhine of North America," a more comprehensive picture of the province's health care program was revealed in talks with officials and advocates of different interest groups. As everywhere, there was strong support for Medicare and fear for its future. Here a sense of the province's medical distribution of services, including the high-tech equipment, came into clearer focus: which facilities were in Fredericton and which in the larger cities of Moncton and St. John; how the provinces' ethnic configuration affects health care (the province is one-third Acadian French, and that creates a need for two hospitals in Moncton—one French, one English); and, finally, what other smaller facilities existed, like the new regional hospitals in French-speaking areas near Edmundston and Campbellton. Here I also learned of the reverberations of Canada's controversial constitutional politics, and how that may impact Medicare's future. In its last provincial election, New Brunswick's Liberal party, which had previously won every seat in the local parliament, lost eight places to a new party, the Confederation of Regions (COR), which campaigned against the bilingualism that is so much a part of New Brunswick's public life.

The position of Medicare in the constitutional debate was well stated in an article by Charlotte Gray in the magazine *Saturday Night:* "For the past quarter-century Medicare has been at the heart of our national identity." The fear she expressed was that the federal government was backtracking on the national commitment to the program. "With every shared federal-provincial programme on the constitutional negotiating table, its [the federal government's] definition of 'national standards' appears increasingly fuzzy."[1] And Charlotte Gray hastens to add that "money is not the problem." She implies it is a question of ideological attitude and the will to support Medicare.

In front of the provincial parliament in Fredericton is a statue of Dr. W.F. Roberts, the man who promoted Canada's first ministry of health in 1918—an act lauded by city fathers in a plaque that reads, in part, "The concept was later adopted in other parts of Canada and, indeed, throughout the world." That first ministry of health is now the New Brunswick Department of Health and Community Services, and in an office around the corner from the statue, I met D.B. "Don" Chevarie, the director of Medicare for the province. The first thing he told me was that Medicare was "one of the most popular programs ever instituted in the country and the people would never allow it to be dismantled."

What Chevarie called "public relations hype" about the lack of certain services he attributed to those involved in negotiations with the single payer (in this case, himself). While he admitted Medicare is costly, he quickly pointed out that it's nowhere near as expensive as health care in the U.S. According to him, the public was so pleased it was willing to pay even more if necessary. He was not specific about the amount of the provincial budget earmarked for health care (the range in Canada seems to be from 34 percent in Ontario to 23 percent in Newfoundland), and he insisted there were still things to be done to better control costs.

To me he sounded like any American insurance executive, exasperated by doctors who bill too frequently. Because the Canadian system is fee-for-service, some doctors do try to increase their incomes by seeing as many patients as possible, as often as possible. Chevarie calls it the "come see me every second day" syndrome. Yet there are now professional review committees, composed mostly of doctors, looking into such practices. On occasion, physicians who overbill are asked to repay the system. As in the U.S., there are professional associations that consider quality questions. The Royal College of Physicians and Surgeons acts as a licensing body and receives complaints. The provincial medical society, on the other hand, acts more as a union and bargaining agent in fee negotiations with the province. Contracts are for three years, and the bargaining with the medical society's economics committee can become heated. Negotiations with hospitals are more complicated. At one time, each institution negotiated for itself, but now the New Brunswick Hospital Association acts as a single bargaining unit. The agreed-upon global budgets are exclusive of salaries. Another committee, including representatives of the various employee unions, parlays with the government to set their pay scales.

Some hospitals run deficits, and in such cases, teams visit the sites. If they find the increases over budget justified—if there was an unexpected rise in patient volume, for instance—the government, as the single payer, will accept the over-budget costs.

On the politically volatile question of waits for service, Chevarie did admit waits for elective surgery, but like all Canadian health officials, strongly emphasized that "all emergency services are taken care of at once." It is the physicians who make the decisions on who gets what services when, they put names on the waiting lists, and Chevarie questioned how often they clear their lists.

Despite their initial opposition to Medicare, doctors now are solidly behind the program, according to Chevarie. In the September elections in New Brunswick, the CMA (Canadian Medical Association) sent questionnaires to candidates, soliciting support for Medicare and demanding to know if they would support it. Some Canadian doctors did move their practices to the U.S. at first, but Chevarie claims many are coming back. His figures for physician incomes seemed high for Canada—$700,000 a year for some, and for others as much as $1 million. There was considerable admiration in Fredericton for the cleverness of the province's minister of health, Ray Frenette, when he tried to set a cap on physician earnings at $400,000 a year. The doctors fought the proposal, and the public was shocked—they never dreamed their doctors made so much money (and apparently few of them do).

Chevarie also explained some of the intricacies of administering Medicare in a single province. There are the problems of those from other provinces who become ill in New Brunswick (their province picks up the bill at New Brunswick rates), and the reverse problems when local people require care elsewhere. Americans, as well as other non-Canadians, are charged the New Brunswick rate for doctors and hospitals, plus a surcharge for capital costs. Local people treated in the U.S. have their bills paid by the province—at about four times the local cost, according to Chevarie. A ticklish point concerns Canadians who work and live in the U.S. and then, when they become ill after many years away, want to come back for their health care. Since their taxes have not contributed to Medicare and they do not indicate that they intend to be permanent residents, they are sometimes turned away. The system gives special consideration to refugees, covered by the federal government, and the native populations of Indians and Inuits (Eskimos). The latter are given Native Health Cards by the Federal government, but their care is paid for by the governments of their home provinces. The natives also receive federal coverage outside Medicare.

Another part of the provincial responsibility is to dispense prescription drugs. A talk with Fay MacKie of the Department of Health and Community Services revealed several interesting wrinkles. Only one province—Saskatchewan—provides prescriptions drugs for everyone under Medicare. In the other provinces, only those over sixty-five have medicines provided. Even in such cases there is a $7.05 dispensing charge unless the individual receives income assistance. Medicare does pay drug costs in special situations—for transplants, nursing home residents, children with special needs, or for those in the care of the province. AZT is covered for AIDS patients, and according to Fay MacKie, New Brunswick had, at last count, sixty to sixty-five such cases. Heavy emphasis is placed on supplying generic drugs, a practice in most provinces—except that New Brunswick differs by having a list of interchangeable drugs to which doctors can add by requesting departmental physicians to review the drug in question. The department also monitors drug utilization to see if any medicines are overused, as was the case recently with a particular tranquilizer.

New Brunswick's two innovative programs—the Extra-Mural Hospital and the Single Entry Point program for Seniors—have already been noted. They exemplify provincial policy, and any discussion with provincial health care officials usually touches on attempts to move more in the direction of home care. The genial director of the Single Entry Point program, Eric Gionet, was, as could be expected, extremely upbeat about his two pilot projects, case management efforts linking existing services and the Extra-Mural Hospital. An evaluation issued in April 1991 backed his contention that the Single Entry Point was fulfilling its purpose. "Over an eleven month period an average per diem of $31 helped to keep 117 frail elderly at home for an average period of 8 or 9 months," reads one of the conclusions. "At the end of the evaluation period, 91 were still living at home."[2] What's more, the goal of reducing waiting lists for nursing homes seems to have been achieved. In the two pilot cases, Fredericton and the Acadian Penninsula, the list was six times shorter than the previous year in the former area and four times shorter in the latter.[3]

Prevention is a buzzword invariably heard anywhere in the world when health policy is discussed. The New Brunswick government holds that it is doing something about it (and intends to do more) in a "draft report" issued in August 1991 by the Premier's Council on Health Strategy. The document begins with an anonymous quote: "If I had know I was going to live this long, I would have taken better care of myself."[4] It then plunges into a thicket of the kind of airy prose that makes government reports so maddening: "If we invest wisely in health promotion and prevention objectives, we can surely hope to reduce the growth of health care and social costs while improving quality of life for more people for longer periods."[5]

Yet, in all fairness, it must be admitted there is valuable information in the report, particularly in the summaries of innovative health promotion and prevention programs from other provinces, as well as a listing of things that have already been done in New Brunswick. Examples include the Injury Awareness and Prevention Centre in Alberta; the Acti-Menu Health Program run by the Provigo supermarket chain in Quebec, which promotes public knowledge of healthy diets; the Ontario Health Innovation Fund ($100 million over four years), which gives grants to non-profit, community-based groups; and local projects like the Student Assistance Program at Fredericton High School, which addresses drug and alcohol problems.

The recommendations section zeroes in on specifics. Targets and strategies for reductions in such public health problems as motor vehicle accidents, head and spinal cord injuries, suicide, hip fractures of seniors, etc. are included. There is a particular attack on smoking. The Minister of Health and Community Services is charged to present a bill calling for the following:

- Addiction warnings on packages of tobacco products and health warnings where tobacco is sold.
- A ban on cigarette vending machines.
- A ban on advertising tobacco products.
- A ban on the sale of loose cigarettes.

The proposed law is a provincial action, but Canada as a whole has been vigorously taking on the tobacco issue. And it has done so from a position of weakness. Canadians were once known as "champion smokers." The percentage of smokers there was higher than in the U.S. for many years. In 1981, Canadians were consuming 3.52 kilograms per capita of tobacco products versus 3.21 for Americans.[6] But by 1989, Canadian tobacco use had been drastically decreased to the point where the kilogram per capita figure was exactly that of the U.S. Much of the reason was the heavy tax on tobacco—in Canada, two-thirds of the cost of a pack of cigarettes is attributed to federal and provincial taxes; in the U.S., only 20 percent. The high cost of Canadian cigarettes, together with other elements of the national plan to reduce smoking (banning ads and emphasizing health warnings) has had its effect. Also, some of the money raised by this high level of taxation finds its way into health care. It is not, as some charge, the other way around—that cigarettes cost so much because of the health care system. High taxation is a deliberate strategy, recognized as such by the tobacco industry, which has protested that it is the target of such discrimination that it may challenge the taxation level on the grounds that it is confiscatory and unconstitutional.

Dr. Warren Davidson liked the idea of cigarettes at seven dollars a pack. I met him in his office in a building adjoining the sprawling Moncton Regional Hospital. His specialty is gerontology (he is chief of geriatrics at Moncton), and he is very interested in health promotion. He is also a thinking doctor, even philosophic, and writes articles with titles like "Metaphors of Health and Aging: Geriatrics as Metaphor." He's liable to greet visitors with the statement that his profession has "sold out to technology. The art of medicine is quickly slipping away."

167

Dr. Davidson thinks the notion of an impending crisis in Canadian (and worldwide) health care due to the increasing numbers of elderly is "complete and utter nonsense." It is true that thirty-five to forty cents of every health dollar is spent on those over sixty-five, and that an even larger amount on those over eighty, particularly in the last year and the last weeks of life. Even so, with a different orientation, the same amount of resources could be better used. He describes those in charge of the present system of health care as "a brotherhood far more powerful than the KKK," and intimates they should be treated with the same scorn. A doctor-driven solution, he said, would be very expensive and would fail. He declared himself a strong supporter of community care and projects like the Single Entry Point.

He referred to a study done in the U.S. and Canada considering different approaches to care of the elderly. Four levels of care were described for a hypothetical eighty-five-year-old grandmother found unconscious and bleeding rectally:

1. Supportive care (keeping the patient comfortable).
2. Limited intervention.
3. Both of the above, plus emergency surgery.
4. Doing everything. Americans, he said, chose 3 and 4, both for the aged loved one and for themselves when they were old and sick. Canadians chose 1 and 2 for the projected relative, while for themselves they wanted more intervention.

In his paper, "Metaphors of Health and Aging," Dr. Davidson enlarges on the theme. He rails against the myth that the aged are "senile, disengaged, inflexible and unproductive." This prejudice, linked to the increasing dependence on health care technology, has led to the dehumanization of elderly patients, over-medicalization and situations whereby "patients with catastrophic and irreversible damage are maintained on artificial life-support systems, such as ventilators and/or tube-feedings."

Dr. Davidson then adds: "With the denigration and loss of the art of medicine, we practitioners, who have married technology, have lost our skills and capacity to decide on, or influence matters of humanity. We have opted, undoubtedly, for the least litigious course: that is, to make no decision other than to treat blindly."[7]

Given the fact that the over-seventy-five group has been shown statistically to consume 35 percent of the Canadian health budget, a new way of thinking about the elderly has to be developed, and Dr. Davidson sees the solution in "the development of geriatric assessment and rehabilitation programs." The essence of such activities, which he says have not been well-developed in North America, lies in "the vigorous promotion of healthy aging, active living, as well as dying with care and dignity."

All Canadians are eligible for Medicare, and there are added benefits for those over sixty-five. Medicines at minimal costs are one. In New Brunswick, there is also the Seniors' Health Benefit Program. Any senior citizen who receives both an Old Age Security pension and a Guaranteed Income Supplement (available to Old Age Security recipients with little or no other income) is automatically eligible for additional health benefits. Those who don't get the Guaranteed Income Supplement can join the program for $39.96 a year. The range of benefits includes syringes and needles for self-injections, diabetic testing supplies, ostomy supplies, eye exams, eyeglass lenses or contacts, hearing aids, foot care, chiropractic treatment, protheses—and 80 percent of the costs of these non-Medicare–covered services will be paid.

The New Brunswick government is close to sharing Dr. Davidson's philosophy. A report issued in April 1991, *Enhancing Seniors' Independence*, seems to borrow his words. The four major thrusts are developing wellness/healthy lifestyles, community living, and a coordinated access and delivery system, and in the description of one of the outcomes it hopes for, the language follows Dr. Davidson almost exactly: "[Changes] will help to dispel the myth that most seniors are sick and a drain on the public purse."[8]

A final image of my visit, which relates to the elderly, is of Fredericton's recreation department building, surrounded by playing fields and tennis courts, where I met Colleen Hanna, the pleasant wife of a doctor, whose job it is to coordinate senior citizen recreational activities. She stressed the importance of recreation and the idea of wellness. "Osteoperosis is preventable," she said. This major problem afflicting older women can be avoided by exercise. "Seniorobics" and "Let's Get Flexible" are two of the provincial fitness programs described in a comprehensive booklet of senior services available at the recreation building.

On the outskirts of Fredericton is the already mentioned Chalmers

169

Hospital, named for Dr. Everett Chalmers, a local physician and, as explained in the institution's orientation manual, "the politician who was most instrumental in obtaining a new hospital to replace the Victoria Public Hospital in existence since 1887."[10] Chalmers opened its doors on September 18, 1976, and still looks relatively new. Built on a thirty-seven-acre site, it has 416,000 square feet on four levels, and a capacity of 487 beds. The layout was criticized in an interview I had with Abel Bourque, a Fredericton accountant and former hospital trustee and financial advisor. He believes hospitals should rise vertically, rather than spread horizontally, in order to save movement from place to place. Kenneth McGeorge, Chalmers' chief executive officer, agreed the design was faulty. He said he had to use motorized vehicles to ship supplies around, and he blamed a federal decision in the late 1960s to use only a single architect. McMaster University Hospital in Hamilton, Ontario, which I would visit later, was designed by the same person. These are four-floor hospitals (potentially eight, because of the spaces left between floors with plenty of room for internal changes). "Over the years many renovations have taken place where entire services have been relocated within the building," says the Chalmers manual. McGeorge doesn't think other new hospitals like it will ever be built—but he also does not think there will be any new hospitals built in Canada. At the same time, no hospitals have been closed, he said. Their roles may change. Some may become long-term care facilities. And in communities with more than one hospital, the government will see to it that the services are rationally distributed, avoiding the duplicate services so often seen in the U.S.

The "Mission Statement" of the Chalmers Hospital begins: "The citizens of the province of New Brunswick, through their Government, are the owners of the Dr. Everett Chalmers Hospital."[9]

What is the governance of a place like Chalmers? There is a board of trustees of distinguished persons, as in any similarly non-profit, community hospital in the United States. In this case, the provincial government makes four appointments, the medical staff two, the board itself two, the Fredericton City Council two, and among the remaining appointments, all ten of the region's referring hospitals have one each. Chalmers serves a designated health region. Under the regionalization approach, the other hospitals serve as feeders. They handle the easiest cases; the tougher ones are sent on to

Fredericton. Except for neurosurgery, open-heart surgery, and transplants, Chalmers does everything. It is also affiliated with two medical schools—Dalhousie University in Halifax and Memorial Medical School in St. John, Newfoundland.

Ken McGeorge spoke with some envy of the extent of regionalization in other provinces, particularly Quebec. There, he told me, regional boards actually receive funds from the provincial government and parcel them out to hospitals. A similar movement is underway in British Columbia, where recalcitrant and overly parochial boards have been dismissed and multiple hospitals consolidated for greater efficiency.

As a hospital administrator under the Canadian system, McGeorge does have complaints, but not about the system as such. Labor rules force him to employ mostly registered nurses rather than aides or orderlies, even though he feels less qualified personnel could do some of the routine work. A case in point, he said, was his own experience last summer when he smashed a finger and went to his own emergency room. He was seen by several nurses and a doctor, was X-rayed, and had other procedures performed. He estimated the cost of his treatment at $250. At the hospital in Bangor, Maine, he argued, he would have been seen by a medic or a single nurse, and the cost would have been less. He faces the same professional turf problems between doctors and nurses. He has no nurse practitioners nor nurse anesthetists.

The overuse of the emergency room is also a problem. The province once tried user fees to discourage frivolous use. Not only were the fees resented, they were also ineffective. Despite the fact that 70 percent of admissions to emergency rooms were for non–life-threatening conditions, crowding did not seem that much of a problem. Last August, waiting time in the Chalmers emergency room was less than an hour.

The biggest problem was waits for elective surgery, said McGeorge, especially for hip replacements when the patient was in no danger and not in serious discomfort.

McGeorge gave me a little history about something called the Red Book, a listing of medically necessary in-patient procedures that would be covered in Canadian hospitals. (Remember that the Canadian system began with hospital insurance.) In the 1970s and 1980s, the Red Book grew. When the system started, no one had foreseen techniques like hip replacements, pacemakers, coronary bypasses, transplants, and neo-natal units. "In the 1980s the Red Book exploded, and was broadened to include everything in the World Health Organization definition—abortion, vasectomies, tubal ligations, breast reconstruction." After saying this, McGeorge added that the contradictory pressure put on governments was to contain costs despite this expanding service, to stay within 25 to 30 percent of provincial budgets. A possible solution, he offered, was to stick with the original Red Book list—a narrow range of coverage—much as insurance companies do in the U.S.

Despite his gripes, McGeorge believes the whole question of waits had been "blown out of proportion." Certainly, some wealthy Canadians went to places like the Mayo and Lahey clinics—"jumped the queue," as the expression goes. He said he did not think this was always a bad thing. For example, he would not be happy with the disruption caused if the K.C. Irving family came to his hospital. It would be like "having the Queen," he said of this prominent New Brunswick family, one of the wealthiest in Canada. He did express surprise that more American firms did not take advantage of cheaper Canadian health care prices. For example, Hospital Corporation of America has an arrangement to bring American patients to the London University Hospital in Ontario. But when the hospital in Kingston, Ontario, which does kidney transplants for half the U.S. price, offered the service to an American Blue Cross-Blue Shield plan, there was no interest.

McGeorge also gave an example of the political undertones often accompanying the charges of underfunding and lack of service that are sensationalized by the press. These charges frequently come from doctors trying to pressure hospitals into adding equipment that will enhance their practices. If they don't prevail, they complain to the press. That occurred in Fredericton in the last provincial election. A Chalmers doctor was also a member of the New Brunswick Parliament and a Minister in the provincial cabinet. A colleague at Chalmers ran against him. The challenger made an issue of underfunding, claiming that patients had died waiting for vascular surgery (average wait forty-eight hours). He raised such a fuss that the premier had to get into the battle to defend his man. In the end the incumbent won.

Chalmers Hospital is big business. Its annual budget is $67 million, and it handles sixteen thousand in-patients, fifty-two thousand emergency room visits, and thirty thousand out-patients. It has 1,250 full-time–equivalent employees and a medical staff of 125. If outward impressions mean anything, the operation seems to work smoothly without any of the visible stresses seen in some urban U.S. hospitals—no patients in beds in corridors, a quiet hospital-like atmosphere, cheery decor, etc.

That Canadian hospitals are not simply the impersonal, governmental institutions as portrayed by foes in the U.S. is attested by a questionnaire I picked up in the lobby of the Edmundston Hospital. In two languages, it asks these and other questions:

YOUR ADMISSION: were you:
1. Personally greeted with courtesy?
2. Admitted with ease and without undue delay?

CARE AND COMMUNICATION:
1. Were your physical, emotional and spiritual needs adequately met?
2. Were you treated kindly and with respect by all personnel (Nursing, Medical and other)? If not, please specify.

DIETETIC SERVICE:
... were you satisfied with:
1. The temperature of the food?
2. The flavor and quality of the food?

COMFORT AND ENVIRONMENT:
1. Were visiting hours satisfactory to you and your family?
2. Was your room kept clean and comfortable?
3. Were the toilet facilities convenient and sanitary?
4. Was noise well controlled?

The completed questionnaire was to be deposited at the nurses' station upon discharge or mailed directly. Signing it was optional. It even had a postage stamp on it.

St. John Regional Hospital is the largest health care facility in the province. It is ten years old, yet looks almost brand-new. People in New Brunswick speak of it with awe. Especially mentioned is the atrium in the lobby; some say the place looks like a luxury hotel.

173

My main purpose in visiting was to see its high-tech equipment at work. It has the only major oncology treatment unit in New Brunswick (Moncton will have one in June 1993), and the machines, as mentioned earlier, are all due to be replaced soon by Toshiba. The new equipment will be housed in a "Centre of Excellence," cheek by jowl with the "Heart Centre" with its cardiac catheters and angio-plasty services available to the cardiac surgeons who perform bypass-es. There is a CAT scan, and an MRI is in the offing, as are a computerized medical information system, what I was told is "the newest Lanyea dictation system," an IVP for kidneys (whatever that is), and a daylight loading system for diagnostic films that will do away with darkrooms. Digital angiography is also coming, and there was ultrasound equipment and umpteen computers in place. It all looked terribly high-tech to my eye.

The last section I visited was the neo-natal unit, where premature babies were in incubators—not many at the time, although they have had up to twenty-six at once. They do everything for these tiny humans except pediatric heart surgery. That procedure is done in Halifax, and infants are sent via air ambulance—Canada has many of them, and the service is paid for by Medicare. Not long ago, an infant weighing only 1 1/4 pounds was successfully transported. One of the babies I saw had weighed 565 grams at birth—little more than a pound. Born July 19, she was almost four pounds by late September, and would be home for Christmas. This is a part of the hospital where Americans come regularly—three or four neo-natals a year are trans-ferred from the hospital in Calais, Maine during the winter, when travel to Bangor (a two to three-hour trip under the best conditions) is treacherous. St. John is only ninety minutes from Calais.

It's hard to know whether or not to be impressed by high-tech medi-cal gadgets. Most likely what I saw in St. John is duplicated in most American hospitals of its size and perhaps in many that are smaller. So my most meaningful impression may have come from my encounter with a young doctor. This clean-cut blond man was apparently in charge of some of the radiology treatments in the oncology depart-ment. As he described his cancer-fighting equipment, it became obvi-ous to me he was not Canadian; his accent was British. I asked why he was practicing in Canada. His answer was forthright. He'd left Britain, he said, because the National Health Service was "disintegrating" under the assaults of the Tory government. He was a great admirer of

Canadian Medicare. Here, he said, doctors were not divided into consultants and GPs as they were in England. Everyone was equal. He ended by saying he would never practice in the U.S. despite the additional money he would make there. He felt treatment there, which depends primarily on the ability to pay, was "morally wrong."

Another hospital I visited was in Ontario. Chedoke-McMaster Hospital in Hamilton is one of the aristocrats of the system, as it would be anywhere else—a university-based teaching hospital located adjacent to the campus of McMaster University in a city of three hundred thousand at the head of Lake Ontario.

I had been given interesting directions: I was to turn onto West Main Street, then drive a few blocks until I came to "a weird building on the right." It was indeed a bizarre-looking structure that loomed up before me. I entered through a huge underground parking complex, then rode up color-coded elevators into a cavernous lobby giving onto bisecting corridors with brightly-lit shops offering a range of goods and services—the Marlin Travel Office, the Optix Optical Centre, a dry cleaner, the expected gift shop, and, in the lobby itself, a snack bar and ice cream parlor. It was not your everyday hospital.

Dr. William Walsh, one of the founders of the hospital and its unique medical school, explained that the travel agency, the dry cleaner, and the soon-to-be-opened super-florist were the hospital's venture into free-enterprise—at least to the extent that the space was rented so the revenues gained might be kept as a sum over and above the global revenue.

I met with Dr. Walsh in his office, actually a clinic he shared with other doctors. There was a comfortable waiting area where soft music played and there was a suggestion box with a sign: "To our patients: we welcome your comments and suggestions regarding our service."

Before we toured the sprawling facility (each floor is the length of two football fields), Bill Walsh filled me in on the history of McMaster.

During the early 1960s, he said, there were projections that Canada would need many more doctors. The federal government had plenty of money in those days and was willing to start new medical schools. The political infighting over a location in Ontario was fierce, but McMaster had a strong reputation for science (it even had its own nuclear reactor), and Hamilton had the right patient population. Built at a cost of $85 million, the hospital opened in 1972, after universal hospital insurance had come into being, but before Medicare.

In an early example of "rationalization" of services, attempts were made through the Hamilton-Wentworth District Health Council to prevent their duplication. Since five hospitals already were in the area, it was decided that Hamilton General would offer the cardiac catheter and open-heart surgery, Henderson General the cancer clinic, St. Joseph's nephrology and respiratory, and Chedoke, which eventually merged with McMaster, geriatrics.

Students get their training in the specialties at the appropriate hospitals, all of which have strong research components and full-time faculty. But the unusual element at McMaster is the way students are trained. Given carte blanche to devise their own curriculum when they began, they were dissatisfied with the then-existing (and still prevailing) mode of medical education, with its heavy emphasis on chemistry, anatomy, and similar technical disciplines. At McMaster, according to Dr. Walsh, the idea was "to start from the end product and work back. We asked ourselves, what kind of doctor did we want in the year 2000?" They decided the need would be for a problem-solver, one who would continually search for information, possess people skills, and be bright and a team player. They devised a program with no prerequisites except a baccalaureate degree; there was no pre-med requirement. To the astonishment of skeptics, at the end of the first year of training it was impossible to tell which students had the extensive science background and which had started from scratch.

The teaching method resembles that of England's Oxford University. There are no lectures, and heavy reliance is placed on tutors who work with no more than six students. Learning is through problem-solving, first on paper, then with simulated patients trained to feign the symptoms of diseases, and finally with real patients. They have a worldwide elective program, which one can enter even in the first year, that sends students off to study abroad. As can be expected, unusual experiences are common. One student arrived in rural Jamaica and had to set a forearm fracture with the aid of a textbook on his very first day. Another student went to Paris to study with the famous Dr. Lamaze, holding a book on obstetrics in one hand and learning French from a volume held in the other.

Tracking graduates shows that half enter family practice. The program is popular; every year there are twenty-five hundred applicants for about a hundred places.

The discussion of medical education brought to mind a major issue concerning the future of American health care: the tremendous debts that burden medical school graduates in the U.S., and often provide the impetus for their pursuit of lucrative specialties. More often than not, young American doctors graduate owing a hundred thousand dollars or more. The figure for his med students and others in Canada, according to Dr. Walsh, is more like ten thousand, and there are student aid programs as well as low-interest government loans. Dr. Walsh also marveled at the difference between his days as a resident and today. He was paid sixty dollars a month; today, Canadian residents earn thirty-five to forty thousand dollars a year.

Dr. Walsh was clearly proud of his school's pioneering approach. He asked if I, by chance, had attended Harvard. When I said no, he chided that venerable institution's medical school for having initiated a similar program, the Harvard New Tract, without giving McMaster any credit. I told him I was not surprised, and he could condemn Harvard all he wanted since I was a Yale man. More seriously, he added that two other medical schools, in Maastricht, Holland, and Newcastle, Australia, were acknowledged replicas of McMaster. The school also maintains an office in the rural Ontario north country at Thunder Bay, and supplies it with students for family practice in that underserved area. At least half the students at McMaster are female, and one year women actually comprised 70 percent of the student body.

Like other Canadians involved in health policy, Dr. Walsh complained that the country was producing far too many doctors. He also described the political problem involved in trying to restrict foreign doctors. Before the collapse of the Iron Curtain, Canada had a flood of Polish emigre physicians. When the government refused to permit them to practice, they staged a hunger strike. This galvanized the large Polish community in the western provinces to apply political pressure and in the end the Poles were licensed.

Research is important at McMaster, and includes work on AIDS. There are also some 300,000 out-patient visits to the hospital every year. Global budgeting has forced the hospital to encourage ambulatory care and day surgery. Faculty members are allowed to have their own clinics, and Dr. Walsh, an internist, does so. Since faculty salaries have not gone up very much, those who teach depend more and more on their clinical earnings. Doctors at the hospital make about $100,000 annually.

177

We talked of the so-called drain of Canadian doctors to the U.S. in search of higher incomes. Like other Canadian doctors to whom I spoke, Dr. Walsh didn't consider that much of a problem any more. Stories were coming back about adverse conditions for physicians in the U.S.—huge malpractice costs, mounting overheads, incredible bureaucracies. He spoke with a sort of wonder of an American friend of his, a senior professor of medicine, who had to call an insurance company to get permission for the treatment of one of his patients. "Who does he talk to—one of his peers, who would understand all the complications of the case? No, he has to get the approval of a student nurse—a twenty-one-year-old kid!"

The Canadian point of view was also expressed by Dr. John Atkinson of Ottawa. He is a prestigious physician, chief of the medical staff at the Ottawa Civic Hospital, chairman of the Ontario Medical Association's Committee on Hospitals, coordinator of the nationwide Canadian Medical Association's Hospital Committee, chairman of the Hospital Medical Records Institution (HMRI), and a former member of the District Health Council in the region encompassing Canada's capital.

The latter two institutions require some explanation. The HMRI, Dr. Atkinson said, tracks 85 percent of all medical records in Canada—in contrast to the U.S., where such tracking is fragmented among the states. It is a private, non-profit organization of hospitals. There is no direct tie to the government, and all records are strictly confidential, a legal requirement. The most important information is contained in what are called CHAPs—Comprehensive Hospital Activity Programs—that break down the kinds of cases hospitals are handling and the intensity of their resource utilization. This provides insight into the cost of, for instance, treating pneumonia or performing a hip replacement. Such data collection is important, said Dr. Atkinson, because in the past hospitals were funded on the basis of patient days; now the government is looking at types and mixtures of cases. Comparisons will show where money can be saved.

District Health Councils are an Ontario phenomenon. They are voluntary bodies, established in seventeen regions within the province, mainly for planning. At the moment they have no fiscal responsibilities, but that may change, according to Dr. Atkinson. Council members are selected by the provincial government, also the source of funding. Through their committees on adult hospital care, pediatrics,

178

mental health, etc., the councils look at the availability of services and advise what is needed and at what cost. A recent concern dealt with pediatric mental health—a function deemed insufficiently covered in Ontario. While the plan offered is only advisory, there are teeth to the process, since no new services or capital construction can proceed without the recommendation of the District Health Council.

A few years ago there was a public furor in Ontario about the lack of open-heart surgery. According to Dr. Atkinson, five provincial cardiac centers got together to set priorities for operations. "The critical care problem in Ontario is gone," said Dr. Atkinson. Some services—including hip replacements and cataract—still require waits, he admitted, but as I heard so often in this country, "with acute care, you will be looked after instantly." For rural areas, he told me, there are hot lines to urban doctors, who consult over the phone or make arrangements to transfer patients by air ambulance.

Concerned about overdoctoring and its effect on costs, Canada is now limiting the number of new doctors. Moreover, postgraduate positions, the gateways to specialization, are also constrained. More than half the country's med school graduates cannot find slots for continuing their studies and become family practitioners.

Our discussion led me to ask about Dr. Ian Munro. He is the current director of the International Craniofacial Institute at the Humana Advanced Surgical Institutes in the U.S. He was born in Great Britain and practiced in Canada before going to work for Humana. He's an outspoken critic of the Canadian health care system who has declared publicly, "I do not think that the Canadian system has worked and it's going to get worse."[10]

Dr. Munro practiced at the Hospital for Sick Children in Toronto, an institution with a worldwide reputation which recently received acclaim for research that isolated the gene responsible for cystic fibrosis. Dr. Munro came to Sick Children's in 1971, prior to the initiation of Medicare and after the beginning of universal hospital insurance. Speaking at a forum in the U.S., he maintained Medicare had ruined this great hospital.

It was an 800-bed hospital and the finest pediatric hospital in North America, bar none. Probably the finest in the world. Over the course of the next few years it became obvious that this excellence could not be maintained.

179

That hospital is now under 500 beds; most of its top doctors have left. People who are dealing with patients there are now so over-rushed that they cannot spend adequate time with their patients. Waiting lists are outrageous. People report to the hospital but are turned back because there are no beds. This is a total turnaround from the policies prior to the government system.[11]

A rebuttal to these charges was issued at the same forum by Peter Ellis, President and CEO of the Sunnybrook Medical Centre in North York, Ontario, another institution at which Dr. Munro had worked.

Although it is hardly my place to defend Sick Kids,' I do believe I should make a point. But rather than talk about Sick Kids,' let me talk about Sunnybrook because Dr. Munro was also on staff at Sunnybrook where he did his adult work while he did children at Sick Kids.' I have to say that he left and we replaced him. And we replaced him with an individual whose international recognition is equal and, in fact, is some ways far more appropriate to the mission of Sunnybrook.[12]

Ellis, also a displaced Englishman, went on to assert how focused the Canadian system was on "receiving the input of the patient and dealing with that input" and he related this to his further references to Dr. Munro.

The Canadian health system attracts a lot of media attention. In fact, Dr. Munro was a master of using the media when he wasn't getting quite his own way in terms of resources. The media appear equally ready to latch onto any story of unprovided services, and so the patient's view has direct impact on the way services are delivered ... Many of the fights that Dr. Munro had with Sunnybrook—and I'm sure he would have continued to have—were the results of his desire to meet the needs of his patients.[13]

Having previously read this exchange, I brought the subject of Dr. Munro up with Dr. Atkinson. He had known him. The man was a world leader in his field, maxillofacial surgery—the reconstruction of faces—particularly for children. The Canadians could not pay him what he could earn in the U.S. nor, apparently, provide him with the resources he required. The term Dr. Atkinson used, not in a pejorative sense, was that Dr. Munro was a "pure entrepreneur," and thus bound to be unhappy with the restrictions of this—or, undoubtedly, any—universal health care system.

As for the Sick Children's Hospital, he saw its problem as stemming from the fact that it tried to do everything—it not only conducted world-class research and dealt with the most complex of pediatric problems, but also provided the run-of-the-mill services of any hospital, like removing tonsils and adenoids. One interesting point he revealed about Sick Kids' was that all of the medical staff had organized themselves into a single group for funding medical services, on the order of an HMO.

Until recently Canada's HMOs were regarded with as much hostility by doctors as they were by the AMA in the days of Dr. Fishbein. The Canadian system, for all the talk of government control, is, as should be obvious by now, dominated by doctors and their attitudes. The idea of abandoning fee-for-service for the type of capped payments that physicians receive under "managed care" does not sit well with them.

Herb Botkin is an HMO fan. He works in the head office of Blue Cross in Ontario and is director of Managed Dental Care of Canada, Inc., a Blue Cross subsidiary. It is a new division of this private, non-profit insurance company—a dental HMO. Since dental care—except where medically necessary—is outside of Medicare, this is a totally private operation and people have to buy into it.

Within Medicare, Botkin said, some attempts are being made to establish managed care models. An HSO (Health Service Organization), a group practice where doctors are on salary, has been organized by three hundred Ontario physicians, and recently the Toronto General Hospital and the Toronto Western Hospital announced their interest in starting an HMO to prove to the government they could save money with it. According to Botkin, they were having trouble getting approval from the Ontario Ministry of Health. The problem was that one governmental branch couldn't agree with the other.

It should be noted that the current provincial government is controlled by the NDP (New Democratic Party), a group considerably to the left. Yet, as was pointed out to me by Dr. Atkinson, political ideology plays a small role in Canadian health care. "The effect is zero. It's apolitical," he said, and noted that despite having had three different parties in office in five years, provincial health policy didn't change one iota.

Herb Botkin had a reason for his impatience with the ministry's dilly-dallying over the Toronto General–Toronto Western proposal. His dental HMO, the first of its kind in Canada, would be affiliated with it and that would help him reach his goal of four thousand contracts.

He sounded very much like insurance executives in the U.S. when they rail against the practices of doctors and hospitals, although the Americans are no doubt motivated by the fact that their companies have to pick up the bills. In Canada, where insurance companies have only marginal markets, I thought his complaints that there is no accountability, no control, no peer review, and no checking of billings might have a more abstract root. Then one particular beef did seem to connect to the bottom line. As of September 1, 1991, according to Botkin, the Ontario government was putting a limit of four hundred dollars a day on what it would pay for health care outside Canada, thereby saving itself a quarter of a billion dollars, but presumably passing an additional burden to the insurers of legions of Florida- and Arizona- and California-bound "snowbirds."

A hot debate was raging in Ontario over this decision, which some saw as depriving Canadians of their right to health care. Others, notably the egalitarian-minded NDP government, viewed it in these terms: If you're rich enough to go south in the winter, you're rich enough to pay some of your health care.

Despite the pervasiveness of the Medicare system in Canada, there are ways to get private care without going to the U.S. David Melnick, a successful Harvard-educated Toronto businessman, told me of his annual visit to a clinic called Laurentian Health. There, for $550, he receives a thorough, half-day checkup. Under the public system, Melnick told me, such a comprehensive physical is not possible. This particular alternative is permitted because it is set up as a physical for life insurance purposes. (Incidentally, Canadian Blue Cross sells life and disability insurance as well as supplemental health.)

Another Blue Cross official, Donald Lennox, a vice-president of the Atlantic Canada Plan, told me of the company's continual search for new business niches. When Medicare went into effect, his staff dropped from 200 to less than 40 people. But within ten years it has risen again to 350. Most of their business is in group policies (primarily small groups)—$120 million opposed to only $14 million for individuals—and the biggest part of the business is in insuring drug costs. However, Medicare mitigates the problem for Blue Cross when it has an AIDS patient. Since hospital and doctor bills are paid and the government even pays for AZT as a treatment, not a drug, the Blue Cross exposure is minimal. Whether Blue Cross is more profitable in Canada because they don't have the huge bills they have in the U.S. was a question never really answered by Botkin or Lennox, both of whom left the impression they would like to be in markets now covered by Medicare.

Since Canadian insurance companies pay for a lot of prescription medicines, the old battle between brand names and generics came up in conversations. A guiding principle these days, according to Lennox, is "interchangeability." Where formerly provinces were apt to demand the use of generics, options are now permitted.

One of the most contentious fights over health care in recent years in the national Parliament occurred over Bill C-22, passed in 1987 after months of rancorous debate. The bill's passage was a victory for the Pharmaceutical Manufacturers Association of Canada (PMAC) over what sounds like its twin, the Canadian Drug Manufacturers Association (CDMA). In fact, the former represents the brand-name producers, the latter the generics. Both claim to be as Canadian as hockey and the maple leaf. The PMAC brags that it is Canada's oldest trade association, founded in 1914 with roots going back a century. The CDMA, for its part, dismisses its rival as "an American-controlled lobby group" of foreign-owned multinational drug corporations, and calls itself the "Canadian generic pharmaceutical industry."[14] Not to be outdone, the PMAC replies through its president, the Honorable Judy Erola, former cabinet minister, that of the four major generic companies in the country, two are Canadian and the other two American-based.[15]

Charges fly back and forth between the two groups. The PMAC insists its annual research and development expenditures have grown from $50 million in 1983 to $211 million in 1989. The CDMA maintains that their rivals promised R & D expenditures of $1.4 billion over ten years and haven't delivered. They insist Canada has the second lowest ratio of R & D to sales in the western world—8.2 percent. (the U.S., at 14.2 percent, is not the highest; that distinction goes to the "socialized" systems in Sweden with 21.8 percent, Britain with 20.9 percent, and Germany with 17.9 percent.) Furthermore, the generic group claims that the PMAC members actually reduced

Canadian manufacturing facilities and eliminated hundreds of jobs. Canada, they claim, is a net importer of pharmaceuticals, and the deficit in this area has reached $600 million a year.

Essentially, Bill C-22 gave the brand name companies ten years of patent rights before generics could copy their products. The PMAC claims this is only partial protection, and "that the restoration of full patent protection for the intellectual property of pharmaceutical researchers is ultimately in the best interests of Canada." The CDMA replies that "prior to the introduction of the multinational monopoly in 1987," annual savings of $210 million were being realized by the competition between brand-name and generic drugs. While the PMAC boasts about its Health Research Foundation, the CDMA continues to lobby for the repeal of Bill C-22.

It should be said that many major American and international pharmaceutical companies do have Canadian branches: Squibb Canada, Ciba-Geigy Canada, Upjohn Co. of Canada, Sandoz Canada, Eli Lilly Canada, Inc., Parke-Davis Canada, Schering Canada, Hoffmann La Roche Ltd., Abbott Laboratories Ltd., etc.

None of my contacts in Blue Cross mentioned the TAPS (Treatment Accounts Processing System) program. As an example of the "public-private partnership" so dear to U.S. politicos, this arrangement is exemplary. It is the result of a combined effort by the federal Department of Veterans Affairs and Blue Cross of Atlantic Canada. Under TAPS, an eligible vet is mailed an identification card by Blue Cross. That card is presented to health professionals or suppliers of health equipment and the bill will be sent to Blue Cross for payment on behalf of the department, which supplies the funds.

Gordon Moore, Chief of Client Services at the Veterans Affairs office in St. John, explained how this supplemental benefits program dovetails with Medicare. Since veteran services predated the Medicare program, a role had to be found when medical and hospital costs were taken over by the provinces. A few veterans' hospitals and homes are left, but the department is trying to stop providing direct health services. Its supplemental benefits are often similar to those for which nonveterans buy private health insurance, such as dental, eyeglasses, prescription drugs, and others not covered by any private insurer, with a strong component for home care. A tug of war does occur with the provincial governments, said Moore. They quibble about who pays what—and about the philosophical, yet financially vital question: Are New Brunswick veterans first considered citizens of the province or are they national veterans?

There are ten to twelve thousand veterans in New Brunswick, and an equal number of potential ones if peacetime service is to be given the same weight as wartime experience. The last official "war" in which Canadians served was Korea. A few were in Vietnam, but only as observers. The overall number of veterans is shrinking, and the mean age is now seventy; the country had about a million veterans from World War II and twenty thousand from the Korean War. At the same time, the caseload is expanding as the veterans age. Moore was candid about gaps in the overall system, problems he had with mentally handicapped seniors who, in places like Nova Scotia, had been deinstitutionalized, and he spoke of waiting lists, but in this case for suitable housing. When some of his vets go to the U.S. they can be served in VA hospitals, and like other snowbirds, they buy health insurance against these risks. But Moore also spoke of Canadians he knew who came home from the States rather than be treated at extra cost. One was "a guy with a bowel condition who flew back from Florida." Another was a woman in his own office who had an attack of appendicitis in Bangor. "She died driving home," he said.

Nurses constitute another major influence on the Canadian scene. Like their U.S. counterparts, they have struck for better pay and working conditions. Shortages of nurses have caused breakdowns in the health delivery system and account for some of those waiting periods for operations. I had been told that the nurses in New Brunswick are not as militant as those in other parts of the country. Certainly Madeleine Steeves, the grandmotherly RN who is labour relations officer of the New Brunswick Nurses' Union, hardly appeared to be a labor agitator. She readily conceded there had been no strikes in New Brunswick, but said nurses had staged job actions in the province between 1969 and 1975 (essentially before Medicare). She insisted that the old saw that "a nurse is a nurse is a nurse," implying total submission to doctors, is a thing of the past. Today's Canadian nurses, while not attempting to be doctors, are "trying to be nurses as we see they should be." This means better education: The goal is a college degree for every nurse entering the profession. Despite much publicity about nurse dissatisfaction, Steeves said that as nurses, she and her colleagues strongly support the five principles of Canadian health care. Like many others, they believe the system should move more in the direction of community health care. They enthusiastically support community health centers and would like to see them open longer hours, and are positively delighted by experiments like the Extra-Mural Hospital. ("Real nursing," she called it).

Nursing shortages are hardly confined to Canada, Steeves told me. American hospitals were doing heavy recruiting up north, and in the early 1980s some Canadian nurses went to England and Ireland but found standards lower than in Canada. Currently there are shortages of critical care nurses (i.e., intensive care), but that is a problem of education. In New Brunswick there are only twenty slots for such advanced training, ten in English and ten in French. Two provincial universities have baccalaureate nursing programs, and some Canadians from the Maritime Provinces attend the University of Maine.

Nursing homes also enter into the picture for Canadian nurses. In New Brunswick, twenty-three such homes are unionized, the largest having two hundred beds. Some are private, some public, and all are registered under the Nursing Home Act. There are also special care homes with no nursing staffs. Some of these, I was told, have lost their licenses, and as in the U.S., there was a possibility of paying for first class accommodations. Steeves mentioned one home that was like a luxury hotel.

Several times during our discussion, Steeves alluded to a book she insisted I must read. Entitled *Second Opinion: What's Wrong With Canada's Health Care System and How To Fix It*, it was co-authored by Michael Rachlis, a Toronto doctor, and Carol Kushner. After buying the book (an apparent best-seller several years ago, it was now difficult to find in bookstores) and reading what the authors had to say about nursing, I could understand Steeves' high opinion of it. The authors expressed her ideas perfectly.

> Dozens of studies have shown that nurses do as well or even better than physicians when given the opportunity to work to their full potential.
>
> We need to put caring back into health care and nursing is an ideal place to start doing that.
>
> We'll have to offer them incentives like the chance to participate in management, paid leave for continuing education, and more autonomy consistent with their training and experience, if we're going to keep them in the system. Unless steps are taken to make nursing more professionally and financially rewarding, we'll continue to lose nurses to other fields.[16]

186

10 JUST SUPPOSE

Among some health care groups in recent years, Canada-bashing has become as popular as Japan-bashing is in Detroit. It's particularly prevalent among those in the health insurance industry. That's understandable, since even the talk of a single-payer system in America is enough to give them splitting headaches and sleepless nights. The industry has launched an offensive designed to convince the American people that our own failing system is the world's best. Any failure in the Canadian system is instantly seized upon and blown out of all proportion. We hear immediately of any poor Canadian who has had the misfortune to die while waiting for an operation. We are told, over and over again, that we Americans will never put up with that sort of thing; we will never fail to have access to immediate medical attention. It is never explained, of course, why 37 to 40 million of us who do not have access to health insurance do not share this so-called national trait.

In Maine, Senator William Cohen arranged a conference on health care in Portland that drew a turn-away crowd. Among the speakers were Carl Schramm, president of the Health Insurance Association of America, and Gail Wilensky, director of the Federal Health Care Financing Administration. Critics in attendance complained the session was little more than a platform for an attack on Canadian health care.

Pfizer, Inc., a leading drug manufacturer (highly profitable pharmaceutical companies have no wish to see our ultraexpensive system change), hired two economists to prepare a report purportedly show-

187

ing that Canadian health care was not as inexpensive as it was made out to be. (Ironically, their methodology was disputed by two employees of the Health Care Financing Administration and that caused a major flap.)[1] In a tradition dating back to before World War I, the heavy artillery of political pressure, public relation sloganeering and the sometimes questionable pronouncements of so-called experts have been wheeled into line in an attempt to discredit a specific course of action that just might be used to deal with the problem of health care in America.

Nor is the Canadian system immune to attack within its own borders, despite its immense popularity. *The Financial Post*, Canada's national business newspaper, ran the following item in September 1991: "The Toronto Board of Health warned recently that some provinces will go to a U.S. style of health insurance in which the user pays most of the insurance fees."[2]

The possible reversion to a pre-Medicare, U.S.-style system of health care is most often raised in Canada as a paranoid-sounding fear, not as a criticism of what they already have. One iconoclastic exception is William D. Gairdner, a forceful Canadian muckraker from the political right. In his best-selling book *The Trouble With Canada*, he pilloried Medicare along with other aspects of contemporary Canadian life. Gairdner, described as a successful Olympic athlete, academic, and businessman, and a former president of the Fitness Institute, argued vociferously for an American-style health care system for Canada, where "user fees" were paid, where all Canadians would be required to buy major medical policies from private insurance companies, where patients would have to pay physicians directly and then be reimbursed, and where "the State must stop telling free citizens how much of their own resources they are allowed to spend on their own health and must also stop blocking their access to better care." But even Gairdner makes a slight bow in the direction of universal access by also recommending, "continue a government service for basic care if that's what the people want."[3]

Those I spoke with in Canada told me that Gairdner was not taken too seriously, but Dr. Gordon Guyatt, director of Residency Programs at McMaster, did see a future scenario which could put Medicare in jeopardy. He linked the danger to the efforts of the current Conservative Mulroney government to institute changes in the Canadian constitution. The bill implementing those changes, C-69, allegedly would eliminate the idea of federal transfer payments to the provinces. The effect on Medicare, according to Guyatt, would be to gut the procedure in the Canada Health Act of 1984 that was used to end extra-billing by physicians—a procedure that imposed a penalty subtracting dollar for dollar the amount of provincial extra-billing from the federal health care subsidies to the provinces. Without the federal payments, of course, there would be no incentives for the provinces to ban extra-billing, and Guyatt's fear is that such an eventuality would lead to two-tiered medicine. That would mean the end of the concept of equal access embodied in the Medicare ideal.

Dr. Michael Rachlis, co-author of *Second Opinion*, approaches Medicare from the same vantage point as Dr. Guyatt. But he does not worry about the continuation of the program. Instead, he is a fierce and unrelenting critic of the program as it presently exists. He is, in other words, a critic on the left, and his tone is invariably accusative:

> ... a massive misallocation of resources, particularly in social spending ...
> ... our system is outrageously inefficient ...
> ... the organization of health services in Canada is in a shambles ...
> ... wasteful ...

Rachlis and his co-author, Carol Kushner, are as critical as Gairdner, but they have found different villains to blame for the system's shortcomings, and offer elaborately thought-out solutions they believe will not only improve Canadian Medicare, but also actually save it from destruction at the hands of inexorable cost-cutters who see nothing beyond dollar signs.

To Rachlis and Kushner, the fatal flaws in Medicare are fee-for-service payments to doctors, the oversupply of physicians, overhospitalization of patients, and the emphasis on treating illness rather than promoting good health. They claim the system is not underfunded and no infusion of new money is needed. Instead—and with rhetoric that sounds positively Reagan-like—they claim that "by trimming the fat from our present system we can generate enormous savings." In their opinion, such savings will amount to $12 billion.[4]

The heart of their proposed cure for the ills of Medicare lies in finding ways to reduce the rates of overtesting, unnecessary surgery, and poor drug prescribing through "constructive processes for peer review"; plus ending turf battles between various groups like doctors and nurses, reducing the dominant role of physicians and increasing the usage of paramedical personnel, cutting down the number of medical students, capping the overall volume of fees paid doctors, encouraging group practice and HMOs, shortening hospital stays, and emphasizing home care and community care. They project a 25 percent saving in hospital costs, a 28 percent reduction in nursing home costs, a 20 percent reduction in expenditures on physicians, and a 50 percent cut in prescription drug costs.

Their next step would be to reallocate the $12 billion in a manner they believe will promote health rather than health care. They promote funding for such non–health care, but health-related items as transition homes for victims of family violence, rape crisis centers, new units of social housing, literacy programs, cash payments to the poor, antismoking programs, new community health centers, home hospital programs like New Brunswick's Extra-Mural Hospital, health care evaluation programs, occupational injury prevention, more fitness and physical exercise programs, etc.

It is not enough to dismiss the Rachlis-Kushner proposals as naive or overoptimistic about certain assumptions. What is important is that these critics have examined a system that successfully offers access for an entire population and then asked, in effect, Is what we have given our people access to appropriate to their needs? Even though their answer is no, they do not then say, in the Reaganite fashion, that the nation should throw out the entire system. Instead, they recommend changing it from within by applying a different method of looking at the entire problem of health care.

Before discussing the implications of the Rachlis-Kushner approach for the situation in this country, one final observation needs be made about Canada. Taxes in Canada are high—there can be no denying that. There is general agreement that health care accounts for about one-quarter of that tax load. Welfare, it should be noted, takes a greater percentage. (In 1985, for example, spending on health in Canada at all government levels was $30.2 billion; for welfare, $49.1 billion.)[5] In recent years, Canadian tax policy under the Progressive Conservatives has favored consumer taxes, thus contributing, along with the strengthening of the Canadian dollar, to the flow of Canadian shoppers to the U.S. The other side of the coin is that concurrently some taxes have been reduced. A Canadian Labour

Congress advertisement in the *Toronto Globe and Mail* recently stated that since the Tories came to power in 1984, personal taxes had gone up 66 percent while corporate taxes had dropped 34 percent.[6] Yet another perspective on Canadian taxes came from *Macleans* magazine. The article was about Americans living and working in Canada who were returning home because of high taxation. The final paragraph is significant:

> But other Americans who are long-time residents of Canada readily acknowledged that they admire Canada's publicly-funded, universally accessible health-care system, and add that they are concerned about having to purchase private health insurance south of the border. Says American Club of Toronto's current president, Stanley Katz, a Brooklyn, N.Y. native: 'Canada was a great place to live, but with the high tax rate and confused economic situation, most people would like to leave. If the United States had a health plan like Canada's, we'd probably all be gone."

Could the United States have "a health plan like Canada's?"

Why not? If Canada's health care system elicits such a sense of loyalty that even hardheaded American business types feel it's worth paying higher taxes to stay under its protective umbrella, why not transpose it to the United States?

Because, opponents counter, we Americans will not stand for a system under which, if we have the money, we might have to wait for nonemergency service—that is, unless we're Americans living in Canada, and then we will put up with a lot of things, including higher taxes, to stay where we're protected by a health care system that guarantees we'll never be impoverished if we come down with a serious illness.

How different is health care in Canada from that in this country?

A few short trips do not make an expert. But my overall impression as I toured Canadian hospitals and talked to Canadian physicians and officials was that I had never left the United States. To be sure, there were differences. The hospitals were somewhat quieter, cleaner, brighter, and less frenetic than many in the U.S. There were fewer people in doctors' waiting rooms. Perhaps the personnel were a bit friendlier, but that, no doubt, was an even more subjective reaction than the sense of being in a "kinder, gentler" country. Yet, when it came right down to it, nothing seemed much different except for the absence of anger and despair over the cost and the inadequacy of one's insurance coverage, the nightmare of dealing with insurance bureaucracies, and that fear of impoverishment from illness that now terrifies more and more of us.

There are, as we have seen, criticisms of Canada's Medicare: There is anger that the system can be wasteful, whether expressed by insurance executives or liberal-minded reformers. There is frustration that funding is insufficient, or that service may not be as immediately available or as extensive as people of means would like it to be.

Since 1912, the U.S. has experimented with many methods of delivering health care to people. We have tested many concepts. But we have never tried an overall national health care policy devoted to the idea of universal access regardless of the ability to pay.

If all other nations were in the same fix, if no country had universal health care, we might have cause for our complacency. We could reasonably fall back on the cliché that our American health care, for those with the money to pay for it, is the most advanced in the world (which it most likely is), and suffer the crisis of rising health care costs in silence without worrying about those who fall through the cracks or remain outside the system altogether.

But there are other models to follow.

For clarity, it should be understood that when we speak of Canadian Medicare, we are speaking of a *single payer*. To further clear the air, let us agree that the old epithet of socialized medicine is no longer germane to the debate, if it ever was.

The framework of the single-payer plan that our northern neighbors have put in place is now more than twenty years old. By all accounts it has tremendous popular acceptance. No political party has dared advocate its repeal, neither the Progressive Conservatives (supposedly analogous to America's liberal to moderate Republicans), nor the Socreds (Social Credits, more to the right), nor the Liberals, nor those further to the left, the New Democrats. While its cost has grown, and it is the most expensive system among countries with national health care, it is still some 30 percent cheaper than the American system. And it is all-inclusive—no one is left out. Finally, because it pays the full cost of the services it insures, no one is left in jeopardy of having a lifetime of work wiped away by medical bills.

American voters must make a political judgment.

That the single payer concept can be transferred to the United States is indisputable. Of course it can. It could have been done years ago, but the American people allowed themselves to be persuaded that it would be too costly, that it was somehow ideologically alien to their basic values, and that it would diminish the quality of their health care.

As a result of our lack of interest, the fragmented, multipayer relic with which we struggle—and which once existed in other countries, including Canada—has become a monster of inefficiency and growing expense. It is today the single most costly and least inclusive system in the world. Like feudalism, which was great for a few privileged *seigneurs* and their families, this antiquated, jerry-built example of social inequity totters toward a destiny where only the wealthiest will have access to the best of care. Because more and more Americans are feeling the financial pinch involved in protecting the health of their families, and feeling less and less secure about the validity of the protection their insurance provides, the outcry has brought the supposedly dead and buried ghost of national health care out of the grave where greedy special interests thought it had long ago been buried with a stake through its heart.

That specter, that phoenix risen from the ashes, now hangs over the last nation in the world to hold out against the idea that all people deserve access to health care.

The Rachlis-Kushner criticism of the Canadian system calls for access to health as well as health care. From an American point of view it appears that without a framework of basic security provided by a national health care plan, such reform efforts can only be wasted.

To put these "reformist" ideas in a wholly different context, it is curious to note that some of these concepts—the emphasis on prevention, on community care, on paramedical providers, on planning, on the active involvement and participation of the public—have been major components of a system of health care generally acknowledged to be poor, if not abysmal—that of the Soviet Union. Indeed, the loudly trumpeted publication of statistics on the Soviet Union showing dramatic rises in infant mortality rates and a significant decline in longevity provided an argument that the entire Communist structure, not just its health care component, was shot through with dry rot. A British doctor, John Fry, writing in the 1970s, and comparing the American, British, and Soviet systems, sounds at times like Rachlis and Kushner when he describes medical practice in the USSR.

> Great emphasis is placed on prevention in all fields of medical care ... the aim of health education is to create a cooperative public, knowledgeable in the basic elements of health maintenance and disease prevention ... A system of paramedical auxiliary care has been built up. In all rural areas there are feldsher-midwife posts staffed by personnel classified as middle-grade medical staff with nursing and medical training, and a midwife responsible for antenatal and post-natal care and supervision of infants ... The polyclinic (not the hospital) is the medical centre in the community.[8]

The point is that the Rachlish-Kushner ideas are not unworkable or ineffective. Rather, the context in which they are placed is the key factor. The Soviets established a health care system that provided access to 280 million people, but it failed the test of quality. The United States provides high quality care, but fails the test of access—it effectively leaves many millions out of the process. The present Canadian structure provides both quality and access, with room within its framework for experimentation with ideas like prevention, community care, paramedical personnel, etc.

"But wait," says the constant doubter. "You speak of the Canadian system as one that combines quality and access. How can you say that when we know that people have to wait for certain services?"

The answer to that question involves certain temptations. The first is to point out that no one challenges the quality of services people receive in Canada. If, as alleged, Canadians are coming to the U.S. for treatment, it is not because they cannot receive adequate care in their own country, but rather because they have to wait to be treated for nonemergencies. It should also be noted that there are particularly desirable specialists in the U.S. just as there are those in Canada sought by Americans: A governor of Michigan, for example, went to Ontario's Schuldeist Hospital, famed for its treatment of hernias.

How extensive is the border-crossing by Canadians? What quantitative studies have been done? In the *New England Journal of Medicine* John Iglehart discusses an investigation requested by veteran Ohio Congressman William Gradison and done by the staff of the

Pepper Commission. Ten major American hospitals were surveyed, including such prestigious institutions as the Massachusetts General Hospital, the Memorial Sloan-Kettering Cancer Center, Johns Hopkins Medical Center, and top-notch medical facilities convenient to the Canadian border. Only two reported treating an appreciable number of Canadians. Buffalo General said 3 percent of its patients were Canadians, and fifty of the one hundred patients receiving monthly lithotripsy treatments were doing so under a formal agreement with the province of Ontario. The University of Washington Medical Center reported that half its in vitro fertilizations (125 of 250) were being done on Canadians at five thousand dollars each. Also, some cardiac surgery had been contracted by Ontario with St. John's Hospital in Detroit. The report to Gradison: "No evidence that substantial numbers of Canadians are seeking care at American medical centers."[9]

Some other figures speak of the length (or shortness) of waits. A study at the Vancouver General Hospital from February to April 1990 showed that half of all *nonemergency* cardiac surgery cases were performed within one week of being booked. Emergency cases were done within hours. The U.S. Government Accounting Office report on Canadian health care surveyed ten Ontario cardiovascular surgery centers. For emergency surgery, there were no waits. Three of the ten reported no waits at all for what was deemed urgent but not emergency surgery. One of ten reported no waits even for elective surgery, and, in any event, there were no waits at all longer than thirty days for any operations.

The GAO also looked at the cross-border situation. It found that during the 1980s about two hundred patients out of five to six thousand cases a year sought heart surgery in the U.S. Even when arrangements were made by the Ontario government with Detroit hospitals, the number in 1990-91 only rose to 350 cases out of 7,650— or less than 5 percent.[10]

A crisis in Ontario between mid-1987 and late 1989, when waits for coronary artery bypass surgery reached their peak, seems to have been the inspiration for much of the adverse publicity directed against Canadian health care. A study of that situation has now been done by C. David Naylor, an assistant professor on the faculty of medicine at the University of Toronto, and it was printed in the fall 1991 issue of *Health Affairs*, which is published by Project HOPE.

By December 1990, when a *Wall Street Journal* story headlined "CANADIANS CROSS BORDER TO SAVE THEIR LIVES" appeared, the situation in Ontario, according to Naylor, had already been ameliorated. By January 1991, he wrote, the cardiac surgery waiting list in the province had fallen from eighteen hundred persons the previous year to about one thousand. "Average waiting times were also down dramatically with elective patients waiting only a few weeks in the hands of most surgeons."[11] The reasons for the improvement were several: The Ontario government had put more money into the system, some patients had been treated with angioplasty as an alternative to surgery, three hundred patients had been sent by contract to the U.S., and the explosive increase in the need for cardiac bypass surgery that had existed in the 1987 to 1989 period had leveled off. Naylor concluded that "given current capacity and waiting times, it seems doubtful that the Ontario government will continue reimbursement for elective open-heart surgery performed in the United States."

But even as intelligent and thoughtful an observer of the political scene as the editorial board of the *New York Times* has dismissed the Canadian system, in part on the question of waits, claiming that women must wait months for a mammogram.[12] Whether this dismissal is simply because they champion their own pet program—a somehow universalized "managed-care" array of HMO-type organizations—is unknown, but the cavalier rejection leads one to wonder whether in dismissing the Canadian system, they have ever examined a standard response of Canadian defenders of Medicare when asked about waits if their system were applied in the U.S. The answer is illuminating: If U.S. spending stayed at the same rate of 12 percent of GNP, as opposed to the Canadian 9 percent, they contend there would be no waits whatever for any health care service.

The other *New York Times* objection—that Canada's health costs are rising at a rate higher than those in Europe and not far below those in the U.S.—also misses a major point: The Canadian health care system covers everyone; ours does not. Even if costs were equal, instead of 12 percent GNP versus 9 percent GNP, the Canadian system would be superior simply because no one is excluded.

A trio of *USA Today* articles puts yet another spin on the question of quality in Canadian health care.

U.S. PATIENTS GO TO CANADA
FOR TREATMENT
TURNING NORTH SAVED
STUDENT'S LIFE
CANADIANS HAPPY WITH
HEALTH CARE

These were headlines in one issue of the "Nation's Newspaper."[13] One story contained the following: "In a slap at the U.S. health care system, which calls itself the best in the world, thousands of U.S. residents are heading north to visit Canadian doctors and hospitals for everything from routine treatment to complicated medical procedures." The quotes from women who had their babies in Sault Ste. Marie's General Hospital are also revealing. "We're good Americans," said one, "but when it's a matter of getting the best medical care, we go to Canada." Said another, "I got my appointment a lot faster than I do with my doctor in Toledo, Ohio." An opthamologist in Canada's Sault Ste. Marie had so many American patients that he opened a second practice across the border in the Michigan Sault Ste. Marie. His comment was that "Americans are finding surgeons and physicians are equally well-trained on the other side of the border."

Such stories are, of course, merely anecdotal. But so too are the tales of those who knock the Canadian system, like that of the famous Mr. Coleman, whose heart bypass operation was postponed eleven times (five or six of those postponements at his own request so he might go to Florida) and who then died. On the other side is the instructive anecdote concerning Rena Sheppard. A twenty-three-year-old college student, she needed a lung transplant to save her life. Public pressure caused Blue Cross-Blue Shield to agree to fund the $200,000 procedure. But Rena could not find a medical center in the U.S. to do the operation; they all considered her condition too risky. She turned to the Toronto Medical Center, and after a wait of several weeks, was operated on successfully and has now resumed her studies. Toronto General, by the way, is "the world leader in lung transplants," according to *USA Today*, and 5 percent of its patients are Americans.

Since I do not favor the vaguely Germanic-style approach of the *New York Times* "managed care" idea, or the "play or pay" attempt to force all businesses to cover their employees, another variant on the German system, or the "private-public partnership" notion of those who say "don't abandon what we already have, but build on it," the question must be something like this: Why do you think it will be easier to adapt the Canadian single-payer system to the U.S., and what advantages does it offer that others do not?

That is a fair question and deserves a thoughtful, detailed answer.

Point 1. Whatever the U.S. does to create universal health care coverage is bound to be expensive. It will require tax increases. That money can either be funneled into what we have, already the most expensive system in the world, or it can be used to displace what people are now paying out of their own pockets—for insurance premiums, co-payments, deductibles, and the other portions of health care costs not covered by insurance.

A single-payer system covering doctor's bills and hospital care, à la Canada, is the *only plan* that relieves individuals of the expenditures they now must make themselves. It is the *only plan* that assures them they will not be bankrupted by medical costs. It is the *only plan* that gives them something in return for their extra tax dollars.

Yes, it may cost $300 billion–plus in new taxes, as opponents claim, but we must subtract from that (or from a more objectively determined amount) the dollars people now pay out of their own pockets for insurance premiums and for the costs their insurance does not cover. And we must factor in the savings to the system resulting from a simplified administration. One savings that perhaps doesn't have a dollar value is the immense aggravation of dealing with insurance company bureaucracies. A recent issue of *Kiplinger's Personal Finance Magazine* set forth an absolutely horrific list of suggestions for winning health insurance claims—horrific in the amount of time, effort, attention, and even expense (for litigation) it takes to force insurance companies to pay what they have promised to pay. In regard to the *New York Times* and its managed care panacea, Kiplinger had this to say:

> Don't expect so-called managed care to lead you out of the red-tape maze. Managed care is supposed to control overuse of health care services but it often means more work for the patient.
>
> You can expect to encounter managed care most often in the guise of something called utilization review (UR). You call a toll-free number to get prior approval for hospital admissions or medical procedures, or to

find out whether you need a second opinion. UR veterans can tell horror stories of getting endless busy signals or languishing on hold for
eternity. But if you don't make the call, you can be hit with a penalty of
as much as $1000.

To avoid being penalized, keep careful records. Call your UR company
three to five days in advance of a hospital stay and ask for written confirmation of approval. Jot down the name of the person you talk to. To
avoid busy signals, call early in the day and never during lunch ...

"Ultimately, the consumer is responsible for making sure contact is
made," says Fran Hackett, director of group medical insurance at
Prudential."[14]

Contrast this rigmarole with the procedure in Canada, where all
one has to do is present a health care card to which he or she is entitled simply by virtue of being a resident.

Point 2. The U.S. and Canada both have federal systems of governance. It is said that Canadian provinces have more powers than
American states, but there is nothing in the U.S. Constitution to prevent states from playing the same lead role in health care. Nor is
there any legal impediment to having the U.S. Federal government do
as the Canadian national government does—set forth the basic standards of benefits to be included in any fundable health care plan,
plus certain broad principles to be followed in order to qualify for an
agreed-upon amount of funding to supplement the state contribution.

At this juncture, the constant doubter (or the health insurance
industry representative) is likely to say, "Aha! There's the rub. The
Canadian federal government started out paying 50 percent of the
cost, and is now down to 37 percent. What's to keep our Federal government from bowing out of the agreement, just as they have failed to
prevent a growing shortfall in Medicare payments or have fallen
behind the needs of the poor in Medicaid?"

That's a good point, and makes for a strong argument. It's true that
the precise percentage of Canadian federal aid varies from province
to province, that the distribution is complicated by the fact that not
just money is granted, but also "tax points"—a kind of revenue-shar-
ing where taxing authority is granted—and that there has been serious concern that the Mulroney government is stepping away from its
commitment to Canadian Medicare. In August 1991, Dr. Michael

Rachlis testified before a House of Commons committee against the proposed Government Expenditures Restraint Act (GERA), which would freeze federal contributions to health care until 1995.[15] A meeting in Winnipeg of provincial health ministers and the federal health minister, Benoit Bouchard, produced a pledge to "uphold universal Medicare and provide adequate funding," and although the Tory government was sticking to a target of maintaining health spending at 9 percent of GNP, New Brunswick health minister Ray Frenette declared himself very encouraged that all parties agreed Medicare must be preserved on the basis of its five principles. "We went into our meetings with a real concern for the survival of Medicare and its role as a unifying force in this country. We came out with a firm consensus of how to ensure a positive future for both."

The key to funding any government program is forceful public support. If the Federal government in the United States has not lived up to its commitments to Medicare and Medicaid, it may be because these programs are not universal. Social Security, a universal program, has not suffered the same fate. So far, in Canada, the GERA bill has only gone through the Senate, a nonelective body whose members hold life appointments. Our senators are far more sensitive to the public. If the entire U.S. population—not just restricted segments—were to bring pressure on Congress to have the Feds live up to whatever agreement was made, particularly for a program that effects every one of them, the chances of the Federal government backing away from its commitments would be lessened. One of the tricks in government is to make the other fellow pay. Under our federal system in the U.S., the Feds try to dump costs onto the states (called the New Federalism), and the states, in turn, will try to shift financial burdens to the localities—the counties and the cities and towns. Within our present health care setup, there are still other targets on which to unload expenses—third-party payers like insurance companies, the providers themselves, and of course the public, whose out-of-pocket charges, in addition to what they already pay in taxes, just go up and up and up. A single-payer system at least restricts to the Federal and state governments the number of levels where cost-shifting can occur.

The Canadian parliamentary system—under which elections are not fixed in time, and governments can be overthrown by losing a vote of confidence—lacks some of our checks and balances. It is easier to get something done in Canada because the majority party selects the executive. Yet the pressure of public opinion has less force than it does in the U.S., where every member of the House of Representatives must stand for election every two years. In Canada right now, for example, the Tories have an abysmal popularity rating—about 16 percent—but party discipline will keep them from losing a key vote, and the time when an election must be called is still several years off. Breakthroughs come slower in the U.S., but tend to be more lasting. Social Security has been around since 1935, and even those who muttered about making it voluntary, as some of the Reagan forces did, never even tried. National health care, once instituted, would certainly have the same staying-power.

As a sideline to point 2: The federal system, under which the states are entitled to go beyond the basics of a nationwide program in their own versions, allows great diversity. No doubt California's requirements and benefits would be different from Maine's, just as British Columbia's are different from Nova Scotia's. That we have more states than they have provinces doesn't mean a thing. Our fifty state units have served admirably as administrative bodies in many governmental programs. They can assuredly do the same for universal health care. It is also argued that Canada does not have the population mix that we do, nor the problems of poverty, and drug culture, AIDS, etc., etc., etc. Yet Canadian Medicare seems to accommodate a population with large numbers of new immigrants; currently ten million residents (out of twenty-five million) are not of British or Canadian stock.[16] Many new Canadians now come from Asia, Africa, or the Middle East. It is no easier to find a native-born cab driver in Toronto or Ottawa than in New York or Washington. Vancouver, apparently, has the second highest drug problem in North America, and the poverty in some sections of Montreal rivals that of the poor neighborhoods of large U.S. cities. And AIDS, proportionately, is just as big a public health problem up north as it is here. Finally, more than 17 percent of Canadian children live in poverty[17] as do 30 percent of unattached individuals under sixty-five and 38 percent of those over sixty-five.[18]

Point 3. The establishment of a single-payer system does not jeopardize the elements of quality that exist in our own system, even though that quality is too often available only to those who can afford to pay the price.

This last argument is a ticklish one. A dentist friend said, when we discussed the issue, "Well, if I try to do extra quality work and perform special services for a patient, I want to be paid for it." To my retort—was it fair that only those with money to pay could be the recipients of his best work—he had no answer. But the truth is that within a single-payer system there are mechanisms established for differentiation—not by the government, which is a current American trend Relative Value Scales), but by the provider's peers, the medical society that determines how to cut up the payment pie they receive from the single payer.

The case of Dr. Ian Munro may indicate some limits. This "super-doc" plastic surgeon was unhappy in England, even though private medicine is permitted outside the National Health Service. He was also unhappy in Canada, where he could not, it seems, garner all the resources he wanted within the hospitals where he practiced. He is now happy in Texas working for Humana, a private, for-profit operation. It is doubtful that, aside from an occasional charity case, very many average Americans can afford to avail themselves of Dr. Munro's services. Can a medical care system be said to have "the best medicine in the world" if its best is reserved only for the smallest, upper-echelon fringe of its population?

Under a single-payer system in the U.S., if it followed the Canadian example, Humana hospitals, like all others, would negotiate with the single payer—in this case the state government. Would quality deteriorate? Dr. Munro would unquestionably say yes, given his criticism of the Sick Children's Hospital in Toronto. Nor would he be alone in his judgment. The mother of one of his patients, a Mrs. Sharron Holmes, also felt that Sick Children's Hospital had gone downhill.[19] But it should be pointed out that long after Canada's Medicare came into being, her son's life was saved at this hospital in Toronto. Mrs. Holmes's complaints only started when Dr. Munro left to go to Texas. She was able to bring her son to the Humana hospital there for continued treatment. She was very pleased with the care, whereas she had become unhappy at Sick Children's. She admitted to being shocked at the size of the bill, but OHIP, the Ontario Health Plan, paid it. Now, she says, she lives with "the daily fear that OHIP is going to pull the rug out from under my son at any time. They may decide, 'Well, we can provide service in Canada equal to what's being provided in the States.'"[20] Mrs. Holmes doesn't believe Canada can provide equal care. But an irony that escapes that good lady is that because of Canada's single-payer system, she, as a Canadian, is receiving specialized care for her son not available to millions of Americans. An American mother in her position with no health insurance cannot make the fine distinctions Mrs. Holmes has made and receive the "best care" for her child.

The same sort of double standard applies to the "safety valve" issue that has been raised against the adoption of a single-payer system. Again, compassion is directed to those Canadians who, tired of waiting for elective procedures, have come to the U.S. for their operations. Where would they go if the U.S. had a single-payer system? That's the wrong question. It should be: Where would they go if Canada didn't have the single-payer system? Where would they go if they didn't have Canadian Medicare to pay the bills, like Mrs. Holmes? If, as now seems evident, "thousands of Americans" are going to Canada for treatment, it seems unlikely that a change in the U.S. system would cause any great dislocation, except perhaps for a super-doc like Ian Munro, who might then want to go back to "socialized" England to practice totally private medicine.

Another consideration: What is happening to our American medical facilities? Many are closing their doors. Will Humana Hospital in Dallas, so dear to Dr. Munro and Mrs. Holmes, remain in existence if the company loses money? As one recent book asserts, "Humana's financial problems, created by overexpansion in health insurance, lower dividends for shareholders in hospital corporations such as American Medical International and an overall decline in the value of corporate hospital stocks suggest that the future of for-profits is less optimistic than was predicted in the early 1980s."[21] HCA, the Hospital Corporation of America, another major for-profit, actually lost $58.4 million in 1987, compared to a $174.6 million profit the year before, and despite the fact that it divested itself of 104 of its less profitable hospitals. Non-profit institutions are doing even worse under the current U.S. system. On the other hand, the single-payer system in Canada has built a safety net under their hospitals.

Would research and technology in the U.S. suffer under a single-payer system? Ronald H. Yamada is a Canadian who works for the MDS Health Group Ltd. of Toronto, a company that provides diagnostic health services throughout Canada as well as in New York, New Jersey, and Pennsylvania. The company employs four thousand people, serves eleven thousand physicians, and reaches 9 million patients a year. It not only exists in Canada under Medicare; it thrives. In a forum at the National Committee for Quality Health Care annual meeting, Yamada spoke of the similarities in the provision of laboratory services and diagnostic services in the U.S. and Canada. "Ordering patterns are very similar. You find that instrumentation and technology are the same. Quality control requirements are the same. Regulatory pressures are the same."[22]

What is different, according to Yamada, is the administrative cost relative to billing: three claims billing clerks to every one million patients in Canada versus forty-four to every million in the U.S. In Canada, bad debt write-offs for his company were 0.5 percent; in the U.S., 5 percent. "More importantly, the complex billing systems in the United States limit, rather than maximize, the effectiveness of cost-saving computer systems."

In regard to research efforts, Yamada produced figures representing overall national (not just health care) research. Canada spends only 1.6 percent of GNP on all research, well below the 2.5 percent U.S. figure. However, the U.S. lags behind France at 2.7 percent, and, not surprisingly, well behind Japan at 3.2 percent. Health care research in Canada, because of the country's small demographic base, is concentrated in such areas as genetics and blood coagulation studies. Yamada's company was working with university-based facilities doing work on projects such as the development of a whole blood substitute (with a worldwide market of $5 billion), devices to aid pain control, new three-dimensional diagnostic imaging services, and the invention of an artificial spinal disk. The company is also providing laboratory management to four community hospitals in Canada, and has a joint venture with a Toronto hospital to commercialize research and to fund additional research with the money earned. This latter arrangement is no different from the one it has with hospitals in the Poughkeepsie area of New York State.

A change to a U.S. single-payer system should have little, if any, adverse effect on current basic health research, now heavily concentrated in the U.S. Institutes of Health and funded separately from the delivery system. An argument put forth at the National Committee for Quality Health Care forum by Wayne I. Roe, president of Health Technology Associates, addressed those areas outside of basic research, now the province of the private sector. He states his objection to any change in the current U.S. situation: "The real fear is that, if we move from a system which is still...a market with multiple decision makers at all levels, public and private, to one where rigid budgetary constraints are being placed on hospitals...that will stifle their ability to fund research and development and have an objectionable impact both in the United States and worldwide."[23]

Roe's statement brought several thoughts to mind. I remembered the epic battle in the Maine state legislature over Certificate of Need as applied to new equipment for the hospital in my small town. I reflected on the numbers of hospitals closing in the U.S. and what effect that has to have on the medical technology market under the present free-market system. And finally, I had to smile as I remembered my visit to the St. John Regional Hospital in New Brunswick, where I was shown equipment (some of it American-made) that was being replaced by the latest state-of-the-art equipment. And where was that being produced? In Japan—in a country with a universal national health care program! It seemed free-market America wasn't even competing.

In the final analysis, the difficulty of transposing a version of Canada's single-payer system on to the U.S. (and it must be noted that some support has been voiced for making an American single payer not the state government, as in Canada, but an experienced private, non-profit insurance company like a statewide Blue Cross-Blue Shield) lies less with the perceived deficiencies of our northern neighbor's health care relative to our own than it does with political realities. How can politicians in Washington and in state houses, who recoil at even the mention of the "T-word," be expected to vote for the tax package needed to make the shift from private to public insurance? The media, with its addiction to sensation, will promptly forget that it has been editorializing about the inadequacies of the present system and the mess it has become and dwell instead on the large-scale tax increase needed to make the change. They will also no doubt neglect, as the concept's opponents do, to subtract what people will no longer be forced to pay out of their own pockets. Nor, I suspect, will they place a value on lifting the fear of impoverishment. The faint of heart in public life will reach even more desperately for the security blanket of incrementalism. "We can't do it all at one time," will be their cry. The special interests whose oxen are being gored will join the fray and use every tactic known to political man—

205

and probably even invent a few new ones—to attempt to defeat the effort. After all, they have been able to do that since 1912. Can't a few more bones be cast to a naive public, a bit more magic dust be tossed in the taxpayer's eyes—and can't it be made to look like something has been done when, in reality, there has been almost no change at all?

Set against the need of the American people for a fundamental change in the way health care is financed is the political culture of our nation's capital. The domination of special interests in the funding of campaigns is no myth, as I found out when I became a candidate for the U.S. Senate. For members of either body of Congress who do not have personal financial resources, donations are the only road to re-election, and trying to eke out nickel-and-dime contributions from the electorate is a feat managed by very few (not to mention the fact that it requires a lot of up-front money even to make the effort). The big givers, therefore, are the most profitable targets, and while they will often give to those who would thwart their interests (when pundits prejudge them to be winners) in the hope of winning a few votes in the future, they still exercise their real fiscal muscle in favor of what they consider their legitimate interests. Health insurance companies want to continue business as it is. They will use every ounce of their influence to defeat a plan as "radical" as the single-payer plan. Other groups will join them, and will be opposed by a coalition on the other side, each member group with its own agenda. The elected public official will be caught in the middle. It is an occupational hazard, and the politician's instinct is to wiggle through somehow with a compromise in place of a bold act.

But there is one thing politician's understand even better than money or compromise. They all understand votes.

The Special U.S. Senate race in Pennsylvania that ended with Harris Wofford's come-from-behind victory over Richard Thornburgh on November 5, 1991, sent shock waves through the good folks inside the beltway. That health care has become a burning issue, a fact known for some time, was that day made an official fact of life.

And, in one sense—that of defining the direction the political response will take—the battle has been joined.

11 MEANWHILE, BACK IN WASHINGTON

There was no way political neophyte Harris Wofford could beat popular Richard Thornburgh. Every political pro in Washington knew that. A Thornburgh victory in the Pennsylvania Senate election was money in the bank—a foregone conclusion.

Election day was a bombshell that echoed through Washington and left the pundits stunned. Wofford not only upset George Bush's former attorney-general, but did so with a resounding 55 percent of the vote. Percentages being to the political *cognoscenti* what race track odds are to touts—the very lifeblood of their calling—there was a frantic scurrying to try to rationalize the results.

On October 17, 1991, almost three weeks before the election, an article in Roll Call, a sort of Beltway Bible, had analyzed the Wofford campaign. The piece had discussed Wofford's TV spots and evaluated the help they had given the former president of Bryn Mawr College and one-time Kennedy staffer (who had been appointed to fill out the term of Senator John Heinz, killed in a plane crash) in narrowing the crushing deficit he initially faced in the polls. The better-known three-time governor of Pennsylvania, Richard Thornburgh, had slipped from a 44 percent lead to a still safe 24 percent.

The *Roll Call* analysis noted that one of Wofford's spots was devoted to health care. This commercial pointed out that our Constitution guarantees a criminal the right to a lawyer. It then went on to say: "But millions of Americans aren't able to see a doctor. They either don't have health insurance or they're afraid medical costs will bankrupt them." Wofford's appeal also said, "Working Americans should have the right to a doctor." It told the people of Pennsylvania that was the reason he was fighting for national health insurance.

Roll Call concluded by noting that while Wofford was still down by twenty-four points in the polls, "Time is ticking and that may prove to be Thornburgh's savior if a close race occurs."[1]

That same day, October 17, Harris Wofford made a speech on the floor of the U.S. Senate. It was entitled, "A Right Not a Privilege: Meeting the Challenge of Affordable Health Care for All Americans."

Wofford spoke of a campaign visit to Philadelphia's Methodist Hospital, where he met Linda Sherk, a twenty-four-year-old Lancaster woman who was in a wheelchair recovering from a back operation. She had dropped her health insurance and had been forced to wait a year and a half to save enough money to pay for her disk operation. Using powerful rhetoric—"If you have your health, you have everything; if you need health care, you stand to lose just about everything ... What would this administration say to Linda Sherk?"—Wofford called for national health insurance. He was not specific. He did not mention "single payer" or "play or pay" or "managed care-competitive." He was content with setting forth eleven principles, and seven of what he called "specific policies." And he did something else that had to appeal to the folks back home. He announced that he had just introduced a bill "to cut off all the special health benefits for members of Congress, until Congress passes a health plan for the country."[2]

A few months earlier, *Money* magazine had reported on congressional health perks in an article entitled "There's a Doctor in the House."[3] The piece began:

> Imagine if you and your family were eligible for this:
> • Automatic health insurance without needing a doctor's exam or having to worry about being socked with higher premiums because of your medical history.
> • The option of choosing among a dozen or so different programs so you can pick the one ideally suited to you.
> • Reasonable premiums of about $80 a month per family.
> • The right to retire after working a mere five years, knowing you and your family are covered for as long as you live.
> • And to cap it all off, you personally get virtually unlimited access to a 30-person doctor's office, its medical lab, pharmacy and ambu-

lance—at absolutely no charge, whether you have a complete physical, fill a prescription or need to be rushed to a hospital.

The catch, of course, is that to be eligible for this particularly generous form of government-run national health insurance, you have to be a member of the U.S. Congress.

A Republican congresswoman from Maryland, questioned about how personally enjoying such privileges might affect her attitude toward extending similar benefits to the rest of the American public, snippily dismissed the free doctors' office as the congressional version of the school nurse's office. *Money* pointed out that this supposedly insignificant office actually cost taxpayers $2 million annually, and was headed by a two-star admiral physician who made $135,000 a year. Some school nurse's office! Incidentally, Rear Admiral Robert C. J. Krasner, the man who runs the office, refused a *Money* request for an interview.

What Wofford's bill proposed was to make House and Senate members participate in the Federal Employees Health Care Benefits Plan, a $13 billion program serving the 2.5 million Federal workers. It's a good plan, but considerably less generous than the one lawmakers enjoy. Not mentioned, and presumably unaffected, would be the health benefits enjoyed, at public expense, by the president and other top appointed officials in the executive branch.

Wofford's intent was to follow the example set with regard to Social Security. "In 1981, Social Security was in deep trouble. In 1982, Congress included itself in the system. And in 1983—Lo and Behold!—the Congress had put Social Security back on sound financial footing."

The Pennsylvania senator's gesture was and will remain, no doubt, symbolic. But even if senators and congressmen were limited to no more than the health benefits given run-of-the-mill Federal employees, they would still be far ahead of millions of their countrymen. Do not think that these elected officials are unaware that the problem is out there. Quite the contrary. It is estimated that there were some thirty separate bills on the subject under consideration before the Wofford upset victory. The shock waves from Pennsylvania are bound to generate still others. Some wags have predicted 100 in the Senate and hundreds in the House—one for each member as lawmakers scurry to cover their posteriors.

All the current bills aim toward the goal of national health care with universal coverage, but they do so from various, and often conflicting philosophical points of view. Among the major approaches are:

- "Play or pay"—the idea of building on the existing structure of employer-based coverage, eventually forcing all employers, regardless of their size, to cover their employees, and then making provision for those who fall outside the employment system.
- "Single payer"—either a Federal-state, Canadian-style system, or a mandate for the Federal government to provide funds to the states for their own systems.
- "Compromise combinations"—a mixture of the above two approaches.
- "Status quo"—a plan that leaves the present system intact and would have the government pick up—at taxpayer expense—those who cannot, for either financial or poor health reasons, fit into the private, insurance-based system. A favorite device is to offer to do this through tax credits and vouchers.
- Competitive managed care" - a concept that has been the subject of much palaver, some of it based on the ideas of Stanford University economist Alain Enthoven and involving HMO-type groups who lower prices in order to entice patients.

In addition, a favorite exercise for some these days is to devise sets of principles by which to judge various legislative offerings—a sort of check list to make sure their particular interests are served. The fifty-five-thousand-member American Public Health Association has done this, as has the College of Physicians, with almost as many members, and very small groups like the New England SERVE committee, funded through the Federal Maternal and Child Health Program, which has issued guidelines for protecting the interests of "children with special needs" (severe disabilities). It seems everybody has an opinion.

The major "play or pay" legislation has been sponsored by Senate Majority Leader George Mitchell. It is officially called "Health America: Affordable Health Care For All Americans Act." The range of co-sponsors of this bill, commonly referred to as the Democratic Leadership Bill, is not large, but includes some heavy hitters. Ted

Kennedy is a co-sponsor, and puts the proposal firmly in perspective since for more than twenty years the Massachusetts senator has been the sole powerful voice speaking out in the lonely fight to keep the issue alive. That Senator Kennedy has taken a number of tactical swerves in the course of his long battle is seen as an indication of the strongest argument for this bill; it is politically achievable, a measure that can muster the support necessary for it to pass—a "realistic" approach.

Another key co-sponsor is Jay Rockefeller. When the legendary Claude Pepper died, putting an end to a career that went back to FDR's first term and the birth of Social Security, Rockefeller assumed the chair of the bipartisan Commission on Comprehensive Health Care, dubbed the "Pepper Commission." By a narrow vote, that group had rejected a single-payer system and opted for a plan similar to the one proposed by Kennedy and California's Congressman Henry Waxman. That plan would have mandated that employers provide coverage for all their workers and their families. Part of the plan included financial help to enable businesses to meet their obligations. Other Pepper Commission proposals included schemes for long-term health care and insurance reform. Having the West Virginia heir to the Pepper reputation as a co-sponsor added even more of the strength of tradition to Mitchell's proposal.

Introducing the measure, Mitchell called it a compromise between those who "argue that the United States should adopt a Canadian model" and those who "argue that tax incentives to businesses with no requirement to provide coverage is the answer."[4] Mitchell also claimed the bill to be in keeping with American traditions and values, and said that any new health care system for the U.S. would have to be in keeping with such traditions and history, just as other nations had evolved their systems in fashions unique to their countries.

The "play or pay" bill, called the culmination of years of work by the Senate Finance and Labor Committees, creates a new public insurance entity called AmeriCare. If employers do not provide their employees and families coverage that meets a basic set of standards, they must contribute a percentage of their payroll to AmeriCare. Thus the concept of "play or pay."

A specific governmental obstacle is also circumvented through the "play or pay" mechanism. This is the Employment Retirement Income Security Act, better known as ERISA, which effectively prohibits states from requiring all employers to cover their employees for health care. Since "play or pay" doesn't legalistically do this, allowing businesses not to provide insurance but to pay a contribution instead, ERISA requirements are bypassed.

Back to the Mitchell bill: Its new entity, AmeriCare, would replace Medicare and Medicaid and be administered by the states. It would cover the unemployed and those whose bosses refuse to play and would therefore have to pay. Premiums would apparently be based on the ability to pay. Basic benefits are for hospital and physician care, diagnostic services, limited mental health coverage, and preventive services like pap smears, mammograms, prenatal care, and various other aspects of child care. The intent of the bill is to ensure that services be covered 100 percent—save for co-payments and deductibles. Subsidies of the premium cost for low-income citizens will be provided by AmeriCare, and no out-of-pocket costs would exceed three thousand dollars annually.

The executive summary of the 349-page legislation reveals other interesting features. Cost-containment is to be achieved by a combination of techniques. It is alleged that cost-shifting (the current method of covering government payment shortfalls by dumping some costs onto consumers by way of increased premiums) will be eliminated because coverage will theoretically be universal. Great weight is also given the elimination of unnecessary care. This is be realized by using the outcomes of medical effectiveness research projects now underway at the Agency for Health Care Policy and Research (for which healthy appropriations are written into the bill), the development of practice guidelines for physicians to be used by insurance companies in determining doctors' payments, and an stepped-up program of technology enhancement. And there is still more. Standardized billing forms are required, and small insurance companies will be made to work together at the state level.

At the Federal level there will be two new structures, a Federal Health Expenditure Board to develop "national health care expenditure, access and quality goals, ...convene and oversee negotiations between health care providers and purchasers to develop patient rates and perform other activities necessary to achieve expenditure goals...developing goals for states and regions that are consistent with national goals," etc.[5] In turn, this Federal body, which has been likened to the Federal Reserve Board as an independent entity with economy-influencing powers, is to work with "state purchasing consortia" that apparently will do the nitty-gritty administration of the act, including the establishment of uniform billing "smart cards," "paperless processing systems," etc.—at least where small insurance companies are concerned. These consortia will also be responsible for utilization review of provider services.

The states have to set up such systems or the Feds will do it for them, but they will get money from Washington to help with the cost. The states, under this bill, are also required to set up Quality Improvement Boards to review the performance of doctors and hospitals, and to establish a regulatory program to determine whether health insurance policies within the state meet the basic standards set by Federal law. The states are also encouraged to provide reinsurance—that is, to cover insurance company losses under model plans prepared by the National Association of Insurance Commissioners (NAIC). These are the same regulators the industry has fought so hard to protect and keep in place for years. Even so, the bill takes the first tentative steps toward some Federal review of the health insurance industry. If a state doesn't set up the required regulatory body, the secretary of Health and Human Services is empowered to establish a toll-free telephone line and complaint system to hear consumer gripes (and presumably to act on them, although that is not spelled out).

The states lose several powers under this bill, chiefly the right to "mandate benefits"—i.e., to insist that insurance companies include specific benefits in any package they market in the state. The Health Insurance Association of America has long maintained that this is the key to small group reform, and the sponsors of the bill have bought their argument. The states are also enjoined from enacting laws that overly interfere with managed care plans. That means they can't stop an HMO from requiring its subscribers to use only the group's doctors. Nor can states, presumably under pressure from doctors, restrict utilization reviews that meet Federal standards.

The Democratic Leadership Bill does make an effort to soften the burden it places on small businesses, which will have to pay 80 percent of the premiums. It includes subsidies for those who will be stretched to make such payments, and lets companies off the hook if 75 percent of their employees are covered. Self-employed persons will get some tax breaks. New businesses will have a two-year grace period before having to plug into the system. Moreover, implementation will be staggered. Not until the fourth year will businesses with between twenty-five and one hundred employees have to participate, and those with fewer than twenty-five workers will have an additional year before they come under the law.

AmeriCare, by then, according to theory, will have covered everyone else—all the poor and those self-employed or unemployed who now fall through the cracks. The state will administer the program with its elaborate mechanism for determining and continuing to determine eligibility. As under Medicaid, the states will pay part of the cost, and will be required to submit plans for Washington's approval in order to receive the Federal share of costs. The executive summary of the bill states that "the cost to the Federal government in the first year of the plan will be approximately $6 billion."[6]

The Mitchell-Kennedy-Rockefeller approach has not exactly generated enthusiasm among partisans of a national health care program. An impromptu and unscheduled debate at the American Public Health Association convention in Atlanta in November 1991 illustrates the dilemma facing those who have been pushing for universal coverage. In this case it involved Dr. Harvey Sloane, former mayor of Louisville and a near-miss candidate for the U.S. Senate in Kentucky in 1990, and Cathy Hurwitt, an activist with the union-backed Citizen Action consumer coalition. Sandwiched between them on a panel entitled "The Politics of a National Health Plan" was Dr. Mary Jane England, President of the Washington Business Group on Health, who articulated the desires—and conditions—of the country's major industries for resolving the health care issue. Both Sloane and Hurwitt are true believers who have fought for national health care for years. At this point they found themselves battling each other—Hurwitt arguing eloquently for the benefits of a single-payer system and Sloane, as president of Health Care for America, a group reportedly formed to lobby for the Democratic Leadership Bill, arguing in less definite fashion for the acceptance of the concept of a universal system. Sloane's frustration was evident as he attempted to steer audience sympathy away from the single-payer idea, asking the audience instead to unite against the "know-nothings" who would take no action at all.

At a time when organizations like the Washington Business Group on Health, as well as the ultraconservative Heritage Foundation, have their own restrictive version of universal health care, it is questionable whether there are really any "know-nothings" left. It is a sad commentary on political realities when natural allies like Harvey Sloane and Cathy Hurwitt cannot get together to support a single piece of legislation.

Cathy Hurwitt and her people believe another bill—best known as the Russo proposal—does offer an answer. Congressman Marty Russo was vice-chairman of the Subcommittee on Health of the House Ways and Means Committee until March 1992, when redistricted out of his seat, he lost a primary battle to another Congressional incumbent. The Chicago Democrat has said that his bill, the Universal Health Care Act of 1991, "incorporates many of the strengths of the health care system that's been so successful in Canada. But it's not a Canadian system, it's an American system."[7]

The Russo bill introduced by Senator Paul Wellstone of Minnesota, now matched in the Senate by a companion measure would provide every American with a health insurance card entitling the holder to a substantial list of benefits. In addition to hospital and physician coverage, those benefits include home care, hospice care dental care, eye care, prescription drugs, preventive care, nursing home services, some disability services, and some mental health care. There would be no co-payments or deductibles. Providers could not charge more than allowed by the program and would be paid, as they are in Canada, through negotiated fees for physicians and global budgets for hospitals. Capital and medical education costs would be handled separately. Administration on the national level would be through the secretary of Health and Human Services, who would establish an overall national health budget and oversee payments to the states for their health budgets. Increases in the overall national budget for health would be tied to inflation and the growth in the Gross National Product. A National Health Trust Fund would be established to receive the monies to pay for the program.

The Russo proposal ducks none of the hard questions. Its author spells out exactly how the program would be funded by a specific set of new taxes.

- A new 6 percent payroll tax on employers.
- An increase in corporate taxes from 34 percent to 38 percent for businesses earning profits of more than seventy-five thousand dollars a year.

215

- Increases in personal income tax rates (now 15 percent, 28 percent and 31 percent to 15 percent, 30 percent and 34 percent, plus the addition of a top rate of 38 percent for incomes over $200,000.
- A long-term care premium equal to the Part B Medicare premium, plus twenty-five dollars a month for the elderly above 120 percent of the poverty line, plus a raise in Social Security taxable levels from 50 percent to 85 percent.
- State payments equal to 85 percent of the state Medicaid effort, plus an annual per capita fee of eighty-five dollars.
- Federal contributions equal to current Federal spending on health care.

The Russo bill also calls for existing Federal programs (Medicare, Medicaid, CHAMPUS, Veterans, etc.) to be folded into the universal program. In addition to the cost-containment measures of global budgets and negotiated fees, outcomes research and practice guidelines would also be included.

Marty Russo's bill has picked up considerable support. At last count, more than sixty House members had signed on as co-sponsors. Despite the fact that AFL-CIO President Lane Kirkland appears to be supporting the Democratic Leadership Bill a number of unions have ignored their leadership and lined up behind Russo. These include such large and powerful organizations as the United Mine Workers, the Machinists and Aerospace Workers, both the major textile unions (ACTWU and ILGWU), the Communications Workers, the Longshoremen and the Electrical Workers. While Horace Deets, Executive Director of AARP, is, like Kirkland, listed on the letterhead of the Alliance for Health Reform, organized by Jay Rockefeller, the National Council of Senior Citizens, mostly retired union members, is solidly behind Russo. Adding more strength to the Russo camp is the Consumers Union and the Consumer Federation of America.

An appropriate question at this point might be, Will the struggle in Congress boil down to a standoff between single-payer and play or pay? Until the presidential election in November 1992 is decided, it is fair to say that no one has the faintest idea. Among the Democrats, if they continue their control of Congress, such a dichotomy might emerge. The House Democratic Caucus has voted overwhelmingly to support universal health care, but without specifying which bill or approach they would back. In January 1992, Democratic members of

Congress held public hearings in their districts all over the country, discussing the issue of health care reform. Senator Kennedy has moved the play or pay bill through his own Labor Committee in an initial partisan vote.

Other ideas between and outside the two main Democratic approaches have emerged as well. Nebraska senator Robert Kerrey, even before announcing his candidacy for the Democratic nomination for president, had offered his Health USA Act of 1991. Kerrey does not tilt to either play or pay or single-payer, but instead blends both into his proposal. He says that "in a time of great economic change, health benefits should be independent of employment,"[8] and then proposes a tax revenue–based system which echoes the Canadian structure. As up north, the Federal government would set minimum standards for any health plan and the state governments would offer the plans. The difference here is that policies would be bought by the states from private insurance companies or non-profit entities. Coverage could not be denied anyone and, once a year, during an "open enrollment" period, people could change plans.

On the Federal level, Kerrey would create an independent commission to "provide general guidelines to states, make recommendations regarding the federally-prescribed minimum benefit package ... coordinate medical effectiveness initiatives, distribute funds to the states and work to standardize and simplify billing."[9]

Kerrey claims his program, if in place, would have saved $11 billion in health care spending in 1991, and more than $150 billion in its first five years. His patchwork of taxes to fund the bill is not dissimilar to Russo's. Attacked as promoting a $300 billion–plus array of new taxes, Kerrey has not backed down, even while campaigning in conservative New Hampshire. As one newspaper story reported, "He said the plan would appeal to tax-phobic New Hampshire residents because it would mean a larger corresponding decrease in costs to residents who would no longer have to pay through their nose for medical costs."[10] In that same New Hampshire interview, Kerrey also emphasized that the single-payer aspect of his proposal was the only way to bring costs under control.

Needless to say, the issue of health care was addressed by all of the candidates vying for the presidential nomination, at least on the Democratic side. All of them had their plans and preferences, ranging from support for the Russo bill (Jerry Brown) to a variation on the

217

Enthoven managed care idea (Paul Tsongas) to different versions of "play or pay" (Bill Clinton, Tom Harkin).

Within Congress itself, the range of plans is equally broad. The single-payer approach of the National Association of Social Workers has been incorporated into legislation sponsored by Hawaii's Senator Daniel Inouye. Congressman Bernie Sanders of Vermont, the only socialist currently serving in Washington, has yet another single-payer–type plan. His bill would parcel out money to states to implement their own single-payer plans. Then there is the Comprehensive Health Care for All Americans Act, introduced by Congresswoman Mary Rose Oakar of Ohio, which is described as "modeled upon the Canadian approach."[11] Still another player is the veteran health care activist Pete Stark of California, whose MediPlan would set up a single agency offering Medicare-type services and long-term care to every American. Trying perhaps to get the best of both possible worlds, Senators Paul Wellstone of Minnesota, Paul Simon of Illinois, and Brock Adams of Washington have proposed to amend the Democratic Leadership Bill by adding a provision to fund single-payer demonstration projects by the states.

Modeled not on Canadian health care but on Great Britain's far more "socialized" system is the plan first presented in 1977 by Congressman Ronald Dellums of California, and offered every year since. His U.S. Health Service Act would create a government-run health service comparable to Britain's NHS, where all health workers are salaried and all health facilities publicly owned.

A report to Congress by the Congressional Research Service of the Library of Congress in November of 1990 used three broad categories to describe the bills extant in Washington: Social Insurance, National Health Service Model, and Mixed Public/Private Model.

Single-payer plans obviously fit in under Social Insurance, which is described as requiring comprehensive universal coverage. Some of the play or pay proposals do the same. The Dellums bill is the one example of the National Health Service Model—not much of an option in this country. That leaves the Mixed Public/Private Model for consideration.

A plan offered by Utah's Republican Senator Orrin Hatch in 1989, anticipating the furor over health care, exemplifies this type. Hatch was promoting an $8 billion package of financial incentives to small employers, plus increased government spending on the uninsured.

He offered it as "an alternative to the $23 billion universal health care plan then advocated by Senator Edward M. Kennedy."[12]

Hatch's plan called for the following changes:

- Ending state mandates.
- Expanding the tax deduction for health insurance premiums for the self-employed from 25 percent of cost to 100 percent and allowing small businesses to recoup one-third of the cost of providing health care to their employees.
- Adding grants to states to come up with programs to insure those who cannot obtain health insurance.
- Budgeting $50 million for prenatal care for low-income women.
- Budgeting $100 million for preventing accidents, for better emergency services, and for paying health care providers for uncompensated care.
- Having the Department of Health and Human Services try to reduce malpractice claims.

The Comprehensive Health Act of 1991, first introduced in September 1990 by Senator William Cohen of Maine, follows the same track. In Cohen's words, the measure "builds upon the existing public-private health partnership to preserve what is good about the American system."[13] It, too, eliminates state mandates in order to allow health insurers to offer "no frills" plans, offers the 100 percent tax deduction to the self-employed for health insurance, and presents incentives to states to create "risk pools" for the medically uninsurable. In addition, tax credits are dangled before middle- and low-income people as inducements to buy health insurance, and more tax credits are used to entice doctors to practice in rural areas and for the encouragement of health promotion and prevention programs. In keeping with Cohen's emphasis on helping people to buy insurance, tax deductions are offered those who buy long-term care insurance.

The costs of malpractice insurance—a concern dealt with in every plan—is here addressed by encouraging states to institute prelitigation screening panels as well as the development of national practice guidelines and care standards.

Malpractice insurance reform seemed for a time to be the sole response of the Bush administration to health care problems. Solve that, the president appeared to believe, and all will be well. But events have outstripped such devotion to minimalism. The Wofford win, the outpouring of media attention on the issue, and the open debate in the Democratic presidential ranks, finally conspired to force the president to react with a plan of his own. He had stalled as long as he could. In his State of the Union speech in January 1990, Bush stated that he would listen to the recommendations of his secretary of Health and Human Services, Dr. Louis W. Sullivan, for ideas on how to deal with soaring costs and the lack of access for growing multimillions of Americans. But the best Sullivan could come up with was the idea that, within a decade, all of the fifteen hundred health insurance companies in the U.S. would issue a single insurance card—not that the card would entitle health insurance to those who couldn't afford it, as was admitted by Carl Schramm of the HIAA. In other words, the Sullivan scheme, announced with great hoopla at a highly publicized "summit" meeting he held with health insurance companies, was immediately seen for what it was—mere window dressing.

So Bush ultimately moved. On February 6, 1992, he formally announced a $100 billion (over five years) proposal, drawing heavily on tax credits and vouchers for the uninsured to buy commercial health insurance. He chose the Greater Cleveland Growth Association as the place to deliver his message and, according to the *New York Times*, "drew but a tepid response from the crowd of Cleveland business leaders who interrupted it only once, when they applauded an attack on rising malpractice costs."[14] One feature that stuck out in the Bush plan as anathema to certain business interests—i.e., the health insurance industry—was a proviso that they not be allowed to exclude anyone on the basis of pre-existing medical conditions. But the big question mark, and possibly the reason for his audience's lack of enthusiasm, was his method of financing. Seemingly his plan was to be paid for by cutting back on Medicare and Medicaid. Business people are well aware that such cost-shifting leads to higher insurance premiums, and is one of the major causes of the current crisis.

Bush's plan, no doubt, will not fare well with Congress, and given the prevailing sense of potential political gridlock on earlier health care reform in D.C., some leading Democrats had already cautiously stepped in with their own versions of "incrementalism"—baby steps that might be easily politically acceptable.

Prominent were the actions in late October of 1991 of two of the most powerful Democrats in Congress—Senator Lloyd Bentsen of Texas, Chairman of the Senate Finance Committee, and Representative Dan Rostenkowski of Illinois, Chairman of the House Ways and Means Committee. Seizing upon the stated Republican concern for small business expressed in bills like those offered by Hatch and Cohen, they, too, proposed that the self-employed be permitted to deduct 100 percent of health insurance costs from their income taxes. They, too—and this did not please the GOP quite as much—called for limitations on the varying rates insurers could set for those small businesses, thus introducing de facto Federal regulation of insurance rates. An alarmed spokesperson for HIAA said his organization would prefer to see the states take such steps in order "to negate the need for Federal legislation."[15]

Another part of Rostenkowski's bill would also allow private insurers to pay providers at Medicare rates, usually lower than those customarily charged. It should be noted that about a month earlier, the Chicago Democrat put in his own House version of the Mitchell-Kennedy-Rockefeller bill. But in a statement perhaps forewarning that "incrementalism" was the only way to make change in the present political climate, Rostenkowski equated his own and Bentsen's solutions with the broader need: "We're trying to end the national scandal where more than 15 percent of our citizens, 34 million Americans, are uninsured."[16]

Hyperbole rolls trippingly off the tongue in Washington. If often means little. Will anything really be done in the foreseeable future to "end the national scandal?" The prospects hardly look promising. The standoff between the administration and the opposition is only part of the problem. With so many ideas on the table, the momentum needed to unite on one has not developed. Legislators find themselves between "a rock and a hard place." They believe the public wants action—a national health care program—but that same public does not want to pay for it, or at least doesn't want to pay very much. They can never forget the monumental deficit, and the budget agreement that restricts any serious new expenditures. The stranglehold of Gramm-Rudman, together with myriad other forces, prohibits bold action that would tread on the toes of some of the nation's most powerful and well-heeled special interests. Real action in the immediate future is going to be exceedingly difficult, if not impossible.

221

But—and this is an enormous "but"—there is a presidential election in 1992. At the time of this writing, in early spring, political strategy is already churning the waters. Democrats in Congress face some tough questions: Is it better to do nothing now? Can the issue be kept alive for the fall campaign? Or should they pass a bill and let the president veto it? Or should they do something minimal and present that to the voters as an accomplishment, as Rostenkowski seems to counsel?

Republicans have the same problem. Restive Senate Republicans announced their own package two days after the Wofford victory. Led by Rhode Island's John Chaffee, twenty GOP senators backed a plan to reform medical malpractice, provide the inevitable tax credits to businesses and individuals that the party favors so heavily, and—what seems new—create a public program outside of Medicaid for the uninsured. The price tag is an un-Republican-like $150 billion over five years, and they didn't say how they'd pay for it. Or can one of the approaches of the GOP's natural allies, the HIAA or the Heritage Foundation, be passed off as a serious attempt to solve the problem? They know the "big-spending" Democrats won't buy that solution, but so what? Maybe the voters will. Amazingly enough, the once reactionary AMA seems willing to go along with the play or pay approach. Listen to Senator Jay Rockefeller talk about the AMA reaction to the Pepper Commission's majority report that recommends such a stance: "The AMA and other physician associations have been incredibly supportive of the Pepper Commission. Indeed, the winning vote in the commission was cast by none other than Jim Davis, a past president of the AMA."[17]

The National Leadership Coalition for Health Care Reform, a major coalition of business and labor groups that includes Chrysler, Xerox, Bethlehem Steel, etc., likes the play or pay notion as well. It has its own version, where a public insurer of last resort called Pro-Health takes the place of AmeriCare. The main difference is that all employers would have to contribute to it, not just those who do not provide worker coverage. Can such support offset the single-payer coalitions? Or is competitive managed care through HMOs, the brainchild of economist Alain Enthoven and his colleague Richard Kronick, boosted by the editorial support of the *New York Times*, about to capture the imagination of the nation's policy-makers and become the dark-horse long shot that will lead the way to the legislative wire? Dr. David Himmelstein of the Physicians For A National Health Program thinks that the race will not be between single-payer and play or pay, but between single-payer and managed care.

The plot has more twists than a soap opera:

Will Bush's plan pass the straight face test?

Will the Democrats pass a bill of their own?

Will it be vetoed?

Will the historic precedent of the mid-1960s, when the almost inexorable merging of different approaches into a single package then thought to be comprehensive and coherent—Medicare and Medicaid—be repeated, and with some irresistible, almost mystical logic of its own produce something that no one can yet envisage?

Will Dan Rostenkowski's statement that "attempting to legislate now would be a terrible mistake" be the prevailing wisdom?

The questions ask themselves with all the suspenseful hype of a soap opera conclusion that urges audiences to tune in again for the next episode.

In such a fluid situation, many cynics believe that nothing at all will happen in the nation's capital—at least nothing of consequence. Instead, they look to the states to be the innovators and problem solvers, pointing out that the Canadian system had its genesis in Saskatchewan.

In truth, there is a great deal going on at the state level—So much so that it will be impossible to deal with all the various avenues of health care reform being explored. But there are highlights and trends to be considered.

12 THE STATES

OREGON

There is no doubt that the proposed state health plan that has attracted the most popular media attention is that of Oregon. The Oregon Basic Health Services Act has made its sponsor, John Kitzhaber, a Roseburg physician and president of the state senate, into a national figure.

Those who throw rocks at the Canadian health care system frequently cite the case of Joel Bondy of Windsor, Ontario. He was a two-year-old cardiac patient who died, allegedly after his necessary surgery was postponed once too often. Those same critics do not like to hear about an equally heart-rending tragedy that was the genesis of the Oregon program. It's not often that a name is attached to any of the countless American horror stories caused when people simply can't afford needed health care. But Oregon has one it can't forget. The name is Coby Howard. It really is Adam Jacoby Howard, but Coby was only seven years old. Coby's family was on welfare and it seemed reasonable to expect that Medicaid would pay for the bone marrow transplant he needed to keep him from dying of leukemia. The only trouble was that the Oregon legislature had voted to stop paying for transplants. They decided to use the money for prenatal care instead. The Howards tried to raise the money to save Coby's life through public appeals. Supporters of their cause even put the boy on TV with instructions to "smile big." It was working; people responded, and they were within thirty thousand dollars of their goal when Coby Howard died.

The people of Oregon were appalled, and with the need for better health care so dramatically publicized, Kitzhaber went into action. He argued that such triage should be done rationally and openly. The question should not be, Who is rationed? but rather, What is rationed?

To accomplish this reasonable goal, a Health Services Commission was established. It was comprised of both providers and consumers, appointed by the governor and given the task to "prioritize health services using criteria based on social values."[1] They were to start with the services most beneficial for improving health, then move down the scale.

In what must be admired as an heroic effort, the commission actually waded into an evaluation of sixteen hundred different medical disorders. In May of 1990, they issued a preliminary ranking of ailment treatments, from those highest on the scale to those lowest. When their rankings were inevitably criticized as being too coldly computer-driven, they convened hearings around the state. Nine months later they produced a refined product based on 808 disorders that had been examined.

Their priority methodology had two poles: social values and clinical effectiveness. To determine the first they used a "Quality of Well-Being Scale" devised by California academics. It seeks to measure intangibles such as "the value society puts on the prevention of death or on the alleviation of a variety of symptoms such as pain, stiffness, depression, visual problems, fatigue, weakness, etc."[2] To determine clinical effectiveness, several technical classifications were used—including the "Physicians' Current Procedural Terminology" and the "International Classification of Diseases"—and these "codes," as they are called, were further broken down into specialities. They were then submitted to twenty-nine panels of physicians to be examined from a variety of views, including efficacy of treatment, cost of treatment, and the duration of the health benefit from successful treatment. Benefit-cost ratios were also established, taking into consideration the "Quality of Well-Being" achieved, the number of years it would last, and the average Oregon cost for the procedure.

It does sound technical, but the eleven commissioners who unanimously approved the plan said they used "common-sense human judgments"[3] in arriving at their decisions. The revised list has, as might be expected, curable conditions at the top—things like various kinds of pneumonia, tuberculosis, peritonitis, appendicitis, and obstructing or gangrenous hernias. At the bottom of the list are trivial conditions (prolapsed urethral mucosa, minor urinary conditions, and benign kidney cysts) and hopeless situations, like terminal HIV diseases and anencephaly (the condition when a baby is born without a brain).

The plan for the use of the list is simple. The legislature will set a budget and determine how many of the 808 disorders can be covered by the available funds. For disorders below the line there will simply be no public financing.

It took several pieces of legislation to create the plan. Kitzhaber's Senate Bill 27 relates to the Medicaid population and postulates that savings from the list of covered procedures will allow the state to enroll every Oregonian below the poverty line. Meanwhile, another law, Senate Bill 935, establishes a play or pay scheme for Oregon employers to either insure their workers or pay into an insurance pool that will protect them. The same list of prioritized services will be applied here.

The theory that drives the whole plan is that this combination of actions will extend health care coverage to all of the state's 400,000 uninsured residents. Kitzhaber says "everybody in Oregon is going to be covered one way or the other and we're doing this with a concise model of how to contain costs."[4]

The most imposing hurdle the concerned Oregon state senator has to clear is the need for a waiver from the Bush administration in Washington. To make such radical changes in Medicaid, Oregon needs the permission of Secretary of Health and Human Services Louis Sullivan. And he is being urged not to grant such a waiver.

There is nothing partisan in the opposition to the Oregon program. One outspoken critic is California congressman Henry Waxman, Chairman of the House Health and Environment Committee. He worries that Oregon is taking a small pie and cutting it into ever smaller pieces.[5] Groups like the Children's Defense Fund, also opposing the waiver, fear that children will be adversely impacted by the rationing.

Whether Kitzhaber will ever receive his waiver is problematic. Congress asked for a recommendation on the Oregon plan from one of its research agencies, the Office of Technology Assessment, and the verdict, delivered in February 1992, was not favorable. The rankings of illnesses were deemed too subjective and liable to deprive some

Medicaid recipients of services they currently enjoy. Under the Oregon plan, as projected, illnesses like viral pneumonia, viral hepatitis, chronic bronchitis, and some types of asthma would not be covered—nor would cancer when doctors asserted the patient had less than a 10 percent chance to live for five years or more. In addition, the technology office criticized Oregon's intention to enroll most of its welfare recipients in HMOs or other forms of managed care. They said "this arrangement might create a financial incentive for doctors to provide too little care because they could keep money not spent on services to patients."[6]

But, if nothing else, the Oregon effort has awakened the public to one aspect of our health crisis that must be taken into account no matter what final mechanism is selected to provide access to the nation's medically unserved people. The preamble to the Oregon Basic Health Services Act defines it as "The Need To Separate Reality From Illusion": "Our current health care system is based on a number of illusions ... They include the illusion that resources are unlimited; the illusion that all medical interventions are of equal value and effectiveness; the illusion that we can satisfy expectation for health care without paying for it; and the illusion that we do not ration health care in 1990."

Of course we ration health care in the U.S. under our so-called free-market system. And, as the Oregonians go on to say: "It is rationing that occurs implicitly, arbitrarily, and by default in a country which spends more per capita and in aggregate on health care than any other nation in the world. It is rationing unguided by any social policy, rationing for which there is no accountability for the consequences. It reflects neither social values nor ethical principles, and does not consider clinical effectiveness."

HAWAII

Hawaii has the reputation of being the state that has done the single best job in filling its need for health care. Only 5 percent—about fifty thousand—of the people in the state are uninsured. And it is all due to a freak of history.

In 1974, the Hawaiian legislature passed the Prepaid Health Care Act. It was the first law of its kind in the country, and under its provisions all businesses within the state, even those with only a single employee, had to provide health insurance. But no other state will ever be able to pass such a law.

The reason, as we have seen, is the Federal Employment Retirement Income Security Act (ERISA). The law was passed in Washington shortly after the Hawaiian statute, and specifically said that no state may regulate employers who self-insure to cover employee health care. After the two pieces of legislation were found to be in conflict, the question of precedence was decided in the courts. Hawaii lost, but won a final victory through congressional action that exempted the state from ERISA.

The terms of the congressional act relieving Hawaii from the ERISA provisions, passed in 1982, forbade the state from making any changes in its 1974 law. Therefore, in order to deal with its still uncovered population, new legislation was needed. This became a high priority of Governor John Waihee, and in April 1990, as the Hawaiian pun has it, the SHIP was launched.

The initials stand for State Health Insurance Program. The program's goal is to fill the gap between the vast bulk of the population covered under the Prepaid Health Care Act and those covered by a broadened (and generous) Medicaid program. In this gap are those who don't fit into either category—mostly working poor with income levels excluding them from Medicaid.

There were many left uncovered by the basic Prepaid Health Care Plan. They were the unemployed, worker's dependents, persons working less that nineteen hours a week, seasonal workers, students, and low-income self-employed. It is estimated that 50 percent of the unemployed on Oahu lack any coverage at all, and there are even higher percentages on the other islands. Native Hawaiians and immigrants are actually those most at risk.

Another unique thing about Hawaii is that there are really only two major health insurers—Blue Cross's Hawaiian Medical Services Association (HMSA) and Kaiser Permanente (an HMO). Between them they cover 68 percent of the population. Employers providing health care for their workers are allowed to choose between two basic plans—a fee-for-service plan and a health maintenance plan. Fee-for-service is the one most often selected, according to John Lewin, Director of the State Department of health.[7]

Community rating for health insurance exists in Hawaii since both large and small businesses form a single pool that spreads risks and keeps rates reasonable. The state maintains a fund to aid employers who are having trouble meeting insurance costs and to assist workers whose employers have gone out of business.

Another Aloha State oddity comes out of the past. Peter Sybinski, Deputy Director of the Department of Health, says that in the early days on the islands, plantation owners had a strong incentive to practice health care prevention and minimize hospitalization so that their workers were able to stay in the fields producing sugar or pineapples.[8] This "out-patient" tradition is reflected in the SHIP program which, according to Lewin, is "heavily weighted toward preventive and primary care, with health appraisals and related tests, well-baby and well-child coverage and accident prevention being fully covered."[9] Hospitalization under SHIP is limited to five days and an expenditure of twenty-five hundred dollars. Elective surgery and high-cost tertiary care has been excluded. Physician visits are restricted to twelve a year, with a five-dollar co-payment for each. The assumption is that if someone in this gap group needs expensive treatment, they will soon "spend down" to the level where they are eligible for Medicaid.

SHIP contracts with HMSA and Kaiser, most of the business going to HMSA on a fee-for-service basis, with a managed care component contemplated in the future. About half the physicians in the state have signed on. Kaiser, on the other hand, will only be taking about a thousand subscribers, most of them Kaiser members who have lost their benefits. SHIP aims to sign up twenty thousand members by the end of 1992. As of July 1991, it had already enrolled half that number.

Prior to its 1974 action, Hawaii had high rates of uninsured, ranging from 12 percent without hospital insurance to 17 percent without physician coverage. At 5 percent the state now not only boasts the lowest level of uninsured in the United States, but also claims the lowest infant mortality rate as well as the lowest death rates from cancer and heart disease. John Lewin equates these facts and the lower insurance rates in the state to "ten years of near-universal access to primary care."[10]

OHIO

"Is the Canadian Health Insurance System a Model for Ohio?" That was the title of the testimony of Eugene Vayda, M.D., before the Ohio House of Representatives on July 14, 1989. Dr. Vayda, a transplanted Buckeye practicing in Toronto, had come to Columbus to support House Bill 425—the Universal Health Insurance for Ohio Act.

Dr. Vayda told state lawmakers: "I am delighted to see my state take national leadership in proposing and hopefully adopting statewide universal health insurance legislation. Our universal program in Canada was enacted only after several of the provinces adopted universal hospital and medical care insurance ... It may well be that a critical mass of state programs such as the one proposed in Ohio may be the path to universal health insurance in the United States."[11]

Representative Robert F. Hagan, a Youngstown Democrat, was the author of the bill, possibly the first of the single-payer bills now popping up in state legislatures. In announcing his measure, Hagan asked and answered the rhetorical question: "Do I expect this bill to fly through the house this session? Of course not. I do fully expect it or something very like it to be law in Ohio in a matter of sessions ... Today we are putting it on the table to start the debate. Today we are starting the organizing. This session we want to start the hearings. This is a bill with very substantial benefits for working families as well as for the poor ... for business as well as labor."[12]

Another medical doctor, Kenneth Frisof, of the Physicians for a National Health Program, described some of the pioneer organizing in the state. The Northeast Ohio Coalition for National Health Care had been formed only the previous year, and already included more than seventy-five individual member organizations. They had staged a successful rally in Cleveland in May, and were on the verge of expanding activities south and west through the rest of Ohio. Their Ohio debate, he told them, "will be attracting a lot of national attention."

The UHIO bill would create the Ohio Health Insurance Plan and administer it with a board of governors. This body, through an executive director and staff, would oversee the Ohio Health Care Trust Fund, from which physicians and hospitals would be paid, capital costs met, prevention activities funded, and medical education subsidized. As in Canada, global budgets for hospitals and negotiated fee-for-service rates for doctors would be used. The funding proposed by Hagan included taxes of 8 percent of payroll on employers and on the self-employed, 1 percent on employees, 2 percent on interest and dividends above a thousand dollars a year, and 10 percent on the sale of alcohol and tobacco. The program was to be phased in over a three-year period.

As predicted, Hagan's bill did not pass into law the first time out. The bill, which initially attracted a dozen co-sponsors, ended in a House select committee formed as a result of Hagan's effort. The chairman of this select committee, the House Speaker pro tem, has stated that he wants a health care bill enacted. Will it be Hagan's ground-breaking plan that leads the nation down "the path to universal health care?"

CALIFORNIA

Or will California be our Saskatchewan?

In the summer of 1990, a Canadian newspaper correspondent in Los Angeles predicted that the state might be on the road to a Canadian-style health care system. Thus far that prediction has not come to pass.

At the time the newspaper made its prophecy, health care bills were flooding the Sacramento legislature. Among them was one sponsored by Oakland Democratic senator Nick Petris. It came close to emulating Canada's single-payer system. Officially entitled the Right To Health Care Act, it is also referred to as the Health Access Plan, particularly by the San Francisco–based consumer coalition, Health Access.

It is said that Health Access was inspired by a patient-dumping incident in Contra Costa County. The coalition was formed to encourage passage of a "no dumping" bill. That coalition now includes over one hundred organizations who, in their few years of existence, have moved boldly to advocacy of a Canadian-style health system.

A report issued by the organization in 1988, entitled *The California Dream, The California Nightmare: 5.2 Million People With No Health Insurance*, has been given credit for sounding the alarm statewide. The preface to the second printing, May 1989, states with some immodesty but, no doubt, a large measure of truth: "When this publication was released in March 1988, legislators, editorial writers, journalists, as well as everyday folks, had little idea of the enormity of California's uninsured problem. Now, thanks to a snowballing public awareness which achieved some critical momentum through the release of this report, the problem as well as possible solutions are high on the public agenda."

In 1989, Health Access proposed, as its highest legislative priority, a bill by Los Angeles assemblyman Burt Margolin that adopted a play or pay approach. That bill had the co-sponsorship of the state's powerful Speaker of the Assembly, Willie Brown, Jr. In a turnaround a year later, a Health Access spokesperson said the Margolin bill would be an improvement, but would do nothing to help the unemployed ineligible for Medi-Cal, the California version of Medicaid.

Health Access had worked up its own Health Access Model Plan (HAP), described as "a concrete proposal for universal, affordable access to comprehensive health care in California."[13]

Instead of Canada's five principles, Health Access had six:

1. Universal coverage.
2. Comprehensive benefits.
3. Progressive financing.
4. Economic efficiency.
5. Publicly guided allocation of health resources.
6. Accountability to consumers.

The Petris bill generally follows HAP lines. Specific details include the provision that small businesses (those with twenty-five or fewer employees) would be partially subsidized for their first three years in existence. The employee payroll tax would be limited to those earning over 250 percent of the Federal Poverty Level. A progressive income tax would be levied on unearned income of fifty thousand dollars or more, and Senior Citizens with income over 250 percent of the Federal Poverty Level would be required to pay a premium equal to Part B of Medicare. The Petris bill covers "all medically necessary health care and long term care."[14]

Health Access, in a mock dialogue in its report, draws a narrow distinction between its proposal and the Canadian system. "Is the HAP like Canada's health system? "Yes and No. Like Canada's system, the HAP guarantees universal access and comprehensive coverage, uses yearly budgets to keep costs down, and allows providers to control their practices. Canada does not have any prepaid plans like Kaiser. The HAP will retain prepaid plans and the consumer's right to choose their health care provider."

"Who will oppose this plan?" The designated villains: the California Medical Association, insurance companies, and the California Hospital Association.

The doctors are said to be interested in protecting their incomes and "positions at the top of the health care pecking order." The insurance companies, naturally, will be opposed because "independent private insurance will not be needed in California" with the exception of coverage for services not covered by the HAP. And the hospitals are expected to fight any reduction of "the portion of health care dollars going to hospitals."

Even so, it is conceded that some individual hospitals and public hospitals (mostly funded by counties) will be receptive to the HAP since it will reimburse them for the uncompensated care they now provide the uninsured. Ten Los Angeles hospitals have already been forced to close their emergency rooms due to this problem.

The power of the opposition in Sacramento (the Petris bill has thus far been successfully stymied) has raised the inevitable subject in referendum-prone California: Should the issue to taken directly to the people? In 1988, a ballot initiative forced insurance companies to roll back rates for property and casualty insurance. The companies spent millions fighting the referendum and lost. They then lost a legal challenge to a ruling that they must repay $133 million to customers.

Health Access approaches any initiative with caution. They are currently involved in preliminary polling to test public response. A referendum is a calculated risk because of the tremendous expense involved, the sure knowledge of the huge sums opponents will spend, and the setback a loss would be to the cause of universal health care, not only in California, but throughout the nation.

On the other hand, a California victory would provide psychological boost of incredible impact. It would far exceed the example of Saskatchewan. Our nation's most populous state, which has seen its health statistics deteriorate in the past two decades—from seventh to fourteenth lowest nationally in infant mortality, from twelfth to seventeenth lowest in low birth weights and from tenth to twenty-ninth highest in pregnant women receiving prenatal care—would be seen as having taken a bold pioneering step toward reversing that trend. Moreover, it would have done it in a comprehensive, rather than piecemeal, manner. Such action would send a message to every state declaring, "If we can do it in California, so can you."

233

MINNESOTA

Minnesota may well beat California to the punch. This midwestern state seems closer to passage of a universal access bill than anyone else. In May of 1991, the Minnesota House passed the Minnesotans' Health Care Plan by an almost two to one vote, 86–47. The Senate passed it by an even greater ratio, 49–19. Then-Governor Arne Carlson vetoed the measure. Action on the veto override has been held over for a new legislature.

Even though the Minnesota bill requires universal coverage it does not propose a single payer. The complex measure is the outcome of the work done by the Minnesota Health Care Access Commission, which delivered its final report to the legislature in January 1991. It reported that 370,000 Minnesotans were uninsured all or part of the year, and 360,000 others had policies that covered them inadequately. It also pointed out that Minnesota had advantages not enjoyed by other states; its percentage of uninsured, 6.5 percent of population, was one of the lowest in the country, and the state's "foundation of HMOs and managed care organizations" was better than most.[15] The Commission, which had labored for fifteen months, had been charged with developing a plan to insure the uninsured at a net cost to the state of $150 million. Their claim was that the Minnesotans' Health Care Plan they devised would cost $144 million—almost exactly on the button. In addition, the commission called for another $140 million to cover the underinsured.

The program would require all state residents to obtain health insurance coverage by July 1, 1997, and policies would have to provide benefits at least equal to the minimums set forth in the bills, incorporating the commission recommendations. Only those unable to receive coverage from employers would receive state coverage, unless the employer programs did not meet basic state standards. Among the most important (and controversial) features was a requirement that all health insurers would have to "community rate."

The politics of the matter boiled down to a contest between three principal health care reform proposals.

1. The Minnesotans' Health Care Plan
2. A Blue Cross bill to make coverage more affordable for small business

3. The governor's plan, an outcomes-based "pilot project" costing $15 million and involving twelve thousand people who would be given incentives to select only treatments deemed necessary, while doctors would be given incentives to deliver only such care.

Parts of the Blue Cross idea were eventually incorporated into the final legislation that emerged from a conference committee. This would allow some small group "no frills" coverage exempt from state mandates. The governor's pilot project was rejected.

Considerably whittled down, the final bill, initially covering thirty-eight thousand people, called for funding by a seven-cent increase in the cigarette tax to pay for start-up costs. Premiums were to be $68 a month for an individual and $204 a month for a family of three. The revised bill's price tag was $37.5 million.

Carlson's veto set off a political outburst. The leaders of the Democratic Farm Labor Party, which controls the legislature, assailed the governor for hypocrisy, claiming the Independent-Republican chief executive had campaigned as being in favor of health care access.

Representative Paul Ogren, House sponsor of the bill and chairman of the nationwide State Alliance for Universal Health Care, blasted Carlson in unusually blunt terms: "The governor is a 24-karat phony ... He is the governor of the rich. He is the governor of the powerful. He is the governor of the insurance industry. He is not the governor of the people. He has no compassion running through his veins."[16]

Carlson, not to be outdone, fired back with equal passion, saying the plan "plays a cruel hoax on the uninsured of Minnesota. In fact, this bill is tantamount to consumer fraud."[17] Carlson claimed the plan would end up costing $500 million a year in the future and the lawmakers hadn't given the "slightest clue" as to how it would be funded.

Insurance and business groups and legislators from his own Republican party had exerted strong pressure on the governor to use his veto on the measure.

But eventually Carlson did sign a bill, establishing HealthRight, a $250 million program to cover all of the state's uninsured. The necessary compromise was that funding would come, in large part, from a 2 percent tax on doctor and hospital revenue, 1 percent on insurance premiums and five cents a pack on cigarettes.

VERMONT

The fear commercial insurers have of mandated "community rating" may have been a prime motivation for their pressure on Governor Carlson to veto the Minnesotans' Health Care Plan. Vermont proves the point. Nowhere has the conflict between "community rating" and "selective rating" been illustrated more plainly than in this small state where a bill requiring community rating in small group insurance has actually been enacted into law.

Impetus for the measure came from an insurance company—Blue Cross-Blue Shield of Vermont (BCBSVT)—and precipitated an industry dogfight. The HIAA ran full page newspaper ads in a vain attempt to defeat the measure. BCBSVT fought equally hard, claiming the bill essential to its survival. Indeed, Vermont's H.176 was attacked as the "Blue Cross bailout bill."

The seeming dichotomy was caused when BCBSVT stuck to its original policy of turning away no potential subscriber. As the commercial carriers cut prices to lure the healthiest of subscribers, BCBSVT lost business. One of its publications declared it had lost 73 percent of its community-rated business since January 1987, and was left with older and sicker groups that used twice the medical services.[18] Faced with losses of $3 million to $4 million yearly, the non-profit company questioned how much longer it would be able to continue to be Vermont's "insurer of last resort."

BCBSVT was referring to non-group individuals and families who can find coverage from no other insurance company. It claimed that in the prior five years it lost $21 million serving these people while, at the same time, their exemption from insurance premium taxes, conditional on their acceptance of such people, was worth only $13 million. BCBSVT also argued that "unlike the commercial industry," it covers any small business in the state on a one business-one rate basis, without regard to the actuarial composition of the employees, and, in particular, their medical condition. Moreover, BCBSVT described itself as one of the few remaining Blue Cross-Blue Shield plans in the nation to do what it does. It claimed to be performing a public function worthy of support.

Were it forced to adopt the same risk avoidance practices of commercial insurers—abandoning market segments, adopting age rating, sex rating, occupational rating (in which certain industries are red-lined and refused coverage), medical exams, etc.—BCBSVT said the legislature would be left with the responsibility of publicly funding a program to deal with thousands of Vermonters who would lose protection and have no place to go.

The BCBSVT statement was emphatic, and highly significant: "The approach, commonly known as 'Risk Pools,' has been established in 23 states and in each and every instance has proven to be a social and economic failure."[19]

The argument carried the day in Montpelier. Three House and three Senate committees considered the bill, and approved it by margins ranging from 6–0 (Senate) to 10–1 (House). The House didn't even bother with a roll call on the measure, passing it by voice vote. The Senate adopted it by a lopsided 23–5.

A top Blue Cross official in Maine, where a similar bill will be proposed, said he thought it had really slipped by in Vermont and caught the opposition napping. The context of his remark was an expression of concern that HIAA was planning to spend $5 million to $8 million lobbying against the measure when it came up before the Maine legislature.

Vermont's action is not universal coverage, but it is most certainly a dagger to the heart of the present mess that favors for-profit insurance companies and leaves it to the public sector to clean up after them.

A single-payer, universal coverage bill has also been introduced in Vermont. The measure, called An Act Relating to Establishment of A Vermont Health Care Program, is the work of Senator Cheryl Rivers of Windsor County. It was hoped, according to Dr. Phil Caper, a nationally known health analyst of Lebanon, New Hampshire, just across the border, that Vermont's "size, homogeneity and their 200 year history of social progressivism gives this a chance of passing."[20] Even the state chamber of commerce had promised its reaction wouldn't be "a knee-jerk: 'Gee, we shouldn't do this.'"[21] And the accession of Lieutenant Governor Howard Dean, a medical doctor sympathetic to national health care, to the governor's office after the death of incumbent Richard Snelling at first seemed to bode well for dramatic action in Vermont.

But Governor Dean threw cold water on the idea while not ruling out a future single-payer approach. His own plan, which he described as "incrementally leading to universal health insurance and cost containment,"[22] would involve an insurance pool run by one or two carriers and guided by a new state agency that would negotiate for lower insurance rates and lower provider prices for pool members—a sort of governmental health insurance company, not unlike that of Australia. Managed care is also to be worked into the program.

In May 1992, a variation of Dean's approach became law. Created was a Health Care Authority with the power to bargain for health insurance for the state's citizens. It is also charged with drawing up a plan to meet the state's health care needs, including a possible single payer approach, and submitting it by 1994.

Resorting to a somewhat diminished incrementalism is not unknown in the history of Vermont's attempts to bring health care to all its people. "The Rise, Fall and Aftermath of Efforts To Provide Health Insurance For The Uninsured In Vermont" is the slightly sardonic title of a presentation on the state's earlier efforts, and how a comprehensive approach ultimately broke into fragments.

In 1988, the legislature established the Vermont Health Insurance Plan Board, promptly nicknamed "the Vermont Pepper Commission." It was to design a health insurance plan for the state's uninsured. The VHIP proposal, once it emerged, offered a menu of programs: a health insurance plan for those who had been without insurance for eighteen months, an interim program for uninsured pregnant women and children, a small business partnership program, insurance reform, student health insurance coverage, and a dedicated health insurance trust. The proposal even spelled out the costs—$1.7 million in the first year, rising to $32 million in the fourth year—and a set of patchwork taxes to fund the plans.

The only program that really resulted was insurance reform (the "community rating" bill) even though a stab was made at providing coverage for pregnant women and children through a program called "Doctor Dynasaur." "Healthy doesn't have to mean wealthy" is the lead of the colorful brochure, complete with drawings attractive to children (a green dinosaur dressed in a doctor's white coat and waving a stethoscope) advertising the plan, now run by the Agency of Human Services.

"If you're a Vermont family with little kids, or expecting a baby, chances are you're eligible for the Doctor Dynasaur program," says the brochure. The income eligibility is tighter for prenatal care than for children's care. The brochure explains:

As an example, a family of four, with a two year old and a household income of under $28,500 would qualify ... if the child:

• had no medical coverage at all

• was covered for *either* physician *or* hospital visits, but not both.

For the mother to receive prenatal care, the family income had to be three thousand dollars lower.

The benefits seem generous: medical office visits, well-child visits, prenatal care, hospital stays, lab tests, psychiatric services, prescriptions, dental visits—all this and more, everything from hearing aids to braces.

A niggling co-payment, two dollars to five dollars depending on family income, is required for well-child visits. One unfortunate restriction is that only children under six are covered; "benefits end with the seventh birthday."

Governor Dean's new bill may make such restrictions moot since "its only immediate impact," according to the *New York Times*, will be to extend state-sponsored health insurance to all children in low-income families.

It is ironic that Vermont Congressman Bernie Sanders's bill in Congress, which would help establish a single-payer system nationwide, is referred to as a "Vermont Plan for National Health Care." The truth is that his Green Mountain State is still a ways from achieving what it wants and what it says it needs to do in health care.

FLORIDA

"FLORIDA HAS A HIGHER PERCENTAGE UNINSURED THAN MOST OTHER STATES."

So reads the caption above a graph in the final report of the Florida Task Force of Government Financed Health Care.[23] At 17.9 percent uninsured, Florida was not only ahead of the United States as a whole (13.2 percent), but also ahead of its sister southern states (16.9 percent). This dubious distinction translates into 2.2 million Floridians without health insurance. The state in 1990 was spending $31.8 billion on health care.

Subsets of these statistics followed. Over 40 percent of Florida's poor were uninsured. Almost a third of young adults lacked health insurance. A disproportionate percentage of Hispanics and non-

239

whites were uninsured (Hispanics, 34.3 percent; non-whites, 26.5 percent, whites, 16.1 percent). The per capita increase in health care costs in the state between 1980 and 1990 were third highest in the nation—from $962 to $2,427. By the year 2000, the per capita figure would swell to $5,520.

The commonly favored method for politicians to deal with such problems—creating a study group—was undertaken twice. Whether by design or not, these were set on parallel tracks by their designations: The Florida Task Force on Government Financed Health Care, and The Florida Task Force On Private Sector Health Care Responsibility.

The task forces' formulas for dealing with the state's health care crisis, delivered in February and March 1991, correspondingly diverged. The government group's major recommendation centered on the notion of providing primary care to all Floridians by 1996, and the creation of a single state agency to have sole responsibility for reforming the health care system. A minority of that commission's members dissented. These included all the doctors and hospital members and one particularly conservative state representative from the business community. Having a single state agency appeared to be the major sticking point.

The private sector group's solution was a minimum benefit insurance plan developed and marketed by the private sector. Employers and employees who couldn't afford it were to get financial help from the state. The only benefits to be covered were the costs of catastrophic illness and, "if feasible," first-dollar coverage for limited preventive services for children and pregnant women.[24]

The philosophy of the free-market enthusiasts was clearly exhibited in the following statement of why they did not go further: "Comprehensive benefit coverage removes the patient from acting as a prudent consumer and insulates them from the economic consequences of their actions."[25] However, they did give a timid nod to governmental coercion by adding that, if at the end of three years, all employers had not voluntarily purchased the minimum benefit plan, "the legislature should consider implementation of a mandatory system."[26]

Even here dissent came once more from the Right. Four members issued a separate statement that said, among other things: "We have particular difficulty with the Task Force's even tentative advocacy of 'play or pay.'"[27] The dissenters declared themselves strongly supportive of report recommendations that encouraged private sector, competition-driven managed care.

The Florida legislature also took parallel tracks. Amazingly enough, given the conservative bent of the "blue ribbon" panels advising them, there was a single-payer bill. Called the Florida Universal Access Plan, it was sponsored by Representative Elaine Gordon, and although unsuccessful, did not die as quickly or easily as one might suspect.

John Wilson, Legislative Chief Analyst of the Florida Senate, in a letter to me, detailed the effort's legislative history:

> During the 1991 Florida Legislative Session, both houses considered a universal health care bill modeled after the Canadian health care system ... it passed the Senate Committee on Health and Rehabilitative Services. The bill died in a subsequent committee of reference and was never voted on by the whole Senate. The House companion bill passed several committees but also was not voted on by the full House of Representatives. Similar bills are being filed in both houses of the Florida Legislature for the 1992 session.[28]

Another bill considered by Florida lawmakers at the same time would have established a play or pay program called Florida Care, and yet another called for the single agency idea recommended by the Government Task Force.

ALASKA

The rugged individualists of the nation's far north are no less immune to our national health care problems than are their countrymen in any other state. According to the latest statistics, ninety thousand Alaskans have no health insurance or government medical aid. Their problem is compounded by geography: 80 percent of the medical facilities in Alaska are located in three cities, Anchorage, Fairbanks, and Juneau.

The man most associated with health care reform in Alaska is state senator Jim Duncan, a Juneau Democrat. His proposed legislation is the centerpiece of the effort to achieve universal health care coverage for Alaskans.

Duncan's bill is not a single-payer system. Duncan calls it an "all-payer system model."[29] His bill, like so many others, is an outgrowth of a task force—the Alaska Health Care Cost Containment Task Force, which Duncan chaired. His bill would create a Health Resources Authority charged with "establishing a system that results in cost efficient payments to providers."[30]

Behind the vague language, the authority's job would be to create a comprehensive group insurance plan, available to all public and private employers who care to join. Ostensibly intended to cover public employees, its extension to the private sector has led private insurers to cry "foul" and "unfair competition."

Duncan denies their contention, arguing:

Insurance companies have viewed the state as "big brother" in this debate. They fear a situation where a state agency will present unfair competition. I agree with the concerns of insurance companies. This is not the intent and their concern is addressed specifically in the legislation. After the authority establishes a pool of private and public sector employers and identifies the uninsured population, private insurance companies will be asked to provide coverage. The authority will issue a request for proposal to all insurance companies doing business in Alaska outlining what the plan must include. The authority can only take on the role of an insurance company if there are no responses or if the proposals submitted by private insurance firms do not meet the criteria outlined in the request for proposal.[31]

Duncan has both defenders and critics. The *Anchorage Daily News* editorialized that "Senator Duncan offers a timely cure" and lauded his approach, noting that state government in thinly populated Alaska is one of the largest buyers of medical care in the state. "When you buy in bulk, you have the power to negotiate a better price. Senator Duncan would take advantage of that buying power to try to hold down both the cost of care and the cost of health insurance."[32]

The *Alaska Journal of Commerce* also chimed in with an expression of support, urging that "it was time to stop talking and do something about the crisis in health insurance and costs of medical care."[33] Both publications predicted strong opposition from the medical establishment, particularly to those parts of the bill restricting fees and establishing utilization standards—and they expressed the hope that the legislature would act and "not just appoint another task force to study the problem."[34]

There was no doubt of the opposition of the medical establishment. The president of the Alaska State Hospital and Nursing Home Association, in his critique, did not really address the bill. Instead, he bored in on the fact that the original Task Force had been formed to consider ways to cut down on the amount the state was paying to insure its own employees, and only as an afterthought had looked at the overall health care problem. Such an approach, he held, was no way to deal with the need for statewide affordable health care. He called for a "diagnosis ... based on adequate information from the state's health providers and consumers"[35]—in other words, another task force. The *Anchorage Times*, in an unfriendly editorial, added, "The Legislature should be looking at the total system to develop a health plan that addresses all citizen's needs."[36] To Duncan's despair (he had met with their editorial board), they persisted in implying that the Duncan bill dealt only with public employees.

The bill has thus far moved through two reference committees and awaits further action in the next session of the Alaska legislature.

NEW YORK

Governor Mario Cuomo held the first of his "Town Meetings On Universal Health Care" in Rochester in June 1991. Four proposals were discussed. Originally, a fifth, the Gottfried Proposal, had been advertised, but its originator, Assemblyman Richard Gottfried of Manhattan, Chairman of the Assembly Health Committee, decided instead to support another plan, the one called New York Health.

An unusual angle to this process was that two of the four proposals were for single-payer plans—New York Health and the New York State Department of Health's UNY*Care. The others were the Hospital Association of New York State's Pro-Health, and the New York Medical Society's American Universal Health Care System.

With no one involved willing to argue against full coverage, the Empire State debate focuses on the specific points each plan tries to make for its method of achieving full coverage in a way that best protects the special interest or philosophical point of view of its sponsor.

Assemblyman Gottfried, attacking the problem from the consumer point of view, stressed the administrative waste that he claimed New

York Health would eliminate. The announcement that he would introduce the bill claimed it would "eliminate more than $5 billion in administrative waste caused by the more than 400 private insurance companies which now provide health care to New Yorkers."[37] This financial estimate was made by Citizen Action of New York, organizers of the New York State Health Care Campaign, and emphasized savings to businesses and local governments. At the same time, broader coverage was promised—broader coverage for everyone. Private insurance would be eliminated, and a system very close to that of Canada's would be instituted. Gottfried's statement in making his announcement did not mention Canada. It simply highlighted what he saw as New York Health's advantages over other proposals: "It provides coverage for everyone, it provides the full range of services, it allows consumers to choose their health care providers, and builds in cost containment."[38]

UNY*Care, the other single-payer system under discussion as part of the roadshow, is more complicated. It establishes a public entity—the Single Payer Authority (SPA)—to serve as an intermediary between third-party payers and providers. It will issue a single enrollment card. The flow chart showing how this will work shows a consumer receiving his card, showing it to the provider, receiving services, the provider billing the SPA, the SPA paying the provider (at the UNY*Care rate), and the SPA billing either the consumer or the third-party payer. An integrated electronic claims processing system is to be instituted to keep everything straight. First, however, a regional demonstration project has to be run to assure the idea's feasibility.

Most importantly, perhaps, the SPA will be a rate-setting agency. It will be the only entity in the state authorized to set rates of reimbursement, and "will assume the role of the single buyer of health care." In its capacity as both single buyer and single payer, it can therefore establish and enforce an overall "health care budget" for the state. In that way it will control medical inflation.[39]

In addition, UNY*Care will provide public coverage for everyone with an income between 100 percent and 200 percent of the Federal poverty level, and will cover all catastrophic medical expenses above twenty-five thousand dollars, thus relieving private insurers of this burden.

Pro-Health, the proposal of the Hospital Association, seeks to address the problems of governmental shortfalls and bad debt/charity losses. The philosophy is clear. The proposal states that "it is more efficient and more realistic to build upon present, existing mechanisms than to create radically new ones for the fulfillment of these goals."[40] The plan answers the question of universal coverage by seeking to expand the coverage of employees by their employers with government subsidies for small businesses "for a limited time," and another subsidy of insurance premiums for those ineligible for Medicaid. It also proposes an expansion of Medicaid eligibility. Pro-Health would determine the minimum benefit package and here, again, employers would have to play or pay. The Hospital Association adds one caveat: "This proposal will have substantial additional costs, including costs of higher rates for physicians and other services, costs resulting from increased demand for services and costs consequent upon paying reasonable hospital outpatient rates without the arbitrary caps imposed by Medicaid as at present."[41]

The New York Medical Society's proposal has no such caveat in its document. Nor does it appear to include any cost-containment measures that would restrict physician income. It does call for ending Medicaid and Medicare, and substituting a basic benefits package costing "in the vicinity of $2500"[42] that would have to be purchased by all Americans not covered by their employers, and for which they would receive tax credits. Vouchers would be given by the Federal government to individuals below 200 percent of poverty for the sole purpose of purchasing such insurance. Limited long-term care would be included in the premium charges, and riders, at extra cost, would be available to those above 200 percent of poverty for extended long-term coverage. Physicians would control utilization review and quality assurance. The plan also envisages a "vigorous Internal Revenue Service pursuit of tax evaders.[43]

NEW JERSEY

Legislators dearly love to pass resolutions. They can be harmless bits of sentiment commemorating the importance of Arbor Day or the birthday of a constituent who is 104 years old—or they can be more substantive, an expression of opinion on a controversial issue, or occasionally, a method for a state legislature to express its wishes to the Congress of the United States.

The latter course was followed by the New Jersey Senate and

General Assembly with regard to health care. While it is true that resolutions are mere pieces of paper with no force of law, it may be argued that by calling on action from the Congress, Garden State lawmakers recognized the limits they faced in attempting to solve the health care crisis.

Like many states, New Jersey started working on the health care problem by establishing a task force. In their case they dubbed it a commission—the Governor's Commission on Health Care Costs. When it issued its report in October 1990, it fashioned a cute acronym to sum up its findings:

> C ost
> A ccessibility
> R esponsibility
> E fficiency
> for New Jersey

The first two recommendations made by the commission were linked to its belief that major action would have to take place in Washington.

> CR1. The United States Congress should enact legislation within the next year for a Universal Health Care System to ensure that all Americans have access to quality health care.

> CR2. Should the United State Congress not enact such a plan, the New Jersey Legislature should consider the passage of a Universal Health Care Plan that ensures that all New Jerseyans are covered through a single payer system and assured access to health care.[44]

This set the stage in Trenton. The first act was Assembly Concurrent Resolution No. 154, introduced on April 22, 1991, by Assemblymen Pascrell and Mecca and thirteen others. It not only called upon Congress to act, but was very specific about the bill it wished to see enacted on the Federal level. It called for the passage of the "Universal Health Care Act of 1991"—the Russo Bill—"which would establish a national single-payer health insurance program."[45]

The "whereases" on the paper detail the thinking that justifies the result. Regarding a single payer, it simply states: "Whereas, a single-payer national health insurance system would streamline administrative procedures and substantially reduce the cost of providing health care." Many other points commonly made by proponents of national health care are also "whereased": the number of uninsured in the country (here estimated in excess of 40 million), the cost in the U.S. (estimated at 11 percent of GNP), the identification of the U.S. and South Africa as the only two countries without national health care, the 1 million New Jerseyans lacking insurance, etc.

The next act in Trenton was to determine the will of the people on the issue. An act—this time a bill, not a resolution—called for a statewide referendum. It was to be nonbinding, however; there was no force of law involved. What the legislature was doing was simply opinion-sampling.

The question was headed: "ENACTMENT OF NATIONAL HEALTH CARE PROGRAM." But instead of being addressed to a specific proposal like the Russo Bill, with its single-payer bias, a much more vaporous approach was taken. In fact, the question was framed in language so innocuous that it could mean anything. In the end it was almost like asking people to vote for motherhood and apple pie.

Shall the State urge the United States Congress and the President of the United States to enact a national health care program which: provides high quality comprehensive personal health care including preventive, curative and occupational health services; is universal in coverage, community-controlled, rationally organized, equitably financed, with minimal out-of-pocket expense to taxpayers; is sensitive to the particular health needs of all persons; and aims at reducing the overall costs of health care?

It is to the credit of the New Jersey legislature that they did not stop there. They did manage to pass a measure containing recommendations from the Governor's Commission. Among achievements of note in this compendious piece of legislation was the creation in the Department of Health of a special fund, the Health Care Cost Reduction Fund. Monies in this fund are to be used for a variety of purposes including three million dollars for local health planning, fifty thousand for a demographic study of hospital patients who incur bad debts, money to eight community health centers so they might stay open evenings and weekends, and expanding Medicaid eligibility. The funds for all this are not to come from the state coffers but from hospitals—0.53 percent of the rate base of every New Jersey hospital. As a final note, in an election that saw a conservative landslide by the State's Republicans running on an anti-tax platform, the national health referendum passed by a 2–1 margin.

WASHINGTON

John Lewin, Hawaii's health commissioner, has made no bones about the fact that the SHIP program, for which he has such high hopes, is based on the state of Washington's Basic Health Plan, adopted in 1987.

Yet matters are somewhat different in Washington than in Hawaii, where only 5 percent of the population was uninsured. To quote a recent legislative finding by the Washington state senate, "A significant percentage of the population of this state does not have reasonably available insurance or other coverage of the costs of necessary basic health care services."[46] So the efforts of the state's Basic Health Plan to cover the working poor have been deemed insufficient to stand by themselves.

Consequently, for the second time in several years, Representative Dennis Braddock, Chair of the Health Services Committee, has introduced a bill to deal with this problem. The first Braddock bill created the inevitable study commission, and the second presented the legislation to implement its recommendations.

The Washington Healthcare Service Act of 1992 aims primarily at the creation of a state-run insurance company. Through a public corporation, the Washington Healthcare Service Corporation, a Healthcare Plan will be offered by the state. By July 1, 1995, it will encompass all present Medicare enrollees, Medicaid recipients, enrollees in the aforesaid Washington Basic Health Plan, plus state and private school employees. A year later, all Washington residents will be enrolled in the Healthcare Plan or an alternative, private insurance plan that meets specified criteria. Among the prerequisites for nongovernmental insurance are the necessity to maintain a monthly enrollment of at least 350,000, no discrimination or preselection of enrollees, and benefits at least equal to those of the Healthcare program.

248

Benefits will include preventive care, provider services, inpatient hospital services, testing and diagnostic services, prescription drugs, etc.

Financing will come from the pooling of funds from existing programs like Medicare and Medicaid, legislative appropriations, employer-paid premiums, employees, the self-employed and (possibly) co-payments. An interesting feature of the proposal is its aim to protect against "improper queuing," which is to say that its board is directed to design strategies to cut down waiting lists. A reserve is provided to fund such efforts. The board is also to establish a "rationing" policy as well as regional health care ethics committees to help guide providers in making tough rationing decisions.

The approach taken in Washington appears to match the Braddock Commission's initial report. That called for use of external managed care plans to deal with the problem of universal access. While the Healthcare program seems—at this stage—to be more of an insurance policy than an HMO, the latter can't be ruled out. The emphasis on managed care may also reflect the state's success with organizations like the Group Health Cooperative, the country's largest *consumer-governed* HMO, with 470,000 members. The organization amassed a $19 million surplus from a $577 million budget in 1990, and also runs twenty-nine medical centers and two hospitals.

MAINE

A study of long-term care insurance released by the state of New York contained the statement that "only Maine has legislation in place concerning long-term care insurance tax credits."[48] But the Pine Tree State has not addressed the problem of universal coverage in any comprehensive fashion. It is typical of the many states that have tried to cope with the crisis by means of patchwork remedies.

Some are innovative and break new ground, like the long-term care tax credits. Others are demonstration programs, like MaineCare, one of a dozen pilot programs funded by the Robert Wood Johnson Foundation through its Health Care For The Uninsured Program. This $6.5 million initiative gave grants to groups in Alabama, Arizona, California, Colorado, Florida, Massachusetts, Michigan, New Jersey, Tennessee, Utah, and Wisconsin, as well as Maine. Most of these groups have concentrated on widening access to coverage for employees of small firms. Almost half of these have been contractors, retailers, real estate personnel, and crafts persons.

A much more extensive effort was made by the Maine Health Program. Funded by the legislature through a patchwork of taxes, including the usual ones on cigarettes and alcohol plus (perhaps a Maine phenomenon) a tax on the sale of used boats, its aim was to cover approximately 21,000 of the state's 150,000 uninsured. A feature of this "package" was the inclusion of money to help hospitals pay for the Medicare shortfall, reflecting the coalition that pushed the bill through—consumers and low-income advocates on one side, hospitals, insurers, and business interests on the other. Resistance came primarily from the governor, who has repeatedly tried to kill the Maine Health Program (while keeping the tax money).

Another step taken by Maine—the creation of a hospital regulatory body, the Maine Health Care Finance Commission—has also been threatened with extinction. Argument rages over whether or not this extreme regulation is useful in containing costs.

The Maine High Risk Insurance Organization is a pool the state has set up, administered by Mutual of Omaha, to cover those who cannot get insurance, and Maine currently has a special legislative committee investigating approaches to universal health care coverage.

The list of activities in all of the fifty states could go on almost endlessly. West Virginia has a Health Care Planning Commission and a legislative Healthcare Oversight Committee. Missouri has the Chatfield Bill, a single-payer measure that was defeated on the House floor by twenty-three votes. Michigan has its Affordable Health Care Plan, presented by Senate Republicans (with tax credits for people to buy a one hundred dollars per month policy). The amounts of time, effort and money being poured into attempts to cope with this consuming issue are unparalleled in American history.

Single-payer plans, considered the most radical (or "comprehensive" according to defenders), were under discussion or consideration in at least fourteen states as of April 1991, and there is reason to believe that number has already risen to more than twenty.

Can one state go it alone in any but the incremental way exemplified by Maine? Under current law, all programs that contemplate receiving funds from Washington would require Federal permission.

Will there be enough grass-roots support to force that permission? What if the Federal government assumes the responsibility for fashioning a truly national solution?

However, should there be gridlock on the Potomac, the ferment in the states might very well result in an elixir that will eventually prove to be the cure for the ills of the nation's health care system.

CONCLUSION

Winston Churchill is once reported to have said, "You can always count on Americans to do the right thing—that is, after they have tried everything else." If he did say that, the health care crisis in our country is living proof of the great Englishman's insight and wisdom.

With the political confusion about health care greater than it has ever been, with a veritable avalanche of proposals filling the halls of government on Capitol Hill and in all fifty state capitals, with economic hard times serving perverse double duty as both a deterrent and a goad to action, the cynical conclusion of the sophisticated observer has to be that despite the mounting urgency of the problem, cautious practical politicians will inevitably do as little as possible. They will follow the path of least resistance. They will make self-serving speeches, fashion clever phrases that make good sound bites for the folks back home, and then, with great fanfare, herald the solution they have fashioned to finally and forever solve the problem.

Of course their solution will do nothing of the kind. It will just be another quick fix that will cause even more strain on our already overburdened, overpriced, inefficient system. It may even, as did well-meaning, half-measure programs like Medicare and Medicaid, end up causing more problems than it corrects. Yet there is hope that, in the words of Gershwin's song, "it ain't necessarily so."

Mr. Churchill had it right: In time, our American democracy does work. We will do the right thing.

Time moves on inexorably. Every day, as economic conditions get tougher, more Americans are forced to cancel health insurance they

253

can no longer afford—or they lose their jobs. In either case, the army of those denied access to health care increases.

Lawmakers are faced with tough questions and are looking at programs that promise relatively simple answers.

Conservatives champion programs that say all that needs be done is to insure the uninsured with government help (tax credits, vouchers, or subsidies). Will such programs answer the problem? Are they affordable? And do they provide security for the average American unless the government pays for everything?

Others offer play or pay proposals which shift more of the burden onto businesses instead of government (but still require a taxpayer contribution). These are the kissing cousins to the conservative answers already offered.

Both notions work on the premise that the existing U.S. health care system, if it can even be called a system, has inherent values worth preserving. They see any changes in terms of additions to what already exists, not substitutions.

This conservative argument elicits a few questions: Is not our present system simply the result of the Churchillian adage above? Have we not spent all our energies so far this century "trying to do everything else?" Can we still maintain that we are morally right in being the only major nation that has been successful in avoiding our responsibility to provide health care to all of our people?

Perhaps the issue is best summed up with a single, ultimate question: Is access to health care an inalienable right like "life, liberty and the pursuit of happiness?" The idea of imposing such a concept through a constitutional amendment has been suggested as one way to resolve the political debate.

Carl Schramm, the chief executive of the Health Insurance Association of America, argues that the present system should be preserved because the health insurance industry has succeeded in covering 85 percent of the population. He claims that is a magnificent achievement, and we should be satisfied with it. Yet it's hard to be satisfied if you are one of the 15 percent left out in the cold.

Others argue that we have the best medical care in the world. They hold that only the free flow of ideas and incentives available under a free-market system can lead to even more innovation and progress. They say nothing concerning the value of such progress if it is not available to the people.

254

Still others argue that Americans will never accept a system where the government provides something to everyone. Those people obviously never heard of Social Security.

As noted earlier, since the nineteenth century we have enjoyed a public school system that has operated under the ideological belief that no one should have to pay to go to a public school. Funding is by general taxation. There is no 185 percent of poverty line above which you have to pay money to send your children to school. Even though our public school system is under attack, Americans still accept the basic assumption that schooling is a right, and not a privilege reserved only for those who can afford it. Is not the health of the nation's people as much of a concern as their schooling?

Our American health care system has grown by haphazard accident. There is nothing inherently American about it. In fact, with its emphasis on employer-provided health insurance, it is eminently German in origin—actually Bismarck's baby. It is a health care answer devised in another age by cynical politicians to deal with a political problem caused by increasing numbers of industrial workers.

One reason I find the Canadian system so attractive is precisely because it is non-European. It is original, and seems far better suited to North American people. Dissenters may cry, "Oh, no! Canadians are much more prone to accept the hand of government than we Americans." While it may be true that the Canadian government does presently offer its people more social services than we do, it is instructive to see how they got that way. Canada's best-selling historian, Pierre Berton, in his book *The Great Depression*, describes the attitude change in that nation because they had no American-style New Deal. During the 1930s, the ideology of those governing Canada was far to the right of even such conservatives as Harding, Coolidge, and Hoover. Canadian political leaders were adamant in their insistence on rugged individualism, which would accept no show of governmental compassion and no official recognition of people's needs.

A Canadian Broadcasting Company radio program called "The Origins of Medicare," aired in December 1990, clarified this point and illustrated the home-grown North American nature of the Canadian health care system. It concerned the Swift Current Health Region in Saskatchewan, the birthplace of Canada's Medicare—a poor region of prairie people who, in the spirit of communal barn-raising and other frontier values, came together during the hard times of the Great Depression, when few could afford even the most basic medical care. They formed a health region. It was a single-payer system that provided care for everyone. It was a simple, practical answer to a common problem. And it was devised by the people themselves. It came to be the model for all of Saskatchewan, and, in time, all of Canada. It was a pure grass-roots effort that came up with an entirely original means of providing health care to fifty thousand people. It was run by local farmers, local doctors, and other local citizens. It was simple, it was nonbureaucratic, and it was rooted deep in the tradition of the pioneer spirit.

What is particularly appealing about the Canadian system of health care, apart from its simplicity and its absence of bureaucracy, is that it creates a structure that provides security. Within that structure the provider of health care can move easily to attend to the first job of any healer, which is to heal.

Unless we erect in the U.S. a structure similar to the Canadian model—one I find preferable to the European models, with their considerable complexity and great bureaucratic involvement—we will twist and turn and waste great sums of money, as we have been doing for decades, in a vain attempt to continue to patch up our present, sick nonsystem.

I firmly believe we can make the transition in this country to a single-payer system. Establishing such a framework will not end our efforts. Internal reforms, like those suggested by Dr. Michael Rachlis for our northern neighbor, will have to be considered. But if there is one major difference between the Canadians and ourselves, it is that we have shown we are more flexible. Managed care—at least the HMO concept—is alive, if not completely well, in this country. If such a concept does not exist in Canada, it has nothing to do with their model for health care financing. It does have something to do with physician hostility. Furthermore, the quasi-medical personnel sought for Canada by Rachlis—nurse's assistants, midwives, paramedics—exist already in the U.S., and would fit easily into the single-payer structure here. I even believe our insurance companies will continue to have a role to play as they do in Canada.

Above all else, there are two overwhelming reasons to choose an American variation of the single-payer system over any other.

256

1. The single-payer system is the only one of all the proposed reforms that guarantees financial security to all the people of the United States. It will never leave anyone untreated, or with crippling bills, as many insurance policies do even when claims are paid without dispute.

2. The single-payer system gives people something for their money. It is true that they will pay more taxes. But they will no longer have to pay insurance premiums, co-payments, deductibles, and other parts of medical bills insurance does not—or will not—pay. When sorted out, the individual American may even save money. Other possible approaches would pour more billions into what is already the most expensive system in the world. They will not relieve the average policyholder of any of the ever-increasing costs.

One more major advantage of the single payer-system: because of the nature of its structure, the system has a built-in cost containment mechanism. Whether the savings of the simplified administration of a single-payer system can end in making our system cheaper is something that will not be known for certain until it is tried. But to continue at our present rate of cost increase is unacceptable—and all other efforts to curb rising health costs have failed miserably.

If, as Pfizer Chemical's Jacques Krasny maintains, Canada's system is not as inexpensive as it seems, the point is still that they do cover all their people. Any comparison has to take into account that growing millions of Americans are either poorly covered or not covered at all.

Dr. Michael Rachlis is very upbeat about the possibilities inherent in a marriage of Canada's streamlined administrative efficiency with the U.S. experience in varieties of cost and quality control. As he told Congress's House Government Operations Committee in June 1991: "The U.S. could implement a national health program which melded the efficiencies ... in public health insurance with the efficiencies ... in managed care. The U.S. has a unique opportunity to build upon its strengths of managed care and clinical guideline development and develop a system which could be a model for the rest of the world."

Since so many experiments have been tried and failed, and since so many millions of people are still not adequately protected from the physical and financial threat of ill health, is it not time to act? Is it not time to finally go to the last alternative—the single-payer system that has proven its worth, and popularity, in the one country in the world that most closely resembles our own?

Let's short-cut the endless process.

The politicians will not do it unless they feel the heat from the people.

"Your money or your health?" How much longer must the American people have to make that awful choice?

NOTES

INTRODUCTION

1. *Health Affairs*, Spring 1991, as reported in the *New York Times*, 19 May 1991. Per capita expenditures from the same source were reported as $2,354 in the U.S., $1,683 in Canada, and $1,274 in France.
2. Congressional Research Service, *Health Insurance and the Uninsured*, 9 June 1988. The AMA's figures were 28.4 million in 1979 and 36.8 million in 1984— a 30 percent jump.
3. Report of the Maine People's Resource Center (citing United Nations statistics), 1 August 1990.
4. Organization for Economic Cooperation and Development (OECD), 1990.
5. Sylvia A. Law, *Blue Cross, What Went Wrong* (New Haven and London: Yale University Press, 1970).

CHAPTER 1: THE FIRESTORM

1. *New York Times*, 13 June 1991.
2. *Christian Science Monitor*, 19 November 1991, 13.
3. *The California Dream, The California Nightmare*, Report by San Francisco Health Access, 1988, 38–39.
4. Report of the Health Insurance Task Force, Ohio Developmental Disabilities Council (Columbus, Ohio, 1990), 19.
5. *Shreveport Journal*.
6. *Health Insurance in Vermont: A Case For Reform*, executive summary, 1–2.
7. *New York Times*, 4 January 1992, 46.
8. *Portsmouth Press*, 30 January 1992, 4.
9. *Miami Herald*, 25 November 1991, 1A, 6A.
10. *Health Care For All News*, vol. III, no. 2 (Spring 1991).

11. This, and all of the following Maine quotes, are from the author's correspondence.

12. *Portland [ME] Press-Herald,* 2 July 1991.

13. United States General Accounting Office, *Canadian Health Insurance Lessons for the United States* (Report to the Chairman, Committee on Government Operations, House of Representatives), executive summary, 3.

14. Ida Hellander M.D., David U. Himmelstein M.D., Sidney M. Wolfe M.D., and Steffie Woolhandler M.D., M.P.H., *Administrative Waste in the U.S. Health Care System in 1991: The Cost to the Nation, the States and the District of Columbia* (Washington, D.C.: Public Citizen Health Research Group and Cambridge, MA: the Division of Social Community Medicine, Department of Medicine, the Cambridge Hospital and Harvard Medical School), executive summary.

15. Humphrey Taylor, "Health Care in Perception: An International Comparison." (Address to the National Committee for Quality Health Care).

16. *New York Times,* 2 July 1991.

17. *New York Times,* 29 January 1991.

18. *New York Times,* 1 May 1991.

19. *Health Care News,* October 1989.

20. Hellander, Himmelstein, Wolfe, and Woolhandler, 3.

21. *New York Times,* 19 February 1990.

22. Private conversation with Dr. Gordon Guyatt.

23. All Statistics in this paragraph are from *Critical Condition: America's Health Care in Jeopardy* (Report by Lewin/ICF, A Division of Health and Sciences Research Inc. to the hospital and pharmaceutical company-dominated organization the National Committee for Quality Health Care, Washington, D.C., 1988).

24. *New York Times,* 28 April 1991.

25. *Boston Globe,* 22 September 1990.

26. *Daily Utah Chronicle,* 17 January 1991.

CHAPTER 2: HOW WE GOT WHERE WE ARE, PART I

1. Hajo Holborn, *A History of Modern Germany, 1840–1945* (New York: Alfred A. Knopf, 1969), 291.

2. Ibid., 293.

3. George Dangerfield, *The Strange Death of Liberal England* (New York: G.P. Putnam's Sons, 1935), 226.

4. Dr. Harold Bauman, *Verging on National Health Insurance Since 1910* (Paper delivered to the Seventh Utah Conference on Ethics and Health, University of Utah, Salt Lake City, 17–18 January 1991).

5. Mark Sullivan, *Our Times: The United States, 1900–1925,* vol. 4 (New York: Charles Scribners Sons, 1932), 38–39.

6. Elmer H. Youngman, ed., *Progressive Principles by Theodore Roosevelt: Selections from Addresses Made During the Presidential Campaign of 1912* (New York: Progressive National Service, 1913), 317.

7. Ibid., 317.

8. *Journal of the American Medical Association,* 17 June 1916, quoted in James G. Burrow, *AMA: Voice of American Medicine* (Baltimore: The Johns Hopkins Press, 1963), 143.

9. Quoted in Bauman, 3.

10. Bernard Mandel, *Samuel Gompers: A Biography* (Yellow Springs, Ohio: The Antioch Press, 1963), 185.

11. Ibid., 542–43.

12. Dr. Harry Gross, *National Health Care: A Pragmatic Perspective* (Dallas: National Center for Policy Analysis, 1983).

13. John C. Goodman, preface to *National Health Insurance: A Pragmatic Perspective.*

14. Rexford G. Tugwell, *The Democratic Roosevelt* (Baltimore: Penguin Books, 1957), 334, 337.

15. Frances Perkins, *The Roosevelt I Knew* (New York: The Viking Press, 1946), 289.

16. Barton J. Bernstein and Allen J. Matusow, Eds., *The Truman Administration: A Documentary History* (New York: Harper and Row, 1966), 117.

17. *New York Times,* 12 February 1961.

18. Arthur M. Schlesinger, Jr., *A Thousand Days: John F. Kennedy in the White House* (New York: Fawcett Premier, 1965), 651.

19. Doris Kearns, *Lyndon Johnson and the American Dream* (New York: Harper and Row, 1976), 250.

CHAPTER 3: HOW WE GOT WHERE WE ARE, PART II

1. Paul Starr, *The Social Transformation of American Medicine* (New York: Basic Books, 1982), 381.

2. Rosemary Stevens, *In Sickness and In Wealth: American Hospitals in the Twentieth Century* (New York: Basic Books, 1989), 288.

3. Ed Cray, *In Failing Health: The Medical Crisis and the AMA* (Indianapolis and New York: The Bobbs-Merrill Co., 1970), 107.

4. Richard M. Nixon, *In the Arena: A Memory of Victory, Defeat and Renewal* (New York: Simon and Schuster, 1990), 168.

5. Barbara and John Ehrenreich, *The American Health Empire: Power, Profit and Politics,* Report from the Health Policy Advisory Center (New York: Vintage Books, 1970), 182.

6. *National Journal,* 16 October 1976, as reported in Starr, 406.

7. Quoted in "Health Policy, the Legislative Agenda," *Congressional Quarterly,* 1980.

8. *Congressional Quarterly Weekly Reports*, 14 October 1989, 2712.

9. *Congressional Quarterly*, 30 September 1989, 2564.

10. *Congressional Quarterly*, 8 September 1989, 2317.

11. *Congressional Quarterly*, 14 October 1989, 2715.

12. Term used in an article by Geraldine Dallek of the National Health Law Program, in *Society*, July-August 1986.

CHAPTER 4: THE FORCES I: The Providers

1. George Bernard Shaw, *The Doctor's Dilemma*, preface (New York: Brentano's, 1909), 5.

2. *New York Times*, 26 July 1991.

3. Ibid.

4. *New York Times*, 29 July 1991, A12.

5. Ibid.

6. All quotes from *Health Access America* (Publication of the American Medical Association), February 1990.

7. *AHCPR Research Activities* Bulletin, no. 141 (May 1991), 2.

8. Ibid.

9. *Health Policy Report* (Publication of the Roche Company, Nutley, N.J.), vol. 4, no. 1 (Spring 1990).

10. Samuel O. Thier, M.D., "Health Care Reform: Who Will Lead?" *Annals of Internal Medicine*, vol. 115, no. 1 (July 1, 1991).

11. Howard H. Hiatt, *America's Health in the Balance: Choice or Chance* (New York: Harper and Row, 1987) 9.

12. Rosemary Stevens, *In Sickness and in Wealth*, 358.

13. *Philadelphia Inquirer*, 28 December 1990, 10C.

14. *Hospital Statistics*, 1988 edition (Chicago: American Hospital Association, 1988)

15. *Philadelphia Inquirer*, 28 December 1990, 17C.

16. *Wall Street Journal*, 26 June 1990.

17. *Not-For-Profit Hospital Tax-Exempt Status* (New Jersey Hospital Association Government Relations Issue Paper)

18. *New York Times*, 21 July 1991, F6.

19. Ibid.

20. Stevens, *In Sickness and In Wealth*, 154.

21. Ibid., 352.

CHAPTER 5: THE FORCES II: The Payers

1. John E. Gregg, *The Health Insurance Racket and How to Beat It* (Chicago: Henry Regenery Company, 1973), 156.

2. The preceding figures are all from Starr, 295–296.

3. All figures from Law, cited above.

4. Rosemary Stevens, *American Medicine and the Public Interest* (New Haven and London: Yale University Press, 1971), 271.

5. Ibid., 271, 272.

6. *San Francisco Chronicle*, 23 May 1990.

7. Gregg, 95, 99.

8. Henry J. Aaron: *Serious and Unstable Condition: Financing America's Health Care* (Washington, D.C.: The Brookings Institution, 1991), 67.

9. *Lewiston [ME] Sun-Journal*, 27 May 1990. Reprint, article by Walter Parker for Knight-Ridder newspapers.

10. *Research Dialogues* (Publication of the Teachers Insurance and Annuity Association College Retirement Fund, New York, New York) no. 27 (October 1990), 5.

11. *New York Times*, 13 February 1991, D3.

12. Huefner, 10.

13. *Wall Street Journal*, 10 July 1990, B1.

14. As reprinted in the *Portland [ME] Press-Herald*, 7 August 1991.

15. *New York Times*, 21 June 1991.

16. *New York Times*, 6 August 1991.

17. *New York Times*, 17 March 1990, 30, as cited in Research Dialogues, 10.

18. Law, 116.

19. Law, 159.

20. *Medicare: Its Use, Funding and Economic Dimensions* (Congressional Research Report, prepared at the request of the Senate Committee on Finance) 1 March 1989, updated 18 May 1989, 4.

21. *Federal Update* (Publication National Conference of State Legislatures) vol. III, no 9 (September 22, 1989).

22. *New York Times*, 13 August 1991, A14.

CHAPTER 6: THE FORCES III: The Consumers

1. *York County [ME] Coast Star,* 6 September 1989.

2. *Questions And Answers About Health Access As An Organization* (Publication of Health Access, San Francisco).

3. Publication of the Louisiana Health Care Campaign.

4. *New Orleans Times-Picayune,* 10 July 1991, B-1.

5. Ibid., B-6.

6. Publication of Minnesota COACT, Minneapolis, Minnesota.

7. Publication of Montana Senior Citizens Association, Helena, Montana.

8. *Economic Notes* (Publication of the Labor Research Association) vol. 57, nos. 7–8 (July–August 1989), 4.

9. *Information and Speakers Manual* (Publication of the Oil, Chemical and Atomic Workers International Union, Denver, Colorado), 4.

10. *Progress Report* (Publication of the National Council of Senior Citizens, Washington, D.C.) (January 1991), 1.

11. *Health Letter* (Publication of the Public Citizen Health Research Group, Washington, D.C.) vol. 7, no. 6 (June 1991).

12. *Modern Maturity,* (December 1990–January 1991), 9.

13. *AARP Highlights,* vol. 7, no. 4 (July–August 1989), 4.

14. *AARP Bulletin,* vol. 32, no. 4 (April 1991), 4.

15. "A National Health Program For The United States, a Physician's Proposal," *New England Journal of Medicine,* 12 January 1989, 102.

16. Ibid., 106.

17. *An Assessment of Selected National Health Program Proposals* (Publication of the American Public Health Association).

18. Dr. Mark W. Wolcott and Dr. Charles B. Smith, "VA Health Care—Its Role In A National Health Care System" (Paper delivered to the Seventh Utah Conference on Ethics and Health, Salt Lake City, January 17–18, 1991), 5.

19. Ibid., 5.

20. Ibid., 17.

21. Ibid., 24.

22. *Wall Street Journal,* 26 August 1991, A12.

23. "Research Activities," *AHCPR Bulletin,* no. 140 (April 1991), 4.

24. Communication to the author, 6 June 1990.

25. Institute of Medicine informational booklet, 3.

26. *Time,* 6 August 1991, 46.

27. Letter printed in the *York [ME] Weekly,* 11 September 1991, 15.

28. Advertisement in the *Washington Post,* 2 May 1991.

29. *Fortune,* 29 July 1991, 4B.

30. *New York Times,* 30 June 1991, 19.

31. Ibid.

32. *The Chronicle of Philanthropy, the Newspaper of the Non-Profit World,* vol. III, no. 13 (23 April 1991), 1.

33. Ibid.

CHAPTER 7: HOW SOME OTHER COUNTRIES DO IT

1. *Boston Globe,* 12 May 1991, 20.

2. Jens Alber, *Structural Reforms in the West German Health Care System* (Paper, Max Planck Institute, Cologne), 2.

3. Marian Dohler, *Policy Networks, Opportunity Structures and Neo-Conservative Reform Strategies in Health Policy* (Paper, Max Planck Institute, Cologne), 236.

4. Ibid., 272.

5. Alber, 19.

6. *Boston Globe*, 12 May 1991, 1.

7. Ibid., 20.

8. Shaw, xvi.

9. Letter to *The Scotsman*, 2 April 1991.

10. Vicente Navarro, *Class Struggle, the State and Medicine: An Historical and Contemporary Analysis of the Medical Sector in Great Britain* (Oxford: Martin Robertson and Co., 1978), 119.

11. Norman Johnson, *Reconstructing the Welfare State: A Decade of Change* (Hempstead: Harvester Wheatsheaf/Simon and Schuster, 1990), 69.

12. Melanie Phillips in the *Guardian*, 23 October 1987.

13. Dr. Julian Tudor Hart, "Transition of Patients From Consumers to Producers: An Agenda For The Next Hundred Years" (Paper for the *International Journal of Health Services*, prepublication copy sent to the author), 5.

14. *The Scotsman*, 14 April 1991.

15. *The Scotsman*, 12 April 1991.

16. *Financial Times*, 28 March 1991, 18.

17. Philippe Rollandin, *Le Sante En Danger* (Paris: Editions de l'Instant, 1987) 140. Translation by the author.

18. Paul Godt, *Policy-Making in France, from de Gaulle to Mitterand* (London and New York: Pinter Publishers, 1989), 192.

19. Rollandin, 135.

20. *Paris-Match*, 16 May 1991, 73–76. Translation by the author.

21. Paul Godt, "Liberalism in the *Dirigiste* State: A Changing Public/Private Mix in French Medical Care," in *From Rhetoric to Reality: Comparative Health Policy and the New Right* (London: Macmillan, 1991), 15.

22. *Figaro-Magazine*, 6 April 1991, 56.

23. *The European*, 29–31 March 1991, 13.

24. *A Journey Through the EC* (Report by the Commission of the European Community, Brussels-Luxembourg, 1988), 45.

25. Stuart Altman and Terri Jackson, "Australia's Health Care Financing System: Lessons for the United States" (Paper by the Dean and Professor of Health Policy of the Heller School, Brandeis University, Waltham, Massachusetts, and a PhD student at the Heller School, respectively), 15.

26. *The Age*, 30 October 1989.

27. *The Age*, 28 November 1990.

28. Ross Gittins in the *Sydney Morning Herald*, 31 January 1990.

29. Democratic Policy Committee, part 1 of 4-part series: *Health Care in Industrial Nations* (Washington, D.C.).

30. *New York Times*, 9 September 1991, A15.

31. *New England Journal of Medicine*, "High Tech Medicine in the Caribbean," "Cuba: A Healthy Revolution," 8 December 1983, 1470.

265

32. Medea Benjamin and Mark Haendel, *Cuba: A Current Issues Reader* (San Francisco: Global Exchange), 63-B.

33. Ibid., 64-B.

34. Sylvia Guendelman, DSW, "Health Care Users Residing on the Mexican Border," in *Medical Care*, vol. 29, no. 5 (May 1991).

35. *South African Panorama* (September 1988), 14.

CHAPTER 8: CANADA

1. Dr. Gordon Guyatt, "Long Version of the Summary of the Development of the Canadian Health Care System" (Paper by member of the Department of Clinical Epidemiology and Biostatistics, McMaster University Health Sciences Center, Hamilton, Ontario 1990).

2. Ibid.

3. Ralph W. Sutherland, M.D. and M. Jane Fulton, Ph.D., *Health Care in Canada: A Description and Analysis of Canadian Health Services* (Ottawa: The Health Group, 1988, 1990), 118.

4. Beth C. Fuchs and Joan Sokolovsky, *CRS Report for Congress: The Canadian Health Care Service* (Washington, D.C: Congressional Research Service, 20 February 1990), CRS 2.

5. Report by the Government Accounting Office. "Canadian Health Insurance" (Washington, D.C.), 29.

6. Ibid., 31.

7. Sutherland and Fulton, 225.

8. Dale A. Rublee, "Medical Technology in Canada, Germany and the United States," *Health Affairs* (Fall 1990), quoted in Neuschler, 29.

9. Personal communication to the author, 17 September 1991.

10. Coversation with the author, 2 October 1991.

11. Sarah Jane Growe, *Who Cares?: The Crisis In Canadian Nursing* (Toronto: McClelland and Stewart, 1991).

12. Growe, 192.

13. Dr. Gordon Ferguson, "Legacy, Accomplishments and Challenges: Opening Plenary" (Presentation at the Proceedings of the First National Home Care Conference, Quebec City, January 14, 1989).

14. Steffi Woolhandler, M.D. and David Himmelstein, M.D., "The Deteriorating Administrative Efficiency of the U.S. Health Care System," in *New England Journal of Medicine*, vol. 324, no. 18 (2 May 1991), 1254–56.

15. *Canadian Social Trends* (Report published by Statistics Canada, Ottawa) (Spring 1988), 3.

CHAPTER 9: TWO TRIPS TO CANADA

1. Charlotte Gray, "Medicare Under the Knife", in *Saturday Night* (September 1991), 10, 12.

2. *Evaluation Report of the Single Entry Pilot Project* (Report of the Bureau de Consultation) (April 1991), 127.

3. Ibid., 129.

4. Ibid., 121.

5. "Health Promotion and Prevention Issues" (Draft Report of the Premier's Council on Health Strategy, Fredericton, New Brunswick) (August 1991), 22.

6. Murray J. Kaiserman, Ph.D. and Byron Rogers, B.A., "Tobacco Consumption Declining Faster in Canada Than in the U.S." in *American Journal of Public Health*, 902–904. (July 1991), vol. 81, no. 7.

7. Dr. Warren Davidson, "Metaphors of Health and Aging: Geriatrics as Metaphor", in G. Kenyon, J. Birren, and J.J.F. Schroots, eds., *Metaphors of aging in science and the Humanities.* (New York: Springer, in press), 11–12.

8. *Enhancing Seniors' Independence* (Report by the New Brunswick Department of Health and Community Services, Fredericton) (April 1991), 31.

9. *Orientation Manual* (Publication of the Dr. Everett Chalmers Hospital, Fredericton, New Brunswick), 4.

10. Ian Munro, M.D., "Rationing by Government Decision" in U.S./Canadian Health Care Systems (Proceedings of the 1990 Annual Meeting of the National Committee for Quality Health Care, Washington, D.C., 30 January 1990), 63.

11. Ibid., 59.

12. Peter Ellis, "Accountability for Service" in *U.S./Canadian Health Care Systems*, 63.

13. Ibid., 65.

14. *The Straight Facts* (Publication of the Canadian Drug Manufacturers Association) no. 5 (1 September 1991).

15. "Challenging The Frontiers of Research" (Special Pharmaceutical Manufacturers Association of Canada advertising section) in *Macleans*, 11 December 1989.

16. Michael Rachlis, M.D. and Carol Kushner, *Second Opinion* (Toronto: Harper Collins, 1989), 247, 306, 307.

CHAPTER 10: JUST SUPPOSE

1. "Peer Review" section, *Health Affairs* (Summer 1991), 152–165.

2. *Financial Post,* 14-16 September 1991.

3. William D. Gairdner, *The Trouble With Canada* (Toronto: General Paperbacks, 1991), 329.

4. Rachlis and Kushner, 295.

5. *Health and Welfare in Canada* (Publication of the Minister of National Health and Welfare, 1989), A7.

6. *Toronto Globe and Mail*, 15 October 1991, 63.

7. *Macleans*, 30 September 1991, 63.

8. Dr. John Fry, *Medicine in Three Societies: A Comparison of Medical Care in the USSR, USA and UK* (New York: American Elsevier Publishing Company, 1970), 24–27.

9. John Iglehart, "Canada's Health Care System Faces Its Problems" (Health Policy Report) in the *New England Journal of Medicine*, 22 February 1990, 566.

10. Figures from the testimony of Dr. Michael Rachlis to the House Government Operations Committee, Washington, D.C., June 18, 1991, 3.

11. C. David Naylor, "A Different View of Queues in Ontario," (Report by Health Access), 116.

12. *New York Times*, 8 November 1991, A26.

13. *USA Today*, 11 November 1991, 1B, 2B, 3B.

14. "How To Fight Your Insurance and Win," in *Kiplinger's Personal Finance* (October 1991), 71.

15. *Today's Seniors* (August 1991), 2.

16. *Maine Sunday Telegram*, 27 October 1991, 11A.

17. Statistics Canada, *Survey of Consumer Finance.*

18. *The Economic Situation of Canada's Seniors* (Report by the National Advisory Council on Aging, Ottawa) (March 1991), 38–39.

19. *U.S./Canadian Health Care Systems* (Report of the National Committee For Quality Health Care, January 1990 meeting) 44–45.

20. Ibid., 47.

21. Joseph L. Scarpaci, ed., *Health Service Privatization in Industrial Societies* (New Brunswick, N.J.: Rutgers University Press, 1989), 28.

22. *U.S./Canadian Health Care Systems*, 80.

23. Ibid., 85.

CHAPTER 11: MEANWHILE, BACK IN WASHINGTON

1. *Roll Call*, 17 October 1991, 14.

2. Copy of speech released by Senator Harris Wofford, October 24, 1991.

3. "Editor's Notes," *Money* (July 1991), 5.

4. *Congressional Record*, 102nd Congress, 1st session, vol. 137, no. 85 (5 June 1991).

5. S. 1227, 170, 171.

6. *Health America: Affordable Health Care For All Americans*, executive summary, 8.

7. *New York Newsday*, 3 June 1991.

8. The Health USA Act of 1991, summary, 2.

9. Ibid., 4.

10. *Portland [ME] Press-Herald,* 5 October 1991, 4B.

11. Beth Fuchs and Joan Sokolovsky, *Health Insurance: Approaches for Universal Coverage* (Washington, D.C.: Congressional Research Service, 28 November 1990), CRS4.

12. *Bangor Daily News,* 24–25 June 1989, 33.

13. *Friday Report* (Publication of the Maine Hospital Association's Research and Education Trust) vol. 18, no. 6 (February 8, 1991).

14. *New York Times,* 7 February 1992, A15.

15. *New York Times,* 25 October 1991, A14.

16. Ibid., A14.

17. Remarks by the Honorable John D. Rockefeller IV to the Massachusetts Medical Society, Boston, 18 May 1991.

CHAPTER 12: THE STATES

1. The Oregon Basic Health Services Act of 1990, narrative, 8.

2. Ibid., Summary, 1.

3. *New York Times,* 22 February 1991.

4. *New York Times,* 9 June 1991.

5. Ibid.

6. *New York Times,* 25 February 1992, A18.

7. Testimony of John Lewin to the U.S. House of Representatives Committee on Ways and Means, Subcommittee on Health, 1.

8. Peter Sybinski, personal interview with the author, Honolulu, Hawaii 21 January 1991.

9. Lewin testimony 3.

10. Ibid., 1.

11. Printed testimony of Dr. Eugene Vayda, 14 June 1989.

12. Press release by Representative Robert Hagen, 12 April 1989, 2.

13. *The California Dream, The California Nightmare,* preface to the second printing, 1989, 1.

14. State Alliance for Universal Health Care Bulletin (no date or page numbers).

15. The Minnesota Health Access Commission, *Final Report to the Legislature,* January 1991, iii.

16. *St. Paul Pioneer Press,* 14 June 1991, 8A.

17. Ibid., 1A.

18. "Concerns Raised About H.176" (Publicly distributed flyer).

19. BCBSVT testimony on H.176, 4.

20. *Valley News,* 14 June 1991.

21. Ibid.

22. *Portland [ME] Press-Herald,* 6 December 1991, 6C.

23. Florida Task Force on Government Financed Health Care, *Final Report*, March 1991, 9.

24. Florida Task Force on Private Sector Health Care Responsibility, *Final Report*, February 1991, 39.

25. Ibid.

26. Ibid., 40.

27. Ibid., 65.

28. Letter from John Wilson, 16 August 1991.

29. Senator Jim Duncan, *2001: A Health Care Reform Odyssey*, 7.

30. Senator Jim Duncan, Opinion column in the *Anchorage Times*, 10 March 1991.

31. Duncan, *2001*, 5.

32. *Anchorage Daily News*, 18 March 1991.

33. *Alaska Journal of Commerce*, 11 March 1991.

36. Ibid., 26 February 1991.

37. Press release issued by New York State Health Campaign, 29 May 1991.

38. Press release issued by Assemblyman Gottfried, May 29, 1991.

39. *Universal New York Health Care: A Proposal, Revision I* (Report by the New York State Department of Health), 10 May 1990, 19.

40. *PRO-HEALTH—A Program For Improving Helath Care for New Yorkers*, revised draft, 24 May 1991, 2.

41. Ibid., 6.

42. News release from the Medical Society of New York, 6.

43. Ibid., 7.

44. Governor's Commission on Health Care Costs, *Report*, 1 October 1990, 9.

45. Assembly Concurrant Resolution No. 154.

46. Senate Bill No. 6020, 1989 Regular Session, 1.

47. Washington Health Care Service Act of 1992, June 7, 1991, i.

48. Senator Tarkey Lombardi, Jr., *How Best To Help: Tax Credits For Long-Term Care Insurance*, A Chairman's Report (Albany, N.Y., 1991), 16.

BIBLIOGRAPHY

Aaron, Henry J. *Serious and Unstable Condition: Financing America's Health Care.* Washington, D.C.: The Brookings Institution, 1991.

Alber, Jens. *Structural Reforms in the West German Health Care System.* Cologne, Germany: Max Planck Institute.

Begin, Monique. *Medicare: Canada's Right to Health.* Montreal: Optimum Publishing, 1987.

Bernstein, Barton J. and Allen J. Matusow, eds. *The Truman Administration.* New York, Evanston and London: Harper Colophon Books, 1966.

Berton, Pierre. *The Great Depression, 1929–1939.* Toronto: Penguin Books, 1991.

Blomqvist, Ake. *The Health Care Business.* Vancouver, B.C.: The Fraser Institute, 1979.

Burrow, James G. *AMA, Voice of American Medicine.* Baltimore: The Johns Hopkins Press, 1963.

Constantine, Stephen. *Social Conditions in Britain, 1918–1939.* London and New York: Methuen and Co., 1983.

Coutant, Daniel and Jean Lacaze. *Hier, une medecine pour demain.* Paris: Syros/Alternative, 1989.

Cray, Ed. *In Failing Health. The Medical Crisis and the AMA.* Indianapolis and New York: The Bobbs Merrill Co., 1970.

Dangerfield, George: *The Strange Death of Liberal England.* New York: G.P. Putnam's Sons, 1961. Reprint, originally published 1935.

Davidson, Warren, M.D. *Metaphors of Health and Aging: Geriatrics as Metaphor.* New York: Springer Verlag.

Dohler, Marian. *Policy Networks, Opportunity Structures and Neo-Conservative Reform Strategies in Health Policy.* Cologne, Germany: Max Planck Institute.

Ehrenreich, Barbara and John-Ehrenreich. *The American Health Empire: Power, Profit and Politics.* New York: Vintage Books 1971.

Fisher, George Ross, M.D. *The Hospital That Ate Chicago.* Philadelphia, London, and Toronto: The Saunders Press, 1980.

271

BIBLIOGRAPHY

Fry, George, M.D. *Medicine in Three Societies*. New York: American Elsevier Publishing Co., 1970.

Gairdner, William. *The Trouble With Canada*. Toronto: General Paperbacks, 1991.

Glaser, William A. *Health Insurance In Practice*. San Francisco and Oxford: Jossey-Bass Publishers, 1991.

Godt, Paul. *Policy-making in France, from de Gaulle to Mitterand*. London and New York: Pinter Publishers, 1989.

————. *Liberalism in the* Dirigiste *State*. London: Macmillan, 1991.

Greenberg, Selig. *The Quality of Mercy*. New York: Atheneum, 1971.

Gregg, John E. *The Health Insurance Racket and How to Beat It*. Chicago: Henry Regenery Co., 1973.

Gross, Martin L. *The Doctors*. New York: Random House, 1966.

Growe, Sarah Jane. *Who Cares? The Crisis in Canadian Nursing*. Toronto: McClelland and Stewart, 1991.

Haggard, Howard W. *The Doctor in History*. New Haven and London: Yale University Press, 1934.

Hart, Julian Tudor, M.D. *Transition of Patients from Consumers to Producers: An Agenda For The Next Hundred Years*. International Journal of Health Services.

Hiatt, Howard H., M.D. *America's Health in the Balance: Choice or Chance*. New York: Harper & Row, 1987.

Holborn, Hajo. *A History of Modern Germany, 1840–1945*. New York: Alfred A. Knopf, 1969.

Illich, Ivan. *Limits To Medicine*. New York and Middlesex, England: Penguin Books, 1976.

Johnson, Norman. *Reconstructing the Welfare State: A Decade of Change*. Hemel Hempstead, Herts. U.K.: Hanester Wheatsheaf, 1990.

Kearns, Doris. *Lyndon Johnson and the American Dream*. New York: Harper & Row, 1976.

Kennedy, Edward M. *In Critical Condition*. New York: Simon and Schuster, 1972.

Law, Sylvia A. *Blue Cross: What Went Wrong?* New Haven and London: Yale University Press, 1970.

Livesay, Harold. *Samuel Gompers and Organized Labor in America*. Boston and Toronto: Little Brown and Co., 1978.

Mandell, Bernard. *Samuel Gompers: A Biography*. Yellow Springs, Ohio: The Antioch Press, 1963.

Means, James Howard, M.D. *Doctors, People and Government*. Boston and Toronto: Little Brown and Co., 1953.

Muller, Mike. *The Health of Nations*. London: Faber and Faber, 1982.

Navarro, Vicente. *Class Struggle, the State and Medicine*. Oxford: Martin Robertson, 1978.

Nixon, Richard M. *In The Arena: A Memory of Victory, Defeat and Renewal*. New York: Simon and Schuster, 1990.

O'Neil, Peter. *Health Crisis 2000*. London: World Health Organization/Heinemann, 1982.

Payer, Lynn. *Medicine and Culture.* New York: Penguin Books, 1988.

Perkins, Frances. *The Roosevelt I Knew.* New York: The Viking Press, 1946.

Rachlis, Michael, M.D. and Carol Kushner. *Second Opinion.* Toronto: Harper Collins, 1989.

Rhodes, Philip. *An Outline History of Medicine.* London: Butterworths, 1985.

Richter, Werner. *Bismarck.* New York: G.P. Putnam's Sons, 1965.

Rollandin, Phillippe. *La Sante En Danger.* Paris: Editions de l'Instant, 1987.

Roux, Jacques. *La Sante En Souffrance.* Paris: Messidor/Editions Sociales. 1989.

Rozovsky, Lorne Elkin. *The Canadian Patient's Book of Rights.* Toronto: Doubleday-Canada, 1980.

Salinger, Pierre. *With Kennedy.* New York: Avon Books, 1966.

Scarpaci, Joseph L. *Health Services Privatization in Industrial Societies.* New Brunswick, N.J.: Rutgers University Press, 1989.

Schwartz, Harry. *National Health Insurance, A Pragmatic Perspective.* Dallas: National Center For Policy Analysis, 1983.

Schlesinger, Arthur M., Jr. *A Thousand Days: John F. Kennedy in the White House.* New York: Fawcett Premier, 1965.

Shaw, George Bernard. *The Doctor's Dilemma.* New York: Brentano's, 1909.

Shernoff, William M. *Payment Refused.* New York: Richardson and Steirman, 1986.

Snyder, Louis L. *Otto Von Bismarck, the Blood and Iron Chancellor.* Princeton, N.J., Toronto, and London: Van Nostrand Co., 1967.

Starr, Paul. *The Social Transformation of American Medicine.* New York: Basic Books, 1982.

Stevens, Rosemary. *American Medicine and the Public Interest.* New Haven and London: Yale University Press, 1971.

————. *In Sickness and In Wealth: American Hospitals in the Twentieth Century.* New York: Basic Books, 1989.

Sullivan, Mark. *Our Times: The United States, 1900–1925,* vol. IV. New York and London: Charles Scribner's Sons, 1932.

Sutherland, Ralph W., M.D. and Jane Fulton, Ph.D. *Health Care In Canada: A Description and Analysis of Canadian Health Services.* Ottawa: The Health Group, 1988.

Taylor, A.J.P. *Bismarck, The Man and The Statesman.* New York: Alfred A. Knopf, 1955.

Townsend, Peter and Nick Davidson. *Inequalities in Health.* Middlesex, England and New York: Penguin Books, 1980.

Tugwell, Rexford. *The Democratic Roosevelt.* Baltimore: Penguin Books, 1969. Reprint, originally published in 1957.

Whitney, Ray. *National Health Crisis ... a modern solution.* London: Shepheard-Walwyn, 1988.

Youngman, Elmer H., ed. *Progressive Principles by Theodore Roosevelt: Selections from Addresses Made During the Presidential Campaign of 1912.* New York: Progressive National Service, 1913.

INDEX

275

279

ABOUT THE AUTHOR

In 1990, Neil Rolde was the Democratic candidate for U.S. Senate in Maine, a campaign in which his strongest issue was the need for national health care in the U.S. A seventy point underdog at the start of his race against a powerful incumbent, Senator William Cohen, Rolde eventually captured 40 percent of the vote in his first try for statewide office.

Previously, he had served sixteen years in the Maine House of Representatives, a number of them on the principal committee dealing with health care. He had also been the House Majority Leader and, prior to his election, was an assistant to Governor Kenneth M. Curtis for six years.

Rolde is a graduate of Phillips Academy, Andover, Yale University, and the Columbia Graduate School of Journalism. At Yale, he won the Dean's Prize for creative writing and was selected for the special Scholar of the House program as a creative writer.

He has published five books, the most recent a narrative history of the state of Maine. He lives in York, Maine, with his wife, the former Carlotta Florsheim of Kew Gardens, New York. They have four daughters and five grandchildren. Rolde has also been active in numerous civic organizations in Maine and New England.